USING TERRI

USING TERRI

The Religious Right's Conspiracy to Take Away Our Rights

Jon B. Eisenberg

HarperSanFrancisco
A Division of HarperCollins*Publishers*

HarperCollins books may be purchased for educational, business, or sales promotional use. For information please write: Special Markets Department, HarperCollins Publishers, 10 East 53rd Street, New York, NY 10022.

HarperCollins Web site: http://www.harpercollins.com
HarperCollins®, ■®, and HarperSanFrancisco™ are
trademarks of HarperCollins Publishers.

FIRST EDITION
Designed by Joseph Rutt

Library of Congress Cataloging-in-Publication Data is available.

ISBN−10: 0−06−087732−4
ISBN−13: 978−0−06−087732−3

05 06 07 08 09 RRD(H) 10 9 8 7 6 5 4 3 2 1

For Linda Hillel
and
in memory of Roslyn August and Bernard Eisenberg

Contents

PART TWO

Where It Went

PART THREE

Where It's Going

Introduction

You may not be aware of it, but a fundamental constitutional right is at risk in America today. It is the right of control over your own body—known as "personal autonomy."

The right of personal autonomy includes the right to make decisions about your own medical treatment. It includes the right to refuse life-sustaining treatment that you don't want—what some people call the "right to die."

The threat to this constitutional right comes from a small but powerful group of extremists on the fringes of American politics. They are popularly known as the "religious Right," and they are richly funded by a group of ultraconservative foundations and think tanks created during the past few decades by a handful of the wealthiest men in America.

These extremists are waging "culture wars"—efforts to turn America into a theocracy where the Constitution is subservient to scripture and all of us are yoked to their religious dogma. They are fighting these wars on multiple fronts—pushing for prayer and creationism in the public schools, and opposing embryonic stem-cell research, women's reproductive rights, and gay civil unions and marriage ... most of today's high-profile social issues.

A key battle in their culture wars was an attempt to keep an unconscious woman's feeding tube attached.

This book tells the story of a sustained effort by leaders of the religious Right to force life-sustaining treatment, in the form of artificial nutrition and hydration, on Terri Schiavo—who was permanently unconscious for fifteen years, who could not eat, drink, think, communicate, or see. The forces behind this effort were motivated by a dogma that cared not a whit whether Terri would have wanted to refuse such treatment had she been able to decide for herself. The culture warriors hold the minority belief that there is no "right to die"—that our bodies belong to God, not ourselves, and that God alone may decide when we will die.

This is the story of a family tragedy that became a national spectacle in the worst way, turning a private matter into a public circus—complete with fulsome politicians, self-aggrandizing preachers, angry demonstrators, and all-knowing TV pundits, each of whom purported to know what was best for Terri Schiavo.

It is a story of law, ethics, and religion: the rights guaranteed by laws across America, the ethical rules that guide doctors and nurses in end-of-life decision-making, and the Judeo-Christian traditions on end-of-life care.

It is a story of ignorance about how it really feels—and how it doesn't feel—to die of dehydration when artificial nutrition and hydration are terminated.

It is a story of money—vast sums of it. Hundreds of millions of dollars are funding a conspiracy—there is no better word for it—to take away our right of personal autonomy. In the *Schiavo* case, the money trail leads from a consortium of foundations with $2 billion in assets, through organizations created by leaders on the religious Right such as Pat Robertson and James Dobson, to the lawyers and activists who fought so relentlessly to keep Terri Schiavo's feeding tube attached.

It is a story of hypocrisy by politicians, such as Republican house majority leader Tom DeLay, who say one thing in public but do the opposite in private; of unprincipled ambition by politicians, such as Florida Governor Jeb Bush, who disregard the fundamental structure of American government when it suits their political needs; of contempt for the American people by politicians, such as Republican senate majority leader Bill Frist, who say something stupid for the whole nation to hear and then deny they ever said it; and of collusion and cowardice by Democrats in Congress who did nothing to stop the national debacle that the *Schiavo* case became.

It is the story of courage and tenacity by a deeply religious Republican judge—George W. Greer of Florida's Pinellas County Circuit Court. Judge Greer stood up to a barrage of litigation tactics the likes of which have never before been seen in American right-to-die litigation—along with calls for his impeachment, death threats, and shunning by his own church—to stay true to the rule of law he swore to uphold.

It is the story of a governor who approached the brink of civil disorder under pressure from religious extremists by dispatching his agents to grab Terri Schiavo from her hospice bed, spirit her off to a hospital, and reattach her feeding tube—after the courts had refused to accede to his wishes—only to be stopped, on two successive days, under threat of being thrown in jail.

It is the story of how twenty judges of the United States District Court, the United States Court of Appeals, and the United States Supreme Court saved America's judicial branch of government from efforts to make it subservient to the legislative and executive branches. The culture warriors tried to tinker with the constitutional separation of powers—the system of checks and balances established by America's founders to prevent any one branch of government from abusing its power. The *Schiavo* case was a civics lesson for a handful of senators and representatives who are bent on upsetting the constitutional balance of American government.

And it is the story of my own family—my cousin, who died like Terri Schiavo, and my uncle, who gave his life to protect our constitutional rights.

It is also a wake-up call for America. The *Schiavo* case was just one battle in the religious Right's culture wars—a battle I watched first-hand, increasingly amazed and appalled as I followed the money trail and saw how far the culture warriors would go. They abused the judicial system with a multitude of delaying tactics and frivolous arguments. They vilified Judge Greer because he wouldn't accede to their demands. They harassed Michael Schiavo mercilessly—and they haven't stopped yet. They engaged in a public relations campaign that proved the adage that truth is the first casualty of war. And they took America to the edge of constitutional crisis with a congressional bill that, though drafted specially for Terri Schiavo with the participation of her parents' lawyer, contained the seed of its own failure.

The culture warriors will keep on fighting to destroy the constitutional right of personal autonomy. They are now using their millions of dollars to fund new attacks on the judicial branch, attempts to change the right-to-die laws from state to state, and various other social causes that fall within the ambit of their far-flung assault on autonomy.

They will succeed unless we do something about it.

PART ONE

Whence It Came

My Cousin Ros

I joined Michael Schiavo's legal team in March 2005 because I understood well his painful task. It is not easy to "pull the plug" on someone you love. I know from personal experience.

In 1998, my cousin Roslyn August suffered a devastating stroke that left her with what doctors called "global aphasia." As one of them put it, "Nothing is getting through to her, and nothing can come out." I spent days at her bedside trying to communicate. I held her hand and asked her to squeeze it. Nothing. I told her to blink if she could hear me. Nothing. I kissed her cheek. Nothing.

Yet she was not in a coma. Her eyes were often open, and sometimes they tracked me as I crossed the room. She seemed lost somewhere between life and death.

On one visit to her bedside, I brought my favorite photograph of her. The photographer had caught her standing in a grove of trees at the base of Yosemite Falls wearing a big, silly grin, facing upward with her arms held up to the sky, as if to say, "How lovely!" I handed her the photograph. She took it in one hand, seemed to look at it uncomprehendingly, and then dropped it and went blank again.

Was she in a persistent vegetative state? None of the doctors ever said. Was she in a minimally conscious state? That diagnosis did not yet even exist. Could she improve? This the doctors could tell me: no. There was nothing they could do.

Except for one thing: They could keep her alive with a feeding tube inserted through her nose into her stomach.

Ros was seventy-nine years old and had been in failing physical and mental health for three years. She was my second cousin once removed: her great-grandparents were my great-great-grandparents. But she was more like a favorite aunt to me than a distant cousin. She had been part of my innermost family circle since my early childhood, and we became good friends in my adult years. The only other relatives with whom Ros had regular contact were a brother in New York City, a niece in San Francisco, and my parents and grandmother in Los Angeles. Ros lived alone in a one-room apartment in Oakland, California—just a few miles from me and my wife, Linda Hillel—subsisting on a small government pension.

Ros often had Linda and me over for dinner. Her cooking was ... well, not so hot. But she did one thing superbly—the Spanish seafood and rice dish, paella. And she was great company. Dinner with Ros was fun.

Ros was a free spirit. She had been married briefly in her youth, and after that she knocked around for years before settling down in Northern California and putting herself through college and graduate school, from which she emerged with a masters degree in social work. She became a psychiatric social worker, employed by a county agency to evaluate mentally disturbed people for government conservatorships. She came to know intimately the world of mental institutions and nursing homes.

Ros retired in her early sixties. She kept close friends. She cultivated many hobbies—weaving, stained glass, poetry, hiking. She traveled widely.

In her seventies, Ros began to slow down. Travel became more difficult. She grew impatient with friends. She became forgetful. She sometimes got lost during her goings about town, which frightened her terribly.

Over the years, our dinner conversations occasionally turned to the subject of death and dying. Ros said she did not want to be kept alive at all costs. We discussed the high-profile "right to die" cases of the day

—Karen Ann Quinlan, the New Jersey woman whose parents disconnected her respirator in 1976; Nancy Cruzan, the Missouri car accident victim whose 1990 case in the U.S. Supreme Court established the constitutional right to refuse tube feeding and other medical treatment; and several local cases that were widely publicized in California. Ros made her position clear: "No machines or tubes for me."

Most Americans feel that way.

Ros even went so far as to get information from the Hemlock Society on how to end her life with drugs, which she planned to buy on a trip to Mexico.

From 1988 through 1996, Ros made several wills appointing me her executor. She had also given me legal power of attorney over her financial affairs should she become unable to handle them, and she executed several advance health-care directives naming me as her surrogate decision-maker. Her most recent health-care directive, on a form I had given her in 1996, said: "I do not want efforts made to prolong my life and I do not want life-sustaining treatment to be provided or continued" under any circumstances "where the burdens of the treatments outweigh the expected benefits."

Ros gave me power over her life and death. But her health-care directive said nothing about feeding tubes. Back then, none of the standard form advance directives did so.

In the fall of 1997, Ros's downhill progression advanced considerably. She became confused, incontinent, and reclusive. She began setting kitchen fires. One day I went to visit her and discovered smoke pouring from her open front door. She had left a skillet of hamburger meat on an open flame. The Oakland Fire Department came and extinguished the smoldering remains.

After a handful of fires, I had her oven disconnected and arranged for daily deliveries of meals-on-wheels from a senior services provider. She asked, "How am I going to make coffee?" I bought her an electric kettle.

I begged Ros to let me place her in an assisted living facility. She was adamantly against it, saying, "I've seen those places. I know what they're like. I'm not ready yet."

But she was oh-so-ready. She just didn't realize it. Or couldn't face it.

Eventually, Ros stopped eating. This was truly alarming, for food had become the central focus of her life, all she had left. She loved to eat, and she ate a lot. After her death, I discovered this entry in one of her journals: "I eat because I experience a lack of control over my world. Eating takes care of all feelings good or bad. It's a safety net psychologically, a spontaneous impulse to eat to achieve control." Control over her life—personal autonomy—meant a lot to Ros. She always knew and did what she wanted. Who wouldn't want to live that way?

On December 24, 1997, I discovered Ros lying on the floor of her apartment, unable to move. She begged me not to call the paramedics, but of course I did. She spent twelve days in the hospital being treated for a severe urinary tract infection. I had her discharged to a skilled nursing facility. After some initial resistance, she agreed to it. There was no fight left in her.

Ros spent three weeks in the nursing home, lying in bed staring into space. She would not read—a lifelong passion—or even watch television. Once, when I caught her in a lucid moment and asked what she was thinking about, she responded, "How I can get out of here."

On January 28, 1998, Ros had her stroke.

Within a few days, the doctors told me that Ros was profoundly brain-damaged. She would never again eat, read, communicate, or even think in any meaningful way. One of the doctors said that I might soon have to decide whether to withhold life-sustaining measures. Ros had been periodically pulling out her feeding tube, which the doctors reinserted. They might have to restrain her to keep it in.

I telephoned Ros's brother Ted in New York and asked him to come to Oakland to help me decide. He and his wife arrived two days later. We had a meeting at the hospital—Ted, his wife, his daughter (the San Francisco niece), Linda and me, Ros's attending physician, and a hospital chaplain. Then we five family members retreated to a local coffee shop, where we spent three hours of tearful agonizing and soul-searching before deciding to remove the tube for good. It was to come out that evening.

Late that night, however, a floor nurse telephoned me at home and said the nursing staff was "uncomfortable" with our decision to remove Ros's feeding tube, and further action would be deferred until a meeting of the hospital's ethics committee three days hence.

I had never heard of a hospital ethics committee. I learned that it's typically an assemblage of doctors, nurses, lawyers, medical and law school professors, and clergy—as many as a dozen or more—who provide advice on ethical questions that arise in the practice of medicine, guided by a mélange of moral, philosophical, and legal principles called bioethics. These days, nearly all hospitals have an ethics committee. Given the nurses' concerns, Ros's attending physician wanted advice before removing the feeding tube.

I was to attend the meeting and make the case for withholding ANH—the doctors' shorthand for artificial nutrition and hydration. Evidently Ros's advance directive wasn't good enough for the doctors, because it said nothing about her specific wishes and nothing about feeding tubes.

This was new to me. I have been a lawyer for twenty-six of my fifty-two years and have represented all sorts of clients—architects, engineers, and doctors; drunk drivers, bar fighters, and prostitutes; billion-dollar chemical and oil companies; and even a multiple murderer. But I had never represented Death.

At the meeting, I told the ethics committee about how Ros had lived her life and what she had said about death and dying. I explained how Linda and I had become Ros's closest relatives and virtually her only remaining friends in her waning years; how I knew the life she had lived and the life she would not want to live; how she would abhor being kept alive in her current condition.

Linda and two of Ros's old friends attended the meeting, too, and said similar things. Ted had returned to New York by then.

I told them how I had gone through Ros's papers the day before the meeting and discovered a note in her handwriting with the address of the Hemlock Society in Los Angeles and what appeared to be a somewhat misspelled recipe for pharmaceutical suicide: "Norflex, orphenadrine, sliokol, barbiturates, morphine, 30–100 mg."

Finally, I concluded: "I am now called upon to speak for Roslyn, who cannot speak for herself. I abhor the idea of speaking as Death's lawyer. Let me speak instead in Ros's voice. Here is what I think she would say: 'I have lost my greatest joy in life—eating. There is an impenetrable wall between me and the people I love, for I can no longer speak to them. My greatest fear in life—institutionalization—has been realized. Please, leave me alone and let me go.'"

And that is what they decided to do.

The doctors told me it would take a week or two for Ros to die, of what they called terminal dehydration. I feared she would suffer. They assured me that she was not cognitive enough to suffer. They told me of medical studies showing that terminal dehydration under such circumstances is not painful and that any possible discomfort can be effectively treated by moistening the patient's mouth and skin and by administering morphine if necessary. I was skeptical. I asked, "Why don't you give her morphine anyway, just in case?" This plainly made them nervous. One of them said, "That could hasten her death, and we can't do anything that seems like euthanasia."

I resolved to watch Ros closely to make sure, as best I could, that she wasn't suffering as she slowly died. I made the doctors promise that they would give her morphine if there were any sign of suffering. But it never seemed necessary.

She died on the tenth day. It was a quiet death, I would even say peaceful.

But it was still difficult to watch. This was, after all, someone I loved, and she was slowly, silently dying. Her urine output, through a catheter, slowed to a trickle and turned dark. Her breathing became shallow. She lay motionless and expressionless while the nurses gently moistened her lips and turned her from time to time in order to prevent bedsores.

One day near the end, I helped a nurse change Ros's bedding, which required us to move Ros around on the bed a few times. I was grateful to be able to have a part, however small, in her care as she gradually slipped away.

On the fifth day, Ros's long-lost brother Alex intervened.

Until Ros had her stroke, I had never even known that she had another brother. She had never mentioned him to me. Ted told me about Alex when I telephoned to inform him of the stroke. Ted said that Ros detested Alex. She and Alex had not seen each other in forty years. Alex was an ultraorthodox Jew; Ros was defiantly nonobservant. Alex was a political conservative; Ros was a passionate leftist. Alex had tried to tell Ros how to live her life; Ros had resented it. Alex was just like their father, and Ros had clashed bitterly with her father.

I guess that's why she had never mentioned Alex.

A few days after the stroke, Alex telephoned me and introduced himself. It was a strange conversation. All he seemed to care about was whether she would be cremated, which he adamantly opposed. His rabbi had instructed him to make sure she wasn't cremated. As it happened, however, her will called for cremation, and she had told me several times that she wanted her ashes scattered. But I figured it was premature to discuss the point, so I said nothing. I gave Alex the telephone numbers for Ros's doctor and nurses.

When the ethics committee meeting was scheduled, I telephoned Alex and invited him to attend. He declined, saying he would defer to my decision on whether to withhold the feeding tube. He didn't seem to care much about it. After the meeting, when I called him and told him what had happened, it still seemed that his only concern was that she not be cremated. This time, however, I told him of her instructions. He became distraught.

Five days later, as Ros lay dying, Alex telephoned one of the nurses and demanded reinsertion of the feeding tube. Her attending physician called me; I called Alex. He told me something had changed. "My rabbi says that as long as the heart beats and she is not dying, she must be fed. Life is sacred." I said, "Do you just automatically do whatever your rabbi tells you?" He seemed surprised by the question. "Of course!"

The conversation turned ugly. I said he had no business insisting on how Ros should die, just like he had never had any business telling her how to live. I said, "She told me what she wants, and I'm her voice now." Alex replied with a warning: "If you don't put that tube back in, I'm going to have a hundred Jews picketing that hospital tomorrow." This was something I never anticipated. Why, I wondered, would a bunch of devout Jews object to letting Ros die?

Years later, I would find out why.

But Alex's threat never materialized. I just told him to "do whatever you feel you need to do," and I heard nothing more from him. The doctors were unsettled by his intervention but decided to ignore it. Five days later, Ros was dead. We had her ashes scattered over San Francisco Bay.

So I know what Michael Schiavo has gone through. He did what I had to do, but in far more painful circumstances, under intense public scrutiny, suffering accusations of murder and abuse and enduring the meddling of religious activists and politicians who knew nothing of his and his wife's wishes and values.

And now I understand Alex better—where he came from, and who was behind him—for Alex's rabbi morphed into a far more potent force in the Terri Schiavo case. Alex was my first battle in the religious Right's cultural war on America. By the time the *Schiavo* case exploded onto the national scene, I understood whence it came and I knew where it would go.

A Family Tragedy

What a cruel irony that Terri Schiavo was named after St. Theresa of Avila, a sixteenth-century Carmelite nun who, at the age of twenty-four, took ill and fell into a coma but then revived, living a productive and spiritual life for another forty-three years.

Born Theresa Marie Schindler near Philadelphia, Pennsylvania, on December 3, 1963, the first of Bob and Mary Schindler's three children, Terri as a child was shy and overweight. The family was suburban, middle-class, Catholic, and by all accounts quite ordinary. Bob was a businessman, Mary a homemaker. Terri wrote fan letters to television stars—her favorite was David Cassidy. She named her gerbils Starsky and Hutch. She liked to draw horses and dogs.

Perhaps the only thing extraordinary about young Terri was her size. In high school, at 5 feet 3 inches tall, she weighed as much as 250 pounds. She would cry when her mother took her shopping for clothes.

Near the end of her senior year, however, she began to diet seriously and lost more than fifty pounds. She enrolled in the local community college and continued to lose weight, dropping to 150 pounds. She came out of her shell, dyed her hair blond, drove a sports car, and started wearing tighter clothes. She made more friends, became more outgoing. She seemed to grow in self-confidence.

At nineteen came her first date—dinner and a movie with a college classmate, Michael Schiavo. They fell in love and within six months were engaged. They married on November 10, 1984.

In 1986, Michael and Terri moved to Florida. So did Bob and Mary Schindler and their other two children, Bobby Jr. and Susan. Michael worked as a restaurant manager for McDonald's, Terri as a clerk for an insurance company.

In Florida, Terri kept losing weight—dramatically. Now 5 feet 4 inches tall, her weight dropped to 110 pounds. Her daily diet regimen included as much as a gallon of iced tea. She was proud of her body. She took to wearing bikini bathing suits. But she still seemed to eat a lot. Once, when asked how she could eat so much and stay thin, she replied that she "must just have a good metabolism." After meals, she would go to the bathroom with a toothbrush, toothpaste, and mouthwash, purportedly to clean her teeth.

There may have been a dark side to the stunning weight loss. Some doctors think Terri had bulimia.

The full name of this eating disorder is bulimia nervosa, and its victims are typically young women. Some 10 percent of college-aged American women are bulimic.

The hallmark of bulimia is "binging and purging"—alternating periods of extreme overeating (the binge) and inappropriate methods of weight control (the purge). Common methods of purging include self-induced vomiting, enemas, excessive use of laxatives or diuretics, and compulsive exercising.

During a binge, the bulimic feels a profound loss of control, which is regained with the purge. But the purge comes at a price. Constant vomiting can erode tooth enamel, damage the esophagus, and cause swelling and soreness in the salivary glands. Bowel function is disrupted. The stomach might rupture. Most dangerously, bulimia can cause heart rhythm irregularities and electrolyte abnormalities—such as decreased potassium levels—which can lead to cardiac arrest.

In the early morning hours of February 25, 1990, at the age of twenty-six, Terri Schiavo collapsed in the hallway of her apartment. Her heart had stopped beating. Tests later showed a precipitous drop in her body potassium.

Michael called 911. By the time the paramedics arrived and re-stored Terri's heartbeat, her brain had been deprived of oxygen—a condition called anoxia—for several minutes. The result was devas-tating brain damage, which caused Terri to slip into a coma.

The paramedics took Terri to Humana Northside Hospital in St. Petersburg, where doctors inserted a feeding tube—specifically, a per-cutaneous endoscopic gastronomy, or PEG. A PEG tube is inserted through an incision in the skin directly into the stomach, delivering a flow of vitamin-enriched liquid sustenance.

Like St. Theresa of Avila, Terri eventually emerged from her coma. Unlike her namesake, however, she never regained consciousness. In-stead, she settled into PVS—medical shorthand for a persistent vege-tative state.

Patients in PVS experience sleep-wake cycles, but they are com-pletely unaware of themselves or their surroundings. They hear nothing, see nothing, and feel no touch; they have no language com-prehension and cannot communicate; they are incontinent in bowel and bladder. The condition can be misleading to the untrained ob-server. Sometimes the patient's eyes are open and may seem to track movement; he or she may occasionally moan or grimace; the patient may even have reflexive reactions to outside stimuli—reactions that could be misinterpreted as purposeful. But they are not; the patient is truly unconscious.

One must be in this condition for at least a month to be diagnosed as PVS. After a year, recovery is unlikely.

Terri spent two and a half months at Humana Northside Hospital. On May 12, 1990, she was discharged to a rehabilitation facility. Over the next several months, she was moved to another hospital, then home to her family, then back to the rehabilitation facility. Despite intensive physical, occupational, and speech therapy, her condition did not im-prove.

The Schindler and Schiavo families shared their grief and their efforts to help Terri. Years later, a report by her court-appointed guardian, Jay Wolfson, would describe Michael and Mary Schindler as "virtual partners in their care of and dedication to Theresa." Wolfson stated, "There is no question but that complete trust, mutual caring, explicit love and a common goal of caring and rehabilitating Theresa were the shared intentions of Michael Schiavo and the Schindlers." In an interview with CNN's Larry King, Bob Schindler told King that Mary and Michael had been "joined at the hip." Michael even went to live with the Schindlers. He also attended nursing school to learn how better to care for Terri.

Being legally incompetent and unable to make decisions about her medical treatment, Terri needed a guardian to handle her affairs. On June 18, 1990, a judge appointed Michael to be her guardian.

Toward the end of 1990, Michael took Terri to California for experimental therapy—implantation of a so-called thalamic stimulator into her brain. The therapy was unsuccessful. A few months later, he took her back to Florida and placed her in another rehabilitation center for further conventional treatment. Again, nothing helped. In mid-1991, Terri was transferred to a skilled nursing facility.

Michael moved out of Bob and Mary Schindler's home in May 1992, but they remained close. By the next year, the Schindlers were encouraging Michael to date other women, and he did. He even introduced his dates to the Schindlers. With their blessing, he had begun to get on with his life.

Is money the root of all evil? Sometimes it seems so. The relationship between Michael and his in-laws began to go sour after Michael achieved success in a lawsuit he filed for medical malpractice. In the late 1980s, Terri and Michael had tried to conceive a child. In the year before her cardiac arrest, they had gotten fertility treatment from an obstetrician, who did nothing to address Terri's dramatic weight loss and failed to give her a blood test that would have detected a potassium imbalance. The malpractice lawsuit resulted in a jury verdict for Michael. In 1993 he received $300,000 and Terri received approximately $700,000. Terri's money was placed in a trust over which Michael had no control. Now there was something for Michael and the Schindlers to disagree about.

And so, in 1993, the fight began. Ten years later, in 2003, Michael told CNN's Larry King that Bob Schindler had immediately demanded a share of the $300,000 that had been awarded to Michael, which Michael refused. Michael told King that Bob "always wanted the money. He wants the money. He wants the control." Similarly, Michael said, Mary Schindler had told him, "We deserve some of this money."

Indeed, Bob and Mary Schindler both had previously admitted in court that they wanted some of Michael's $300,000. But Mary also complained to Larry King in 2003 that "after the money came in" in 1993, Michael "wouldn't do anything" for Terri, and "she hasn't had any therapy" since then.

Michael had indeed stopped Terri's rehabilitative therapy by the time he won the malpractice lawsuit. By then, he later said, he had given up all hope for her recovery.

The rift between Michael and the Schindlers became bitter and irreparable. They stopped speaking to one another. In July 1993, the Schindlers formally challenged Michael's guardianship of Terri, asking the guardianship judge to appoint a legal guardian—called a guardian ad litem—to determine whether Michael had abused Terri. The guardian ad litem determined that there had been no abuse; on the contrary, Michael had acted appropriately and attentively. According to the guardian ad litem, Michael had been so demanding of the staff at Terri's skilled nursing facility as to be "a nursing home administrator's nightmare," and Terri received special care and attention from the staff because of his persistent advocacy.

In early 1994, when Terri got a urinary tract infection, Michael decided—with the treating physician's approval—not to treat the infection, and he imposed a "do not resuscitate" order. But Michael relented after the skilled nursing facility opposed his decision. After that, Terri was transferred to another facility.

The years passed with no improvement in Terri's condition. But Michael remained her most regular visitor.

The litigation over whether to remove Terri's feeding tube—technically, the beginning of what has come to be known as "the Terri
Schiavo case"—started in May 1998, when Michael filed a petition in
the probate division of the Pinellas County Circuit Court, which over-
sees guardianship proceedings, asking the court to authorize removal of
the PEG tube. But the wheels of justice grind slowly. The case did not
go to trial until January 24, 2000. The judge was George W. Greer.

Judge Greer had to decide two issues: whether Terri was truly in
PVS, and what her wishes regarding continued tube feeding would be
if she could express them. Terri had left no written instructions about
her medical care.

On the first issue—Terri's medical condition—two physicians testified that Terri was in PVS. Their testimony was backed up by
computer-assisted tomography (CT scans) showing an empty space in
her brain where there should have been a cerebral cortex. Her cerebral
cortex was virtually gone, replaced by spinal fluid. Even the Schindlers
acknowledged that Terri was in a diagnosed persistent vegetative state.

On the second issue—Terri's end-of-life wishes—Michael and the
Schindlers disagreed bitterly.

On Michael's side, three witnesses testified: Michael, his brother
Scott Schiavo, and his sister-in-law Joan Schiavo, to whom Terri had
been close in the mid-1980s. Michael told Judge Greer about things
Terri had said to him on occasions when they were watching something on television depicting people on ventilators or tube-feeding.
She had told Michael that she didn't want to be kept alive "on anything artificial" and she did "not want to live like that." Michael also
spoke of a time in the mid-1980s when Terri's grandmother was caring
for Terri's severely brain-damaged uncle. Terri had told Michael, "If I
ever have to be a burden to anyone, I don't want to live like that."

Michael's brother Scott recalled Terri's comments to him in 1988,
when his grandmother was being kept alive on a respirator after she
was "pretty much gone." Terri had said, "If I ever go like that, just let
me go. Don't leave me there. I don't want to be kept alive on a machine." And Scott's wife Joan testified about the time when they saw a

movie about someone in a coma after a diving accident, with tubes coming out of his mouth and arm. Terri said she "would not want to go through that" and "would want the tubes and everything taken out."

On the Schindlers' side, the court heard testimony from Mary Schindler and an old friend of Terri's. Mary testified that when Terri was somewhere between seventeen and twenty years old, during television news reports about the Karen Ann Quinlan right-to-die case, Terri had said something to the effect that "they" should "just leave her alone." But on cross-examination, after being shown contemporary news reports about the *Quinlan* case, Mary admitted that Terri could only have been eleven or twelve years old at that time. Terri's friend also testified about similar conversations with Terri about the *Quinlan* case, but Judge Greer concluded that this must have occurred in the same time frame as Terri's conversation with her mother— when Terri was just a child.

The Schindlers also gave disturbing testimony, both in pretrial depositions and during the trial, that suggested the extremes to which they might go to keep Terri alive. As Jay Wolfson put it in his 2003 guardian ad litem's report: "Nearly gruesome examples were given, eliciting agreement by family members that in the event Theresa should contract diabetes and subsequent gangrene in each of her limbs, they would agree to amputate each limb." (The Schindlers later claimed they never intended to imply a desire to keep Terri alive "at all costs.") Wolfson also noted, "Within the testimony, as part of the hypotheticals presented, Schindler family members stated that even if Theresa had told them of her intention to have artificial nutrition withdrawn, they would not do it."

After the trial concluded, Judge Greer issued a thoughtful, lengthy, and detailed written opinion in which he concluded that Terri was indeed in PVS and would want her feeding tube withdrawn.

On the medical issue, Judge Greer found "beyond all doubt that Theresa Marie Schiavo is in a persistent vegetative state," and "the medical evidence before this court conclusively establishes that she has no hope of ever regaining consciousness." He found that "without the feeding tube she will die in seven to fourteen days," and "the unrebutted medical testimony before this court is that such death would be painless."

Addressing the Schindlers' insistence that Terri seemed to be responsive to them, Judge Greer said "the court is not unmindful that perceptions may become reality to the person having them. But the overwhelming credible evidence is that Terri Schiavo has been totally unresponsive since lapsing into the coma almost ten years ago, that her movements are reflexive and predicated on brain stem activity alone," and that "she suffers from severe structural brain damage and to a large extent her brain has been replaced by spinal fluid."

As for Terri's end-of-life wishes, Judge Greer found "that Terri Schiavo did make statements which are creditable and reliable with regard to her intention given the situation at hand." He noted the statements by Terri about which Michael, Scott, and Joan Schiavo had testified, and he found that "these statements are Terri Schiavo's oral declarations concerning her intention as to what she would want done under the present circumstances." Judge Greer concluded that "the testimony regarding such oral declarations is reliable, is creditable and rises to the level of clear and convincing evidence to this court."

The judge's opinion, dated February 11, 2000, ended with the following disposition: "ORDERED AND ADJUDGED that the Petition for Authorization to Discontinue Artificial Life Support of Michael Schiavo, Guardian of the Person of Theresa Marie Schiavo, an incapacitated person, be and the same is hereby GRANTED and Petitioner/Guardian is hereby authorized to proceed with the discontinuance of said artificial life support for Theresa Marie Schiavo."

The feeding tube was to come out. But that wouldn't actually happen for another fourteen months. The litigation frenzy had begun.

The Schindlers appealed Judge Greer's ruling to Florida's intermediate appellate court, the District Court of Appeal. Appeals can take a long time. This one took a full year. Meanwhile, the removal of ANH was put on hold—"stayed," in legal parlance. Finally, on January 24, 2001, the appellate court upheld Judge Greer's decision.

The Court of Appeal's written opinion was as carefully crafted as Judge Greer's. First, the court reviewed the evidence and concluded that "the evidence is overwhelming that Theresa is in a permanent or persistent vegetative state.... Over the span of this last decade, Theresa's brain has deteriorated because of the lack of oxygen it suf- fered at the time of the heart attack.... At this point, much of her cerebral cortex is simply gone and has been replaced by cerebral spinal fluid. Medicine cannot cure this condition."

Next, the court acknowledged the care Michael had lavished on Terri: "Michael has continued to care for her and to visit her all these years.... He has become a professional respiratory therapist and works in a nearby hospital. As a guardian, he has always attempted to pro- vide optimum treatment for his wife. He has been a diligent watch guard of Theresa's care, never hesitating to annoy the nursing staff in order to assure that she receives the proper treatment."

Finally, the court addressed the true issue in the case—what Terri's wishes would be. As the court put it, "the difficult question" that faced Judge Greer was whether Terri "would choose to continue the con- stant nursing care and the supporting tubes in hopes that a miracle would somehow recreate her missing brain tissue, or whether she would wish to permit a natural death process to take its course and for her family members and loved ones to be free to continue their lives." Judge Greer had settled on the latter. The appellate court said: "After due consideration, we conclude that the trial judge had clear and con- vincing evidence to answer this question as he did."

Thus Judge Greer's decision was affirmed. Three months later, the Florida Supreme Court refused to hear the case. So did the U.S. Supreme Court. The appellate jurisdiction of those courts is discre- tionary: they don't have to accept a given case for review.

Once the highest courts of Florida and the United States refused to intervene, Judge Greer's removal order took effect. On April 24, 2001, Terri's PEG tube was clamped, cutting off her supply of ANH.

The Schindlers immediately struck back. They filed a motion in the guardianship proceeding before Judge Greer, seeking relief from his judgment based on new evidence they claimed to have discovered—a purported assertion by Michael's former girlfriend that he had told her that he and Terri had never discussed her end-of-life wishes. When Judge Greer denied this motion, the Schindlers filed a new lawsuit against Michael in a different division of the Pinellas County Circuit Court—the general civil division—making the same claim. This procedural maneuver enabled the Schindlers to go before a different judge, Frank Quesada. They asked Judge Quesada for an emergency injunction requiring the resumption of ANH, which he granted. Two days after the PEG tube was clamped, the clamp was removed and ANH was restored.

The case went back to the Court of Appeal. With the filing of the separate lawsuit, the case had become a procedural mess, which the appellate court sorted out in a written opinion filed on July 11, 2001. The court held that the Schindlers were entitled to challenge Judge Greer's judgment based on newly discovered evidence, but that their motion before Judge Greer had been procedurally untimely and their evidentiary showing before Judge Quesada had been insufficient to support his injunction. They had failed to present an affidavit from the former girlfriend, instead merely offering affidavits by Bob Schindler and a private investigator containing hearsay statements about what the former girlfriend had purportedly told them—which is not enough proof in a court of law. The appellate court sent the case back to Judge Greer, giving the Schindlers time to file another motion for relief based on new evidence. The decision required Judge Quesada to transfer the Schindlers' separate civil lawsuit over to Judge Greer.

Back before Judge Greer, the Schindlers litigated with a vengeance. They not only refiled their motion for relief from the judgment but also filed motions demanding disqualification of Judge Greer from further hearing the case, removal of Michael as Terri's guardian, and another medical examination of Terri by doctors selected by the Schindlers. Now the Schindlers changed their position regarding Terri's medical condition. Armed with affidavits by seven physicians, the Schindlers claimed that Terri was not in PVS after all and that her ability to eat and speak could be restored by a new "cardiovascular medication style of therapy."

All of this was for naught. Judge Greer denied the motions, and once again he ordered removal of the feeding tube.

Once more the case went back to the Court of Appeal, resulting in another stay preventing the cessation of ANH. In a third opinion, on October 17, 2001, the appellate court gave the Schindlers another ray of hope.

The court upheld Judge Greer's rejection of new testimony by two former friends of Michael's and the husband of one of them, concluding that the new evidence was insufficient to change Judge Greer's original ruling. But the court, while expressing "skepticism" about the claim of hope for Terri's improvement through new medical treatment, concluded that the physicians' affidavits were enough to require a new evidentiary hearing before Judge Greer. At this hearing, the Schindlers were to present testimony by two physicians of the Schindlers' choosing; Michael was to present rebuttal testimony by two physicians of his own choosing; and the trial court was to appoint a fifth, independent, physician to examine Terri and testify about her condition.

Again, the Florida Supreme Court refused to intervene.

About those wheels of justice grinding slowly. . . . The new evidentiary hearing was delayed for a year. It finally took place over a ten-day period in October 2002.

Not surprisingly, the Schindlers' two physicians testified that Terri was not in PVS, while Michael's two physicians testified that she was. One of the Schindlers' physicians, Dr. William Hammesfahr, said that Terri could benefit from new "vasodilation" and "hyperbaric" therapies, but he never claimed that those therapies could restore Terri's cognitive functions, and he admitted that they could not replace dead brain tissue.

The deciding vote was cast by the court-appointed physician, Dr. Peter Bambakis, a clinical professor of neurology at Case Western Reserve University and a board-certified neurologist at the Cleveland

Clinic Foundation in Ohio. Dr. Bambakis said Terri was indeed in PVS. She would never improve.

Critical to the hearing were four hours of videotapes made in the summer of 2002, depicting medical examinations of Terri and visits by the Schindlers to her bedside. These videotapes became central to the Court of Appeal's decision when the case next went back up on appeal. And snippets from the videotapes later became a rallying point for the religious Right when the case became a national spectacle.

Three weeks after the hearing, the Schindlers renewed their nine-year-old suggestion from 1993 that Michael might have abused Terri. They filed a motion before Judge Greer asking for time to collect evidence of abuse, again seeking Michael's removal as Terri's guardian.

Once again, however, Judge Greer sided with Michael. The judge concluded that Terri remained in PVS and that the Schindlers had failed to present evidence of any medical treatment that offered a promise of improvement in Terri's cognitive functions such that she would wish to continue tube-feeding and undergo new treatment. On November 22, 2002, Judge Greer rescheduled the removal of Terri's PEG tube.

Yet again the Schindlers appealed. By then, a few new players had arrived on the scene, filing amicus curiae (friend of the court) briefs in support of the Schindlers. One was Rita L. Marker, the head of an antieuthanasia organization called the International Task Force on Euthanasia and Assisted Suicide. Another was a group of disability rights organizations headed by a disabled activist, Diane Coleman of Not Dead Yet. These friends of the court would be heard from further in the years to come.

And yet again the removal order was stayed—for another seven months, until the Court of Appeal issued its fourth written opinion in the case, on June 6, 2003.

This time, there seemed to be no hope left for the Schindlers. The Court of Appeal affirmed Judge Greer's removal order. And the appellate court was extremely careful, independently reviewing the testimony and the videotapes.

Normally, under rules of appellate procedure followed throughout the United States, appellate courts do not conduct what is variously called independent, or de novo, review of the factual evidence presented at a trial. The idea is that because trial judges and juries see and hear the witnesses firsthand, whereas appellate judges review only a written transcript of the trial, the former are better positioned to decide which witnesses are credible and which are not. As Judge Greer succinctly put it in his original 2000 opinion, as the trial judge he "had the opportunity to hear the witnesses, observe their demeanor, hear inflections, note pregnant pauses, and in all manners assess credibility above and beyond the spoken or typed word."

Thus, after facts are determined at a trial, an appellate court does not attempt to second-guess those factual determinations. Instead, the appellate court restricts the scope of its review to determining whether the evidence presented by the party who won—assuming the judge or jury believed that evidence—was sufficient to support the trial court's judgment. This is called review for substantial evidence. It is a basic rule of the appellate process, and there are few exceptions to it.

In posttrial proceedings—such as the Schindlers' motion for relief from the judgment based on newly discovered evidence—a similarly deferential standard of appellate review applies, called review for abuse of discretion. The trial judge is afforded considerable discretion in determining whether to grant such relief, and—once again—an appellate court normally does not second-guess the trial judge or otherwise attempt to redetermine the facts. Instead, the appellate court restricts the scope of its review to determining whether the trial court abused its discretion when ruling as it did. Reversal for abuse of discretion is as rare as reversal for insufficiency of the evidence.

The applicable standard of review on this latest appeal was the abuse of discretion standard, and the Court of Appeal quite easily concluded that Judge Greer had not abused his discretion. The appellate court was especially impressed by the wealth of evidence supporting

Judge Greer's ruling, concluding, "It is likely that no guardianship court has ever received as much high-quality medical evidence in such a proceeding." Plainly, from a strictly appellate perspective, the evidence was sufficient to establish that Judge Greer had not erred in denying the Schindlers' motion.

But the Court of Appeal went further. The court said: "Despite our decision that the appropriate standard of review is abuse of discretion, this court has closely examined all of the evidence in this record." In other words, the judges had conducted an independent review of the evidence after all. They watched the entire four hours of videotapes, studied Terri's brain scans, and pondered the physicians' testimony. The judges concluded that "if we were called upon to review the guardianship court's decision de novo, we would still affirm it."

The judges also made some highly personal comments of a sort rarely seen in appellate opinions: "Each of us, however, has our own family, our own loved ones, our own children. From our review of the videotapes of Mrs. Schiavo, despite the irrefutable evidence that her cerebral cortex has sustained the most severe of irreparable injuries, we understand why a parent who had raised and nurtured a child from conception would hold out hope that some level of cognitive function remained. If Mrs. Schiavo were our own daughter, we could not but hold to such a faith." But, the court said, "this case is not about the aspirations that loving parents have for their children. It is about Theresa Schiavo's right to make her own decision, independent of her parents and independent of her husband. . . . It is the trial judge's duty not to make the decision that the judge would make for himself or herself or for a loved one. Instead, the trial judge must make a decision that the clear and convincing evidence shows the ward would have made for herself."

Terri's decision, the judges concluded, would be to remove the PEG tube. Judge Greer's order was affirmed. The Court of Appeal ordered him to hold another hearing for the sole purpose of rescheduling the removal of ANH. Once more, the Florida Supreme Court refused to intervene. Judge Greer rescheduled the removal for a date a few weeks hence.

In their desperation, the Schindlers went to federal court. The previous litigation had taken place in the Florida state courts. Federal courts hear only cases that involve issues of federal law or disputes between residents of different states. Guardianship proceedings of this sort rarely invoke federal jurisdiction; they are nearly always heard in state courts.

The Schindlers filed a federal action on August 30, 2003, requesting an immediate stay of the scheduled tube removal. And now another new player arrived on the scene—Florida governor Jeb Bush. His lawyers filed a brief in the federal action supporting the Schindlers, suggesting that Terri might be able to ingest food and water on her own, without a feeding tube. The federal judge, however, quickly dismissed the action, ruling that there was no federal jurisdiction. Back the Schindlers went to the Florida Court of Appeal, asking the court to block Judge Greer's removal order. The court refused to do so.

By now, the Terri Schiavo case had gone before two judges of the Pinellas County Circuit Court; there had been nine applications to the state court of appeal, yielding four formal written opinions; on three occasions the Florida Supreme Court had refused to intervene; and on one occasion the U.S. Supreme Court had refused to do so. The case had been very heavily litigated—more so than any other right-to-die case in the history of the United States. The Schindlers had lost, and lost again, and lost yet again. Nearly two dozen judges had no doubt that Terri was in PVS and would not want artificial nutrition and hydration to be continued any longer.

On October 15, 2003—the feast day of St. Theresa of Avila—Terri's feeding tube was removed.

The Right to Die

Can it be legal for a doctor to remove a patient's feeding tube? The answer is yes. Just as there is a constitutional right to life, there is also a constitutional right to die.

It all started with Karen Ann Quinlan.

In 1976, at the age of twenty-two, Karen lay unconscious in a hospital bed in New Jersey. A year earlier, friends had called the police after she had stopped breathing for two extended periods of time. Rushed to the hospital, she was placed on a respirator—a machine that provides air to the lungs, completely taking over the spontaneous breathing function. She was also given ANH through a nasogastric feeding tube threaded through her nose into her stomach.

Karen was in PVS. The cause was anoxia—the same prolonged lack of oxygen to the brain that afflicted Terri Schiavo. It was never determined for certain why Karen had stopped breathing. Her physician had initially suspected a drug overdose, but that was never confirmed. There were traces of barbiturates, Valium, and Librium in her bloodstream, but they were within a normal range.

While Karen was on life support, her weight dropped from 115 to 75 pounds. Her extremities became rigid and deformed. She would occasionally blink her eyes, grimace, cry out, or make chewing motions, but she had no awareness of her surroundings. The doctors determined that she would never be restored to cognitive life.

Karen had previously told her mother, her sister, and a friend—contemporaneous with the terminal illnesses of several relatives and friends—that she would not want to be kept alive by "extraordinary means." After much soul-searching, Karen's parents asked her doctor to disconnect the respirator. He refused to do so. At the time, there was no legal precedent for it.

Karen's parents went to court, asking for judicial approval of their decision. They got it. In the first American "right-to-die" case, the New Jersey Supreme Court held there is a constitutional right to terminate medical treatment. The court based its ruling on the right of privacy guaranteed by the U.S. Constitution. This right is not explicitly mentioned in the Constitution, but the U.S. Supreme Court has recognized it as arising from the "penumbras" of specific guarantees in the Bill of Rights—which the court defines as "emanations from those guarantees that help give them life and substance."

Further, the New Jersey Supreme Court ruled that, because Karen was incompetent, "the only practical way to prevent destruction of" her right to terminate medical treatment was to permit her family to exercise that right on her behalf, making their "best judgment" as to what she would decide. The court commented that if the family's decision was to disconnect the respirator and let Karen die, "this decision should be accepted by a society the overwhelming majority of whose members would, we think, in similar circumstances, exercise such a choice in the same way for themselves or for those closest to them."

This was a unanimous decision by all seven of the court's justices, each of whom placed the exercise of the right to die within the mainstream of American culture.

The Quinlan case garnered widespread public interest. Because this first right-to-die case involved a machine—a respirator—it became common to refer to the withholding of life-sustaining medical treatment as "pulling the plug."

Ironically, however, Karen did not die when the plug was pulled. It was believed she would not last for long—the New Jersey Supreme Court had speculated that "removal from the respirator would cause her death soon, although the time cannot be stated with more precision." But she survived a long time indeed—nearly ten more years. She continued to breathe on her own, and her feeding tube was never removed. She died of pneumonia in 1985.

Fourteen years after the *Quinlan* decision, the U.S. Supreme Court weighed in on the right to die in *Cruzan v. Director, Missouri Department of Public Health*. The court recognized the right to die as a constitutional right but not as part of the right of privacy.

Twenty-five-year-old Nancy Cruzan was the victim of a car accident that left her anoxic for a number of minutes. By the time her breathing was restored, she had sustained permanent brain damage. She went from a coma to PVS, where she remained, kept alive by a feeding tube.

After many months, when it had become apparent that Nancy had no chance of improving, her parents asked hospital employees to terminate her ANH. As in *Quinlan*, they refused, and the parents had to go to court. Evidence at trial indicated that Nancy had previously told a roommate that if sick or injured she "would not wish to continue her life" unless she "could live at least halfway normally."

Years later, the case arrived in the U.S. Supreme Court on a narrow legal issue—whether Missouri could impose an elevated standard of proof for the judicial determination of Nancy's wishes. In civil cases, the usual standard of proof is "preponderance of the evidence," meaning more likely than not. Were that the standard in *Cruzan*, Nancy's parents would have had to prove only that Nancy more likely than not would want to have her feeding tube removed and be allowed to die. Sometimes, however, in special cases, civil courts require a higher standard of proof—"clear and convincing evidence"—which lies somewhere between preponderance of the evidence and proof "beyond a reasonable doubt," the standard applied in criminal cases. The Missouri Supreme Court had imposed the "clear and convincing evidence" standard and concluded that Nancy's comment to her roommate did not meet this standard.

In the 1990 *Cruzan* opinion, written by Chief Justice William Rehnquist, the U.S. Supreme Court held that the states may—but are not required to—require proof of end-of-life wishes by clear and convincing evidence. Thus, the Missouri Supreme Court had acted lawfully in holding Nancy's parents to that standard of proof.

The *Cruzan* opinion is more significant, however, for its recognition of a constitutional right to refuse medical treatment. Unlike the New Jersey Supreme Court in *Quinlan*, the U.S. Supreme Court in *Cruzan* placed the right to die not within the United States Constitution's right of privacy but within the Due Process Clause of the Fourteenth Amendment, which says that no state shall "deprive any person of life, liberty, or property, without due process of law." In other words, the right to refuse medical treatment is a constitutionally protected liberty interest. Justice Rehnquist called this the right of "bodily integrity"— that is, personal autonomy.

The case then returned to the trial court, where additional witnesses testified as to Nancy's prior statements regarding her end-of-life wishes, and the trial judge determined that the evidence now satisfied the "clear and convincing evidence" standard of proof.

Nancy's feeding tube was removed, and she died two weeks later. Her gravestone reads: "Born July 20, 1957. Departed Jan. 11, 1983. At peace Dec. 26, 1990."

Quinlan and *Cruzan* are perhaps the most widely known of the right-to-die cases, but there have been many others nationwide—more than fifty involving patients in PVS. One, *Superintendent of Belchertown State School v. Saikewicz*, arose in Massachusetts in 1977, just a year after *Quinlan*.

Joseph Saikewicz, a profoundly retarded sixty-seven-year-old man with an IQ of 10, had leukemia, for which chemotherapy would normally have been medically indicated. A court-appointed guardian recommended against the chemotherapy because of Joseph's inability to comprehend the treatment and because of the fear and pain he would have suffered.

The Supreme Judicial Court of Massachusetts held that incompetent persons such as Joseph Saikewicz have the same right as competent persons to decline potentially life-prolonging medical treatment. In deciding how that right is to be exercised on behalf of incompetent persons, the court traveled the same path as *Quinlan*. The decision is to be one of "substituted judgment," whereby a surrogate decision-maker—such as the parents in *Quinlan* or the court-appointed guardian in *Saikewicz*—would make his or her best judgment as to what the patient would decide if competent. The Massachusetts court concluded that Joseph himself, if he were competent, would decide against the chemotherapy.

Thus, in America's first two right-to-die cases—*Quinlan* and *Saikewicz*—the notion of substituted-judgment decision-making quickly became firmly established in the law.

In a prescient passage that seems a tailor-made rebuke to the political and religious meddlers in the *Schiavo* case, the Massachusetts high court observed that end-of-life questions "seem to us to require the process of detached but passionate investigation and decision that forms the ideal on which the judicial branch of government was created. Achieving this ideal is our responsibility and that of the lower court, and is not to be entrusted to any other group purporting to represent the 'morality and conscience of our society,' no matter how highly motivated and impressively constituted."

A controversial 1986 California case, *Bouvia v. Superior Court*, attracted the attention of disability rights activists fearing a path toward involuntary euthanasia of disabled persons. Elizabeth Bouvia was a quadriplegic who suffered from severe cerebral palsy. She was confined to a bed in a public hospital, completely immobile except for movement in a few fingers of one hand and some slight head and facial movements. She received morphine injections for severe arthritic pain. Her life was sustained by a nasogastric feeding tube. She wanted to die. But when she asked her physicians to remove the feeding tube, they refused. When she went to court, the trial judge likewise rebuffed her.

This case was different. Elizabeth Bouvia was nowhere near terminally ill, and she was entirely competent. Given enough proper care and attention, she might be able to make a satisfying life for herself.

The California Court of Appeal held that Bouvia, like anyone else—competent or otherwise—had a right to refuse medical treatment even though she was not terminally ill. And, the court said, the decision was uniquely hers: "It is not a medical decision for her physicians to make. Neither is it a legal question whose soundness is to be resolved by lawyers or judges. It is not a conditional right subject to approval by ethics committees or courts of law. It is a moral and philosophical decision that, being a competent adult, is hers alone." The court disclaimed the philosophy of preserving life at all costs: "We do not believe it is the policy of this state that all and every life must be preserved against the will of the sufferer."

The court ordered Bouvia's feeding tube removed. But again, as sometimes happens in these cases, there was an ironic postscript. Once the tube was removed, Bouvia changed her mind about dying and resumed normal eating.

Perhaps one of the reasons the *Bouvia* case was so controversial, and so infuriated some disability rights activists, was that the appellate court chastised the trial judge for failing to consider Bouvia's "quality of life." Those are provocative words. A life that one person would not consider worth living might be considered by another person to be very much worth living. The appellate court was on solid ground in stressing that the decision was Bouvia's alone, but less so in straying into the "quality of life" thicket, where subjective notions of "quality" are debatable.

Doctors and nurses, however, have rights, too. One of them is the right not to do something they find morally repugnant. In the 1988 case of *Conservatorship of Morrison*—where a hospital balked at removing a nasogastric feeding tube from a ninety-year-old patient in PVS—the California Court of Appeal held that "a physician has the right to refuse on personal moral grounds to follow a conservator's direction to withhold life-sustaining treatment, but must be willing to

transfer the patient to another physician who will follow the conservator's direction."

The *Morrison* case marked my first personal involvement in right-
to-die litigation. At that time I was a staff attorney for the authoring
judge, Justice Donald B. King. I helped him draft the opinion.

In 1993, the California Supreme Court addressed the right to die in
Thor v. Superior Court, where a prisoner serving a life sentence had
become quadriplegic as the result of a fall and refused to be fed. A
prison physician sued in an attempt to get a court order authorizing
forcible tube-feeding. The California Supreme Court confirmed the
prisoner's right to refuse medical treatment, holding that "under California law a competent, informed adult has a fundamental right of
self-determination to refuse or demand the withdrawal of medical
treatment of any form irrespective of the personal consequences."

The *Thor* opinion stressed "the long-standing importance in our
Anglo-American legal tradition of personal autonomy and the right
of self-determination." The court acknowledged that "the state's
paramount concern is the preservation of life," but admonished that
"the state has not embraced an unqualified or undifferentiated policy
of preserving life at the expense of personal autonomy. . . . [F]or self-
determination to have any meaning, it cannot be subject to the
scrutiny of anyone else's conscience or sensibilities. It is the individual
who must live or die with the course of treatment chosen or rejected,
not the state." And in balancing the interest in preserving life against
the right to refuse medical treatment, the latter "ordinarily outweighs
any countervailing state interest."

The justices seemed sensitive to the concerns of the disability rights
activists, making a point of explaining, "Clearly, many individuals
with profound disabilities courageously confront and overcome daunt-
ing physical challenges to lead productive and satisfying lives, reflect-
ing the vast potential and determination of the human spirit.
Nevertheless, this fact does not dictate a similar choice for others."

Thor is representative of right-to-die cases nationally, of which there have been many—for example, the 1990 case of *Guardianship of Browning*, where the Florida Supreme Court said that "an integral component of self determination is the right to make choices pertaining to one's health, including the right to refuse unwanted medical treatment." Echoing a theme that harks back to *Quinlan*, the *Browning* opinion stressed that "it is important for the surrogate decision-maker to fully appreciate that he or she makes the decision which the patient would personally choose."

These were the guiding legal principles in Florida when the *Schiavo* case came along.

But what if the patient is incompetent yet conscious? Take my cousin Ros, who in retrospect seems to me to have fallen a bit short of PVS. It wasn't just the eerie feeling I got when her eyes tracked me as I crossed her hospital room—PVS patients can sometimes seem to do that. What about the time I handed her that photograph and she took it from me? She did not seem to be entirely unaware of her surroundings, although she seemed not to comprehend them. I think Ros was in what doctors call a "minimally conscious state"—a condition of severely impaired consciousness and cognition, somewhere between PVS and normal consciousness. The courts have struggled with several such cases.

An especially difficult one was *In re Martin*, a 1995 Michigan case where thirty-seven-year-old Michael Martin had languished in a minimally conscious state, sustained on a gastronomy tube, for eleven years after suffering a severe head injury in a car accident. Michael had some ability to communicate and follow simple instructions. He could move his right arm and leg on command, and he sometimes responded to simple yes or no questions with appropriate motions of his head. Other times, however, he was completely unresponsive. His wife and children wanted the feeding tube removed, but his mother and sister opposed it. The dispute landed in the Michigan Supreme Court, which adopted the "clear and convincing evidence" standard of proof and found such proof to be absent in that case.

The problem for Michael Martin was that, although he had told two co-workers before the accident that he did not want to "live like a vegetable," the court concluded that he was not, strictly speaking, a "vegetable," since he had not been diagnosed as being in PVS. And the court went even further, requiring evidence of prior statements by Michael that foresaw his subsequent medical condition: "Only when the patient's prior statements clearly illustrate a serious, well thought out, consistent decision to refuse treatment under these exact circumstances, or circumstances highly similar to the current situation, should treatment be refused or withdrawn." Because Michael had not expressly anticipated the details of his minimally conscious condition, the court refused to authorize the withdrawal of ANH. The tube stayed in.

A single judge dissented, arguing that "when laypersons express a desire not to be a 'vegetable,' they usually are not referring strictly to a persistent vegetative state." Rather, the judge said, the "popular understanding" of a nonvegetative life involves a "spectrum" of basic human functions of independent living.

The majority opinion in *Martin* enunciated a theme that later became a rallying cry in the *Schiavo* case: "If we are to err, we must err in preserving life." But in the period between *Martin* and *Schiavo* came the fallout from Robert Wendland's truck accident.

Robert Wendland was a forty-two-year-old auto parts salesman with a wife, three children, and a drinking problem. On the night of September 29, 1993, he rolled his truck while driving drunk and sustained severe head injuries.

After languishing in a coma for sixteen months, sustained by a jejunostomy tube—a device similar to a PEG in which the feeding tube is threaded through the stomach and attached to the inside of the small intestine—Robert emerged into a state of minimal consciousness. He was paralyzed on his right side; he required a tracheostomy to breathe; he could not speak or swallow; and he was incontinent. But he definitely was not in PVS. Gradually, after a great deal of therapy, he progressed to a point where he could perform simple tasks with constant prompting. He could pick up designated objects with his left hand; sometimes he would catch a ball thrown to him; and he occasionally gave yes or no answers to simple questions by pressing buttons on a device designed for that purpose—although his answers were often inconsistent or wrong. He could operate an electric wheelchair in a rudimentary fashion. But he remained totally unresponsive to his wife and children.

On three occasions in early 1995, Robert pulled out his feeding tube. The third time this happened, his wife, Rose Wendland—who had been appointed his legal conservator—asked that ANH be withheld. The children, now ages sixteen, fourteen, and ten, concurred.

Rose came to this decision based on comments Robert had previously made in the presence of her, their children, and his brother during and after the death of Rose's father in the summer of 1993—a lingering death hastened by the removal of a respirator. When the respirator was removed, Robert told Rose, "I would never want to live like that, and I wouldn't want my children to see me like that, and look at the hurt you're going through as an adult seeing your father like that." Robert also said he thought Rose's father "wouldn't want to live like a vegetable." And just five days before Robert's accident, when his brother confronted him about his heavy drinking and expressed concern that "you're going to end up in the hospital like a vegetable," Robert replied, "If that ever happened to me, you know what my feelings are. Don't let that happen to me. Just let me go. Leave me alone." According to Robert's daughter Katie, who was also present, Robert added that "if he could not be a provider for his family, if he could not do all the things that he enjoyed doing, just enjoying the outdoors, just basic things, feeding himself, talking, communicating, if he could not do those things, he would not want to live."

Robert's attending physician and the hospital's ethics committee approved Rose's decision. But Robert's mother, Florence, strongly objected. Florence was convinced that Robert enjoyed her visits with him, and she believed it was God's will for him to remain alive. She later told *Time* magazine, "The Lord could have taken him the night of the accident, but he didn't." To this Rose countered, "The good Lord *did* take him. We're keeping him alive artificially."

Florence went to court to halt the withholding of ANH. The judge, Bob W. McNatt, was troubled. He acknowledged Robert's 1993 comments, and he expressed a "strong suspicion" that Robert would have wanted to die under his present circumstances. But Judge McNatt concluded that the evidence of Robert's wishes was not "clear and convincing." On this basis, Judge McNatt forbade the removal of Robert's feeding tube, calling the ruling the "absolutely wrong decision for all the right reasons" and wondering aloud "whether here today I am preserving Robert's life or if I am sentencing him to life."

The case went to the California Supreme Court on the issue of the applicable standard of proof for patients who, like Robert, are not in PVS but are minimally conscious. Rose's attorney, Lawrence Nelson, argued that the standard should be "preponderance of the evidence"; Florence's attorney, Janie Siess, argued that the standard should be "clear and convincing evidence."

The case attracted national attention, bringing out many of the same religious and cultural issues—and many of the same players—that were to emerge later in the *Schiavo* case. Rita Marker and another anti-euthanasia activist, Wesley J. Smith, each filed amicus curiae briefs, as did Not Dead Yet, the disability rights group headed by Diane Coleman.

And there seemed to be some very interesting funding behind Florence. According to an article in *People* magazine, an anti-abortion organization called Life Legal Defense Foundation had "spent more than $200,000 supporting Florence's lawsuit."

In January 1999, I received a telephone call from James M. Braden, a San Francisco attorney with whom I had previously worked on an antitrust appeal. Jim had been named as Robert's court-appointed appellate attorney, independent of Larry Nelson's representation of Rose and Janie Siess's representation of Florence. Jim wanted my help with some thorny issues of appellate procedure—my specialty.

When Jim described the case, I became far more interested than in just chatting about the procedural issues. This case was my cousin Ros redux. I made an open-ended offer of my services on a pro bono basis. Eventually, Jim and Larry seized on the idea of my representing some bioethicists and filing an amicus curiae brief on their behalf, explaining the bioethical underpinnings of the right to die. With the help of local bioethicist Susan Rubin, we assembled a group of forty-three renowned bioethicists from across the nation. Six major health-care organizations joined the bioethicists. When the case hit the California Supreme Court, I wrote and filed their amicus curiae brief.

I also wanted to see Robert Wendland—up close and personal. Jim and I visited him, along with his wife, Rose, on May 20, 2001.

When we entered Robert's room, he was lying on his back in bed, eyes half-closed, his right arm and leg contorted and constricted. Jim took Robert's left hand and tried to introduce himself, but Robert just stared upward, not reacting. I then approached Robert and called his name several times. He never changed his gaze. I took his hand; again, no hint of a response. Then he abruptly pulled his hand away. When I tried to take it again, he took a swipe at me—his first reaction to any of us. Rose then warned me to be careful because Robert had recently bitten an attendant.

We spent about an hour in Robert's room conversing with Rose, mostly about her children and the legal issues in the case. Robert's gaze never changed, even when Jim turned off the blaring television. Robert frequently picked at his upper lip and nose. Every few minutes he made noises that sounded like he was choking on his saliva. Sometimes his tongue lolled out and he seemed to be in some discomfort. Only once or twice did he show any notable facial expression—during a particularly nasty bout of choking, when he looked scared.

Back at my office two days later, I wrote the following note for my *Wendland* file: "Upon two days' reflection, I think of Robert Wendland as a blank canvas. People fill in the blank space with what they need or want to see. Rose needs to see the empty shell of a lost husband of whom she can let go. Florence wants to see some remnant of a son whom she can hold on to. The right-to-lifers want a poster boy to further their agenda. The disability rights people see danger ahead. I just saw the blank canvas. Not being, but nothingness."

I visited Robert twice more that summer. Both times were like the first.

On July 17, 2001, while the case was still pending in the California Supreme Court, Robert died of pneumonia. The court chose to issue an opinion anyway. Three weeks after Robert's death, the justices decided unanimously that the "clear and convincing evidence" standard should apply and that Judge McNatt was right in concluding that this standard was not met, because Robert's 1993 comments "did not describe the precise condition in which he later found himself." Thus, if Robert had not died, the court would have ordered him kept alive.

But the court made its ruling very narrow, saying that "our decision today affects only a narrow class of persons: conscious conservatees who have not left formal directions for health care and whose conservators propose to withhold life-sustaining treatment for the purpose of causing their conservatees' deaths." The court said its ruling would not apply to "permanently unconscious patients, including those who are comatose or in a persistent vegetative state," or "persons who have left legally cognizable instructions for health care," or "persons who have designated agents or other surrogates for health care," or "conservatees for whom conservators have made medical decisions other than those intended to bring about the death of a conscious conservatee." In each of those latter situations—including PVS patients and minimally conscious patients who have named a surrogate without giving formal instructions—the "preponderance of the evidence" standard applies in California.

Some of my bioethicist clients were distressed by the *Wendland* ruling, worried that it requires a degree of proof that can rarely be met in the "real world"—where people at best speak in common, everyday language about their end-of-life wishes, not in legalese or medical terminology. One of the bioethicists wrote to me, "The decision is a disaster for those of us taking care of 'real' patients who generally do not utter meticulously crafted 'clear and convincing' instructions as to their preferences under all possible end-of-life circumstances." Others wondered about how doctors should now proceed in the relatively common situations where a PVS patient has no advance written directive, surrogate, or conservator—situations for which the *Wendland* opinion gives little guidance. A few expressed relief that the court had at least prescribed the usual civil standard of proof for most right-to-die cases, where the patient is in PVS or comatose.

Of special interest to me is how the California Supreme Court responded to the "err on the side of life" mantra that Siess and her supporters had taken up—a theme later sounded in the *Schiavo* case. The court said that "the decision to treat is reversible. The decision to withdraw treatment is not. The role of a high evidentiary standard in such a case is to adjust the risk of error to favor the less perilous result." Simply put, the court was saying that the risk of error is avoided by imposing the higher standard of proof—meaning there is no need to err on the side of life, or in any other way, if the standard of proof is rigorous enough. That's a compelling answer to the "err on the side of life" mantra.

Wendland was the last of the highly publicized right-to-die cases prior to *Schiavo*, by which time the right to die had become firmly established in case law nationwide—whether rooted in the Fourteenth Amendment to the U.S. Constitution, as in *Cruzan*, or in state constitutional rights of privacy (as in the California and Florida cases), or in the common-law tradition guaranteeing personal autonomy.

Over the past thirty years, most states have enacted legislation governing the exercise of the right to die. For example, California's Probate Code provides that "a person may direct that life-sustaining treatment be withheld or withdrawn under conditions specified by the person and not limited to terminal illness, permanent coma, or persistent vegetative state." This includes withholding or withdrawing ANH, and it includes persons in a minimally conscious state. You can use an advance written directive to give an "agent" the power to make health-care decisions for you or you can orally designate a "surrogate" to do so. The agent or surrogate must make decisions in accordance with your "wishes to the extent known" or otherwise in accordance with your "best interest."

The Florida statutes contain similar provisions, along with explicit guarantees that "every competent adult has the fundamental right of self-determination regarding decisions pertaining to his or her own health, including the right to choose or refuse medical treatment," and that an incompetent person has the same right to refuse medical treatment as a competent person.

In Texas, a 1999 law—signed by then-governor George W. Bush—allows advance directives to require the withholding or removal of life-sustaining treatment, including ANH, in the event of incompetency caused by an irreversible condition. The law also allows a surrogate to make that decision for an incompetent patient who has not given an advance directive. Thus President Bush's own Texas law would have treated Terri Schiavo precisely the same as she was treated by Florida law.

The Uniform Health-Care Decisions Act—legislation that has been adopted in many states—provides that "a surrogate shall make a health-care decision in accordance with the patient's individual instructions, if any, and other wishes to the extent known to the surrogate. Otherwise, the surrogate shall make the decision in accordance with the surrogate's determination of the patient's best interest."

Finally, most states that have addressed the burden of proof issue have, unlike California, adopted the "clear and convincing evidence" standard for determining all patients' end-of-life wishes. That is the standard in Florida, and it is the one that was applied in the *Schiavo* case.

Thus, over a thirty-year period, courts across the country—from the New Jersey Supreme Court in *Quinlan*, to the Supreme Judicial Court of Massachusetts in *Saikewicz*, to the Florida Supreme Court in *Browning*, to the California Supreme Court in *Thor*, and even the U.S. Supreme Court in *Cruzan*—have firmly established the legal right of all Americans and their surrogates to refuse medical treatment. It has become entirely legal to pull the plug on comatose, PVS, minimally conscious, and wholly competent patients—if that's what a competent patient wants or what a surrogate decides an incompetent patient would want. Autonomy is the law of the land.

But is it ethical?

The Bioethicists

The right to die isn't just legal; it is also firmly established within an ethical framework developed by doctors, nurses, philosophers, and theologians for resolving ethical problems that arise in the practice of medicine—a discipline called bioethics.

Bioethical issues run the gamut: embryonic stem cell research, cloning, euthanasia, reproductive rights, treatment of severely disabled infants, equal access to health care, medical research on humans and animals, and future problems we cannot even anticipate. Some of these issues are perplexing and controversial, rarely garnering unanimous agreement among those who study them. Often the goal of bioethicists is to achieve not unanimity but consensus—that is, wide acceptance.

Perhaps the most common issue that medical practitioners encounter is whether to forgo or discontinue life-sustaining treatment. Each year, feeding tubes are inserted into tens of thousands of patients in American health-care facilities, and the tubes are subsequently removed with considerable regularity. A study of end-of-life care in a Detroit hospital revealed that 20 percent of patients placed on ANH eventually chose to have their feeding tubes removed. The removal rate for respirators is even higher—the Detroit study had it at 65 percent.

As we will see, on this issue the bioethicists have achieved a degree of consensus approaching unanimity. Yet many doctors still fear legal consequences. One survey of 295 physicians indicated that 96 percent worried or even modified their practice because of fear of lawsuits arising from their treatment of terminally ill patients, and 45 percent said they might refuse a family member's request to comply with a formerly competent patient's stated preferences to have life-sustaining treatment withdrawn, in large part for fear of being sued.

Bioethicists have identified, for the guidance of health-care practitioners confronting bioethical issues, four central values of equal importance—beneficence, professional integrity, justice, and personal autonomy.

Beneficence means promoting a patient's well-being. The goal of medicine, pure and simple, is to help people.

Professional integrity means balancing the rights of patients against the personal moral and religious beliefs of the health-care providers. It is generally accepted that no doctors or nurses should have to do something they find morally repugnant—which is why the California Court of Appeal in *Conservatorship of Morrison* said the doctors in that case could not be forced to remove the conservatee's feeding tube. But a physician who refuses as a matter of conscience to follow a patient's or surrogate's instructions must be willing to transfer the patient to the care of a physician who will.

Justice means giving everyone reasonable access to health care while at the same time ensuring that when medical resources are limited in availability they are fairly distributed. This value can sometimes place limits on a patient's or surrogate's freedom to demand treatment that might be ineffective or prohibitively expensive.

Personal autonomy is where bioethics intersects with the law. Just as the right of personal autonomy—control over one's own body—is firmly embedded in American constitutional law, case law, and statutory law, it is also a tradition of medical practice and ethics. It gives you the right *not* to have medical care, if that is your choice. The value of autonomy puts the patient in control of health-care decision-making.

Thus, for example, if you are diagnosed with a dangerous and aggressive cancer, you cannot be forced to undergo chemotherapy. If you want to decline the treatment because you fear that the limited time it might extend your life would not justify the degree of pain you might suffer, that is your choice. Even if a course of treatment can only help you and has little or no objective downside—say, a blood transfusion or a simple but life-saving surgery such as an appendectomy—you can choose to forgo it, and the doctors can't force you. Jehovah's Witnesses can refuse a blood transfusion based on their belief it is prohibited by the injunction in Leviticus 17:14 that "ye shall eat the blood of no manner of flesh," and Christian Scientists can refuse an appendectomy based on their belief in spiritual healing through prayer, even if it means certain death.

If, like Terri Schiavo, you lack decision-making capacity, the bioethical value of autonomy gives an appropriate surrogate the right to make health-care decisions on your behalf. The bioethicists have developed three models for surrogate exercise of an incompetent patient's right of personal autonomy: advance directive, substituted judgment, and best interests. The guiding principle is that the surrogate should choose as the patient would choose if he or she were able. These guidelines are not restricted to patients in a coma or PVS but apply to anyone who is cognitively impaired, including the minimally conscious.

The "advance directive" model applies to patients who have previously given an advance directive describing their preferences. The advance directive can be written or oral. If it addresses the situation presented—for example, if a patient wrote that under no circumstances should he or she be put on a respirator—the surrogate must follow that instruction.

The "substituted-judgment" model is invoked where there is no advance directive, but the patient has otherwise made known his or her preferences or values—for example, in prior conversations with relatives or friends. This model focuses on the patient's subjective wishes—what he or she, rather than someone else in particular or an average person generally, would want. This is the same notion of substituted-judgment decision-making that was legally pioneered in the *Quinlan* case. The decision-makers rely on their knowledge of the patient's lifestyle, values, and prior comments about end-of-life wishes—the way I relied on what I knew of my cousin Ros's life and what she had said to me about the *Quinlan* and *Cruzan* cases—to try to choose as the patient would have wanted.

The "best interests" model is the last resort. It applies in only two situations: when nothing is known about a formerly competent patient's preferences or values (for example, he or she said nothing to friends and relatives about end-of-life wishes) and when the patient has never been competent (for example, the patient has always been profoundly retarded, like Joseph Saikewicz). This is an objective standard. In these situations, the surrogate must decide as a reasonable person would decide in the patient's best interests, selecting within a range of choices that the average person would make.

In short, it is entirely ethical for health-care professionals to withhold life-sustaining medical treatment—including a feeding tube—at the direction of a patient or the patient's surrogate. And these four bioethical models have become the law. They are codified by legislation in many states, including California and Florida.

The *Schiavo* case implicated the "substituted-judgment" model for surrogate decision-making. Terri Schiavo had given no advance directive, written or oral. Her husband, Michael, had to make health-care decisions for her, guided by his knowledge of her preferences and values.

If a patient has never designated a surrogate, who should the surrogate be? The bioethical preference is for a close relative or friend. Family members, especially, will usually have the most knowledge about the patient's preferences and values.

Bioethicists have constructed a hierarchy of preferred surrogates. At the top of the list is the patient's spouse; at the bottom are professional "public" guardians and conservators employed by the state for that purpose. In between are adult children, parents, adult siblings, other close relatives, and close friends—usually in that order. The law generally follows the lead of bioethicists in this regard. For example,

Florida statutes adopt this hierarchy, which made Michael Schiavo his wife's preferred surrogate. So does the Texas law signed by then-governor George W. Bush.

The law of Florida is unusual in that it allows a patient's surrogate to refer a health-care decision to the county circuit court, which then becomes the surrogate. In Michael's role as Terri's court-appointed guardian, he served as her surrogate for eight years, until May 1998, when he filed a petition in Pinellas County Circuit Court asking the court to make the decision whether to remove Terri's feeding tube. At that point, Judge Greer became Terri's surrogate. It was his job to determine what Terri would want.

A problem with this tidy framework of three bioethical models for surrogate decision-making is that most people don't execute written advance directives. Young adults rarely dwell on preparing for sickness and death. Many people of all ages fear talking or even thinking about death and dying. Those of modest financial means can ill afford a lawyer to help with the paperwork and may not know how easy it is to get their hands on a ready-made form to fill out as an advance directive. Some religious and cultural traditions in our diverse society shun anything having to do with death or dying, while others place a high value on sustaining life at virtually any cost.

The numbers are hard to guess at, but studies suggest that no more than 10 to 20 percent of Americans give advance directives, written or oral. And even where there are written directives, they often are not made available to health-care providers, languishing in a secure but forgotten place outside the patient's medical record. Some advance directives might be too general or uncertain or say nothing about the specific issue presented—as with my cousin Ros, whose advance directive said little other than naming me as her surrogate. The "advance directive" bioethical model is not often invoked.

Equally uncommon are last-resort "best interests" decisions under the third bioethical model. Usually something is known about a patient's preferences and values—if not evidence of prior conversations about end-of-life wishes, then at least some knowledge of the type of life the patient chose to live when competent. The study of end-of-life care in a Detroit hospital showed that a best interests decision was required for only 18 percent of incompetent patients.

Thus, most surrogate decision-making happens under the "substituted-judgment" bioethical model—as happened in the *Schiavo* case.

Terri Schiavo's comments to Michael, Scott, and Joan Schiavo about her end-of-life wishes were enough for Judge Greer to conclude on clear and convincing evidence that Terri would have wanted her feeding tube removed. She had spoken in a manner typical of how most of us speak about the prospect of having our lives sustained by respirators, feeding tubes, and the like—in plain, everyday language. Those who abhor the notion might say, "I wouldn't want to live like a vegetable," "I don't want to be kept alive by machines and tubes," "I want to die with dignity." Those who would want such measures to be taken might say, "Life is precious," "People shouldn't play God," "Do everything possible." In either case, the preference, when expressed, is usually stated in what lawyers and doctors call lay terms—not in legalese or medical terminology.

Paradoxically, Robert Wendland had said pretty much the same things as Terri Schiavo, in very similar language, yet the California courts said that his statements did not rise to the level of clear and convincing evidence. It is difficult to reconcile the *Wendland* and *Schiavo* cases in this regard. Sometimes judges just see things differently among themselves.

One of the more prominent recent issues arising from substituted-judgment decision-making has been the withdrawal of feeding tubes from PVS and minimally conscious patients. The diagnosis of PVS was not defined until the early 1980s, and it was standardized only in 1994. The diagnosis of minimally conscious state, or MCS, was not widely recognized until quite recently. Nobody knows exactly how many PVS patients there are in the United States at any given time; estimates range from ten thousand to thirty thousand. The numbers for MCS patients are anybody's guess. But all PVS and MCS patients require artificial nutrition and hydration.

Throughout the 1980s, bioethicists debated questions regarding the withholding or withdrawing of feeding tubes. Ultimately, a strong consensus emerged: ANH is a life-sustaining medical treatment like any other, and as such it may be refused by a patient or a surrogate. Withholding or withdrawing ANH is not euthanasia—the direct and deliberate killing of a patient. Nor is it physician-assisted suicide—a patient's voluntary ending of his or her life with the assistance of a doctor, usually by taking a fatal drug. The difference is that euthanasia and physician-assisted suicide require the active intervention of someone other than the patient, while forgoing life-sustaining treatment is passive: the doctors simply omit to take action that would extend the life of the patient, allowing death to occur naturally. And bioethicists make no distinction between withholding treatment in the first place and withdrawing treatment that was previously initiated. Morally and ethically, they are the same.

The law once again has taken its lead from bioethicists. Many states now define medical treatment, for purposes of exercising the right to refuse it, as including ANH, and they treat withholding and withdrawing the same. For example, the California statutes define a "health care decision" as including "directions to provide, withhold, or withdraw artificial nutrition and hydration."

That makes sense. We are not talking about normal consumption of food and water here. ANH is an invasive procedure—sometimes requiring surgery, as in the case of a PEG or jejunostomy tube—that enables the delivery of a vitamin-enriched and often medication-laden formula directly into the stomach or small intestine. It can have nasty side effects, such as infection and aspiration pneumonia. For those who are capable of feeling it, it can be physically uncomfortable. That is undoubtedly why my cousin Ros and Robert Wendland pulled out their feeding tubes. Some patients on ANH require physical restraints to keep them from pulling their tubes out.

ANH is a product of modern medicine, but it is a mixed blessing. According to bioethicists, sometimes it is best done without.

How is a substituted-judgment decision made? Not without help. There are various safeguards in place within the health-care professions to ensure against an unethical decision. Chief among them is the hospital ethics committee.

Since 1992, the Joint Commission on Accreditation of Health Care Organizations—the national entity that gives accreditation to American hospitals—has required all health-care facilities to establish formal procedures for promulgating ethics policies and deciding specific ethical issues. This usually means creating an ethics committee by drawing members from various disciplines. Committee members commonly include doctors, nurses, social workers, hospital administrators, lawyers who specialize in health-care issues, and clergy.

Doctors and nurses who face an ethical question in the course of their hospital practice can seek guidance from the hospital's ethics committee—as did my cousin Ros's doctor when the nurses expressed discomfort with the decision to remove her nasogastric tube, and as in the *Wendland* case, where a twenty-member ethics committee reviewed and approved Rose Wendland's decision to remove her husband's jejunostomy tube. With such close review, the ethics committee ensures that bioethical guidelines are followed.

Another ethical safeguard is the patient ombudsman—a disinterested advocate for patients in nursing homes and assisted-living facilities. California, for example, has legislation requiring a local ombudsman to review a decision to withdraw life-sustaining treatment and, if appropriate, refer the decision to other government agencies for further review. That happened in the *Wendland* case, where the local ombudsman joined the hospital ethics committee in approving Rose's decision.

Finally, an inherent safeguard in any substituted-judgment decision to withhold life-sustaining treatment is the attending physician's overarching ethical duty. An ethics opinion of the American Medical Association states that a physician must not accept a surrogate's decision to forgo treatment if the physician believes that the decision is "clearly not what the patient would have decided if competent" or is "not a decision that could reasonably be judged to be in the patient's best interests."

Just who are these so-called bioethicists anyway?

Some are scholars—for example, James Walter, professor and chair of the Bioethics Institute at Loyola Marymount University in Los Angeles. Professor Walter has advanced degrees in theology, philosophy, religious studies, and Christian ethics. In addition to teaching at Loyola Marymount, he has served extensively as a bioethics consultant to several hospitals. He publishes prolifically on bioethical issues—whole books, chapters in books, and articles in professional journals.

Some are medical practitioners—for example, registered nurse Sally Nunn, a member of the faculty at the University of Pennsylvania Center for Bioethics. Ms. Nunn cofounded and for years chaired the ethics committee at a New Jersey hospital, where she was also director of bioethics. She, like Dr. Walter, has also served extensively as a bioethics consultant. She also organizes major bioethics conferences.

Some are clergy—for example, Father Kevin O'Rourke, a Dominican priest at the Neiswanger Institute for Bioethics and Health Policy, which is part of the Strich School of Medicine at Loyola University in Chicago. Father O'Rourke headed the bioethics program at St. Louis University Medical Center for twenty-one years. He also served on the Vatican Council for Health Care Workers for ten years. He has advanced degrees in canon law and theology, and publishes extensively on health-care ethics, including two popular textbooks. Father O'Rourke ministered to the family of Nancy Cruzan, guiding them through the decision to remove her life support.

And some are full-time private consultants—for example, Dr. Susan Rubin of the Ethics Practice in Berkeley, California. Dr. Rubin has advanced degrees in philosophy and bioethics from Georgetown University's Kennedy Institute of Ethics. She advises community hospitals and long-term residential facilities, helping them set up ethics committees, providing bioethics advice on specific cases, and assisting in education, training, and community outreach. She also publishes widely on bioethics issues—books, book chapters, and journal articles.

Each of these bioethicists, and hundreds like them in hospitals throughout the United States, help to safeguard the fundamental value of personal autonomy that lies at the heart of American law and culture.

Autonomy, though cherished by Americans, is not a universally held value. Its opposite is paternalism—the notion that doctors, or your family, or clergy, or even politicians, know what's best for you and should control your medical care. Paternalism is disfavored in America, but in many other countries it still holds sway.

In Japan, for example, where one's family and social group are considered more important than the individual, patients are expected to place their trust entirely in their physicians and family, letting them make health-care decisions on the patient's behalf. Death and dying are taboo subjects and are not often openly discussed. Many physicians oppose the very idea of advance directives, which are rare. In fact, physicians usually won't even tell patients that they have a fatal disease but will tell only family members. Thus patients often lack the information they would need to exercise personal autonomy even if they wanted to do so. This state of affairs is changing—recent polls have shown that the majority of Japanese would prefer to be told if they have a life-threatening condition—but the change is slow in coming.

Europe is a somewhat different story. Autonomy is not yet transcendent, as it is in America, and advance directives remain uncommon, but paternalism is nevertheless on the wane. For example, recent legislation in France, passed in response to the case of a young man who had asked to be allowed to die after a car accident left him paraplegic and blind, allows the withholding or withdrawal of medical treatments that are "useless" or "disproportionate" or "serve no other purpose than the artificial support of life." The French law includes feeding tubes within the types of medical treatment that can be withheld or withdrawn. Spain, in contrast, forbids a surrogate from withholding or withdrawing ANH unless the patient authorized it in a written advance directive. At the other end of the spectrum, the Netherlands permits physician-assisted suicide, which takes personal autonomy to its extreme.

In the world's poor countries, however, the right to die just isn't much of an issue, because only the wealthy few can afford the expense of sustaining a relative in a health-care facility for an extended period of time. Even in places such as India, where the law technically forbids physicians from denying a patient any life-sustaining treatment, as a practical matter the patient dies when the money runs out.

The right of personal autonomy is a luxury we Americans are fortunate to have.

5

The Word of God

I was surprised when two groups of Catholic health-care providers, the Alliance of Catholic Health Care and Catholic Healthcare West, signed onto my amicus curiae brief in the *Wendland* case. The Alliance's members operate some one hundred hospitals and residential health-care facilities, and Catholic Healthcare West operates some fifty hospitals—all Catholic institutions. Why would these people support the removal of Robert Wendland's feeding tube? In my ignorance, I had assumed that the Catholic Church would oppose any removal of ANH, much like it opposes abortion.

How wrong I was.

On December 1, 2000, while the *Wendland* litigation was still pending in the California Supreme Court, the Most Reverend Stephen E. Blaire, bishop of the Diocese of Stockton (the Wendlands were Catholic) issued a short public statement about the case, saying something I didn't quite understand at the time: "The moral question regarding the withdrawal of artificial hydration and nutrition is complicated. The church has a presumption in favor of maintaining such care if it does not entail an excessive burden or is not considered extraordinary care."

"What," I wondered, "does that mean?" It sounded like the church's "presumption" in favor of ANH could be overcome by showing that ANH would be an "excessive burden" or "extraordinary care." Was that the case with Robert Wendland? Is that why I had two major Catholic health-care groups on my brief?

Bishop Blaire's statement also addressed the legal issue then pending before the California Supreme Court—whether the standard of proof for determining Robert's wishes should be "clear and convincing evidence" or "preponderance of the evidence." The statement said, "The 'clear and convincing' legal standard pertaining to surrogate decisions regarding end-of-life issues may be rigorous beyond the Church's teaching."

Did this mean the Catholic Church would support the removal of Robert's feeding tube upon proof of his wishes by a preponderance of the evidence? It certainly seemed so.

I was a bit taken aback. So were the forces behind Florence Wendland. It turned out they had asked California's Catholic bishops to file an amicus curiae brief supporting Florence and had been rebuffed. They became livid when they learned that I had succeeded where they had failed, and that the Catholic hospitals were with me, not them.

On June 7, 2001, shortly before Robert died, Bishop Blair issued another statement, in which he further explained the church's teachings: "The Catholic Church teaches that the presumption must be in favor of life. Included in that is a presumption in favor of nutrition and hydration. Life is good, a precious gift from God, but not an absolute or ultimate good. Life is sacred and must be respected, but does not have to be preserved or prolonged at all costs. . . . The 1980 'Declaration on Euthanasia' from the Vatican's Congregation for the Doctrine of the Faith teaches that medical treatment can be withheld or withdrawn (after all proper consultations) if this treatment is of no benefit to the patient, carries a risk or is burdensome."

The forces behind Florence struck back. Catherine Short, the legal director of Life Legal Defense Foundation—which was reported to have funded Florence Wendland's lawsuit to the tune of more than $200,000—publicly condemned Bishop Blair's second statement as a "half-hearted apologia for the involvement of Catholic hospitals in the effort to starve Robert Wendland to death." She charged the Catholic hospitals with "using the current drift of our laws toward euthanasia as the starting point for further erosion of the sanctity of life ethic."

What was going on here? Plainly I had a lot to learn.

The *Wendland* case exposed a rift in the Catholic Church—a rift that had widened to a gulf by the time the *Schiavo* case heated up. The rift is between traditional Catholic teachings going back more than four hundred years and a revisionist stance that now seems on the verge of prevailing.

In 1557, a posthumous publication by Spanish Dominican theologian Francisco di Vittoria set the stage for four centuries of Catholic philosophizing on the moral obligation to use food to preserve life. Vittoria reasoned, "If a sick man can take food or nourishment with a certain hope of life, he is required to take food as he would be required to give it to one who is sick. However, if the depression of spirits is so severe and there is present grave consternation in the appetitive power so that only with greatest effort and as though through torture can the sick man take food, this is to be reckoned as an impossibility and therefore, he is excused, at least from mortal sin." In today's language, this means it is not a sin to stop eating if one is so sick and depressed that it has become an excessive burden.

Vittoria also addressed the question of whether there is a moral obligation to adopt a special diet to prolong life. His context was eggs versus chickens and partridges. In his time it was common to eat the former but not the latter. He concluded, "Chickens and partridges, even if ordered by the doctor, need not be chosen over eggs and other common items, even if the individual knew for certain that he could live another twenty years by eating such special foods."

If there was no moral obligation in sixteenth-century Spain to eat "special foods" such as chickens and partridges to prolong life, how can there be a moral obligation in America today to take "artificial" nutrition and hydration in order to prolong life? Isn't a vitamin-enriched and medication-laden liquid formula delivered by a feeding tube directly into the stomach or small intestine a "special food" like Vittoria's chickens and partridges?

Building on Vittoria's musings, in 1595 another Dominican moralist, Domingo Bañez, proposed a distinction between "extraordinary" and "ordinary" means of preserving life, with only the latter being a moral obligation. Bañez's measure for determining whether treatment is extraordinary or ordinary is the proportion to which the treatment benefits the patient compared to the burden imposed.

Vittoria and Bañez dominated Catholic moralist thinking all the way through to the 1950s, when Jesuit Gerald Kelly and Archbishop Daniel A. Cronin summarized the Catholic tradition in writings that restated the extraordinary-ordinary distinction as a disproportionate-proportionate dichotomy, the outcome of which depends on a comparison of benefits and burdens. By this time, medical advances had muddled the distinction between extraordinary and ordinary treatment, because "extraordinary" measures such as kidney dialysis and artificial respiration had become routine. It therefore has become necessary to distinguish between what is *medically* ordinary and what is *morally* ordinary. The decision whether to use a measure to prolong life must be informed by a determination of whether the measure is morally ordinary or extraordinary, by using Bañez's balancing test— the comparison of benefits and burdens.

Thus, Kelly opined in 1950, "apart from very special circumstances," respirators and feeding tubes "not only need not but should not be used" when a terminal coma is diagnosed, because "their use creates expense and nervous strain without conferring any real benefit." And in the case of a terminally ill cancer patient on ANH and in severe pain, "the relatives and physicians may reasonably presume that he does not wish the intravenous feeding" and may discontinue it.

Cronin summarized the Catholic tradition in a 1958 dissertation: "Even natural means, such as taking of food and drink, can become optional if taking them requires great effort or if the hope of beneficial results (*spes salutis*) is not present." If a patient's condition is irreversible, medically ordinary means are to be treated as morally extraordinary and may be dispensed with if that is the choice of the patient or a surrogate. As Cronin said, "The wishes of the patient, expressed or reasonably interpreted, must be obeyed."

This became official church doctrine in 1980, in the Declaration on Euthanasia by the church's Congregation for the Doctrine of the Faith—the overseer of Catholic doctrine on matters of faith and morals—which was headed by Joseph Ratzinger, the current Pope Benedict XVI, from 1981 until he became pope. The 1980 declaration adopted the benefits-burdens test of proportionality, stating that a patient may choose to forgo treatments that "impose on the patient strain or suffering out of proportion with the benefits which he or she may gain from such techniques" or that impose "excessive expense on the family or the community." The declaration explained that the traditional extraordinary-ordinary dichotomy "is perhaps less clear today" because of medical advances, and so "some people prefer to speak of 'proportionate' and 'disproportionate' means. In any case, it will be possible to make a correct judgment as to the means by studying the type of treatment to be used, its degree of complexity or risk, its cost and the possibilities of using it, and comparing these elements with the result that can be expected, taking into account the state of the sick person and his or her physical and moral resources." This is what Bishop Blaire meant when he said, with regard to Robert Wendland, that medical treatment could be withdrawn if it imposed an excessive burden.

Thus, by 1980, the benefits-burdens test of proportionality and the distinction between morally (not medically) extraordinary and ordinary treatment had become fully recognized as official church doctrine. Under this approach, ANH can be refused as disproportionate and morally extraordinary if its burdens outweigh its benefits. And the refusal can be by proxy—that is, by surrogate decision-makers who are guided by their knowledge of the patient's preferences and values.

But this is not quite the same as the legal and bioethical approach, which places an overarching value on personal autonomy. The Catholic tradition forbids a proxy from doing anything that crosses the line

into conduct that the church considers immoral—like euthanasia—
even if the patient clearly would have wanted it. As Catholic bioethicist Father Kevin O'Rourke has put it, "The Church's teaching on
proxy consent differs from the statements (although not always the
practice) of some courts and certainly differs from the thought of many
contemporary ethicists who use the person's autonomy as the absolute
criterion for proxy decision-making." For the Catholic Church, autonomy is not king.

How has this Catholic tradition manifested itself in hospital practice?
    There are many Catholic hospitals in America. Approximately six
hundred are members of the Catholic Health Association of the
United States. They are guided by the "Ethical and Religious Directives for Catholic Health Care Services"—commonly called the
ERDs—published by the U.S. Conference of Catholic Bishops. Part 5
of the ERDs addresses "Issues in Care for the Dying." Its introduction
states, "We have a duty to preserve our life and to use it for the glory of
God, but the duty to preserve life is not absolute, for we may reject
life-prolonging procedures that are insufficiently beneficial or excessively burdensome." ERD 58 states, "There should be a presumption in
favor of providing nutrition and hydration to all patients, including
patients who require medically assisted nutrition and hydration, as
long as this is of sufficient benefit to outweigh the burdens involved to
the patient."
    Thus America's Catholic hospitals have embraced the Catholic
tradition, allowing the withholding or removal of ANH under the
benefits-burdens test of proportionality.
    There are, however, Catholic dissenters to this tradition. Through-
out the 1980s, following the 1980 Declaration on Euthanasia, some
Catholic theologians insisted that nutrition and hydration, even if artificial, should always be obligatory. These are the deontologists—ad-
herents of a theory of ethics called deontology, which holds that moral
principles are absolute and must be obeyed without regard to individual circumstances. Deontic, from the Greek word for "obligation,"

means "duty"—here, the duty to obey the absolute principle that ANH is always morally required.

This explains the antiabortionists' backlash against Bishop Blaire in the *Wendland* case. They are part of a revisionist movement within the Catholic Church to repudiate the traditional benefits-burdens proportionality test in favor of a deontic ethic of preserving life at any cost. As Catholic bioethicists Thomas Shannon and James Walter have put it, "The rhetoric of the right to life movement focuses on the obligation to maintain biological life under virtually any and all conditions." Shannon and Walter criticize this approach as being "close to committing idolatry by making biological life the only value to be considered."

Father O'Rourke says that "although prolonging life is usually a value because living humanly draws us closer to God, on some occasions prolonging life becomes an impediment or obstacle to returning God's love." He posits that "to pursue the spiritual purpose of life, one needs a minimal degree of cognitive-affective function," and "if cognitive-affective function is irreparably lost, mere physiological function need not be prolonged because such therapy is ineffective to achieve the spiritual purpose of life."

Where did Pope John Paul II stand on this?

In his 1996 encyclical letter "Evangelium Vitae," John Paul II seemed to embrace the four-hundred-year tradition: "Euthanasia must be distinguished from the decision to forgo so-called 'aggressive medical treatment,' in other words, medical procedures which no longer correspond to the real situation of the patient, either because they are by now disproportionate to any expected results or because they impose an excessive burden on the patient and his family." He added that "it needs to be determined whether the means of treatment available are objectively proportionate to the prospects for improvement. To forgo extraordinary or disproportionate means is not the equivalent of suicide or euthanasia; it rather expresses acceptance of the human condition in the face of death." This was the traditional benefits-burdens proportionality test.

But the encyclical letter added, "In such situations, when death is clearly imminent and inevitable, one can in conscience 'refuse forms of treatment that would only secure a precarious and burdensome prolongation of life, so long as the normal care due to the sick person in similar cases is not interrupted.'" Did this mean that ANH could be refused only "when death is clearly imminent"? Was ANH the sort of "normal care" that could not be interrupted? On these points the letter wasn't clear. And so debate within the church was fueled.

The dissenters seem poised to prevail. On March 20, 2004, Pope John Paul II shook the world of Catholic ethicists with a speech in Rome to four hundred participants in a conference called "Life-Sustaining Treatments and Vegetative State: Scientific Advances and Ethical Dilemmas." In the speech, the pope said that "the administration of food and water, even when provided by artificial means, always represents a natural means of preserving life, not a medical act," and that it "should be considered, in principle, ordinary and proportionate, and as such morally obligatory." Thus, he said, withdrawing nutrition and hydration is "true and proper euthanasia by omission"—a sin.

Is this speech a binding papal pronouncement? Does it put the dissenters in control and revise the Catholic tradition? Neither of these questions is easily answered—although, as we will see, they became a central focus of the Schiavo litigation.

The pope's speech ranks low in the established hierarchy of papal pronouncements. It is what's called an "allocution"—a word derived from a Latin term used in ancient Rome to denote a military commander's speech to his soldiers before or during a battle. In the church, an allocution formally means an address by the pope to a gathering of cardinals. Less formally, it is used broadly to describe an address made to any group of persons—like the four hundred participants in the conference of March 20, 2004.

An allocution is not considered to be "ex cathedra"—literally "from the throne" or "chair." When the pope speaks ex cathedra, he speaks for the church in his role as its supreme head. Ex cathedra pronounce-ments are treated as infallible and binding on all Catholics. In contrast, in an allocution, the pope speaks not as the head of the church but in his private capacity as a moral theologian. An allocution is authorita-tive, but technically it is not binding as church doctrine.

Other papal pronouncements can be ex cathedra and thus binding. At the top of the list is a type of ordination called a papal constitu-tion—a decree by the pope that has the force of law. Lower down is the encyclical, a sort of papal letter addressed to church authorities—for example, John Paul II's 1996 encyclical letter "Evangelium Vitae." These pronouncements bear considerably more weight than allocu-tions—they are ex cathedra, allocutions are not.

But just how authoritative is the 2004 allocution on tube-feeding of PVS patients? There is plenty of disagreement on that issue.

At one end of the spectrum is Father John Paris, a professor of bioethics at Boston College, who told the *St. Petersburg Times* that the allocution is "not an authoritative teaching statement," and "I think the best thing to do is ignore it, and it will go away."

Somewhat more equivocal is Franciscan father Maurizio Faggioni, who told the Catholic News Service that the allocution is "a speech that has a clarifying function. It is authoritative without being defini-tive." Father Faggioni noted that, as an allocution, it "is not an 'ex cathedra' pronouncement. It's not infallible, and it's not an encyclical. But it is not a casual teaching, either." Similarly, Father O'Rourke has written to me that "I do think the allocution has some authority. Clearly it is not a definite statement (infallible), but it does seem to be an authentic teaching (assent of intellect and will should be given, if a person does not have substantial opposition to the teaching)."

At the other end of the spectrum is Richard M. Doerflinger, deputy director of the Secretariat for Pro-Life Activities of the U.S. Confer-ence of Catholic Bishops. He says that the 2004 allocution has ended the former "lack of clear and unambiguous guidance at the level of Church teaching" and puts any argument for withdrawal of ANH from PVS patients in direct conflict with church doctrine.

Evidently, the rift within the church is so wide that Catholic theologians cannot even agree as to the authoritative status of the allocution.

Nor can they agree as to the allocution's substantive meaning. All seem to concur that it departs from the traditional benefits-burdens proportionality test in declaring that ANH for PVS patients must "in principle" be considered "ordinary and proportionate." According to Professors Shannon and Walter, that means ANH always provides a benefit. The Reverend Thomas A. Reese, former editor of the Jesuit magazine *America* (until his removal shortly after the ascension of Benedict XVI), says this veers from Catholic moral tradition.

But would the allocution entirely eliminate the benefits-burdens test? Shannon and Walter seem to think so; they call the allocution "a major reversal of the moral tradition of the Catholic church in assessing whether a particular medical or other intervention is morally obligatory, particularly in the determination of whether this intervention is ordinary or extraordinary treatment." Ronald Hamel, the senior director for ethics at the Catholic Health Association of the United States, evidently agrees, observing that the pope has redefined ANH as "always being a benefit because it sustains life." But Father O'Rourke thinks the allocution just puts the benefit side of the equation in stasis—ANH is always beneficial, but it still can be withheld if it is excessively burdensome.

Bishop Elio Sgreccia, John Paul II's top bioethics advisor and vicepresident of the Pontifical Academy for Life, which had sponsored the 2004 conference, told the Catholic News Service that some have wrongly interpreted the allocution as making ANH obligatory in all circumstances. Rather, he said, the allocution leaves a "margin of judgment" to the doctors to decide whether patients are being nourished and their suffering alleviated.

Monsignor John Strynkowski, executive director of the U.S. Conference of Catholic Bishops' Secretariat for Doctrine and Pastoral Practices, said the allocution requires further "study"—meaning, evidently, that the experts are still debating what it means.

Meanwhile, what about ERD 58, the rule for America's Catholic hospitals allowing the withholding or removal of ANH under the benefits-burdens proportionality test? For the time being, it remains unchanged. In a news release dated April 1, 2004, the Catholic Hospital Association of the United States announced that while the allocution is being "carefully considered" in dialogue among "sponsors, bishops, and providers," the "guidance" in the current ERDs "remains in effect."

But change seems inevitable. Within days of John Paul II's death, even before the election of Joseph Ratzinger as Benedict XVI, the Congregation for the Doctrine of the Faith—then still headed by Cardinal Ratzinger—announced that a new papal document on bioethical issues is in the works. The details of the upcoming document remain secret, but nobody should be surprised if the church goes further down the revisionist path of repudiating the traditional benefits-burdens proportionality test in favor of an absolute rule that ANH is always morally obligatory.

Such a shift in Catholic doctrine will put America's Catholic hospitals on a collision course with American law.

The potentially explosive question is whether Catholic hospitals will disregard a patient's advance directive or a surrogate's substituted-judgment decision against providing ANH. The law says the hospital must comply with the decision or transfer the patient to a facility that will. But what if no other facility can be found—for example, the patient lives in a small town where there are no other hospitals? What if the patient is not in a stable enough condition to be safely and comfortably moved? What if the church takes the position that such transfer amounts to complicity in euthanasia and is itself forbidden?

If the hospital cannot or will not transfer the patient to another facility and instead continues to provide ANH against the patient's or surrogate's wishes, the result could be a monumental lawsuit, setting up a confrontation between the patient's constitutional right of autonomy and the hospital's right of religious freedom.

Another troublesome question is whether the hospital must advise patients upon admission that it will not honor any requests to withhold or withdraw ANH, and whether that would even be legal. And what about non-Catholic patients in Catholic hospitals? In some communities, the local Catholic hospital is the only one around. Will the hospital hold non-Catholic patients to its own moral standards?

Terri Schiavo's parents and their attorneys had no doubt about what the pope's allocution meant; they called it "the word of God" requiring that Terri be kept alive.

The timing of the allocution was propitious and probably no coincidence. By this time, the *Schiavo* case had gained international attention. In October 2003, Governor Bush had ordered the reinsertion of Terri's feeding tube—six days after its withdrawal—and Michael Schiavo had sued the governor, claiming "Terri's Law" was unconstitutional. The lawsuit was still pending at the time of the allocution.

The Schindlers' lawyers went back to Judge Greer, asking him to reconsider his decision in light of the allocution because, as they put it in a written motion filed with the court, "Terri has now changed her mind about dying." The motion argued that "as a practicing Catholic at the time of her collapse ... Terri does not want to commit a sin of the gravest proportions by forgoing treatment to effect her own death in defiance of her religious faith's express and recent instruction to the contrary."

Their argument, in other words, was that Terri would obey the pope's allocution and choose to keep her PEG tube in place. Never mind that Catholic theologians couldn't even agree among themselves as to the authoritativeness of the allocution or how it affected the church's tradition on withholding or withdrawing ANH. For the Schindlers' lawyers, the allocution was another arrow in their quiver of legal maneuvers. At the hearing on the motion, one of their attorneys even argued that the allocution voids the advance directives of all Catholics.

Judge Greer didn't buy it. He resolved the issue by referring back to the Court of Appeal's opinion of January 24, 2001, upholding his judgment, in which the appellate court observed that Terri "had been raised in the Catholic faith, but did not regularly attend mass or have a religious advisor who could assist the court in weighing her religious attitude about life-support methods." According to Judge Greer, "Nothing has changed. There is nothing new presented regarding Terri Schiavo's religious attitude and there still is no religious advisor to assist this or any other court in weighing her desire to comply with this or any other papal pronouncement."

In other words, the Schindlers had failed to show that Terri would have paid any attention—or even understood—an obscure papal allocution on a fine point of Catholic moral doctrine. The judge left Catholic canon law to the church. The Schindlers' subsequent appeals on this point were similarly unsuccessful.

The ongoing debate among Catholics on the morality of withholding or withdrawing life-sustaining treatment is representative of thinking across the spectrum of Judeo-Christian traditions.

Jewish ethicists are also divided. Traditionally, the active ending of a human life was absolutely forbidden, and passive measures such as removing an impediment to death were permitted only in the case of a *goses*, a deathbed patient expected to die within seventy-two hours. At the extreme today are the Orthodox, who, like the revisionist Catholics, take the position that all life is sacred and must be preserved whatever the circumstances, so that life-sustaining treatment must never be withheld or withdrawn. That's what was behind my cousin Ros's brother Alex, whose ultraorthodox rabbi had instructed him that "as long as the heart beats and she is not dying, she must be fed."

Most Jewish moralists take a more moderate position, concluding that, despite the sanctity of human life, there is no duty to preserve it under all circumstances at whatever cost. For some, the proper course of action is to be determined by reference to benefit versus risk to the patient—rather like the Catholics' traditional benefits-burdens proportionality test. Thus, if a patient is terminally ill, medication and life-sustaining measures such as respirators may be withheld or withdrawn.

Feeding tubes are more complicated. As in the Catholic tradition, personal autonomy is not transcendent in the Jewish tradition: our bodies are not our own but the property of God, and as such they must be properly cared for, our lives appropriately preserved, notwithstanding the legal proclamations of personal autonomy set forth in *Quinlan*, *Cruzan*, and their progeny. Many rabbis conclude that there must therefore be a strong, perhaps insurmountable presumption in favor of basic sustenance, including ANH. But others say this presumption can be overcome by a benefits-risks analysis, analogizing feeding tubes to blood transfusions—which, unlike Jehovah's Witnesses, the Jews do not treat as the forbidden "eating" of blood. If one does not "eat" blood by taking it intravenously, arguably one does not "eat" food by taking ANH through a surgically attached feeding tube. Thus feeding tubes may properly be withdrawn or withheld—on the patient's direction or on the instruction of a surrogate in consultation with doctors, family, and clergy, relying on knowledge of the patient's preferences—because that is not a deprivation of food.

Even more difficult is the question of providing ANH to PVS patients who are not terminally ill. The Jewish tradition prohibits judgments based on quality-of-life assessments, meaning that we may not withhold or withdraw ANH from a PVS patient simply because we personally would not want to live that way. But some say that even in these circumstances it is morally acceptable to forgo ANH, on the theory that ANH is like medicine and as such may constitute an inappropriate medical intervention where the patient's condition is incurable. That is the position of Rabbi Elliot N. Dorff, rector of the University of Judaism in Los Angeles, who argued that, for Terri Schiavo, ANH was properly viewed as medical treatment that could properly be withdrawn given the lack of hope for her recovery.

Even evangelical Christians are divided. Some loudly insisted in the *Schiavo* case that Terri Schiavo's "right to life" required ANH absolutely and regardless of her circumstances. Others, however, more quietly follow the mainstream Catholic and Jewish traditions of risk-benefit proportionality. For example, Scott B. Rae, a professor of Christian ethics at Biola University, an evangelical Christian institution in La Mirada, California, has written that ANH may properly be withheld or withdrawn if it is "more burdensome than beneficial to the patient." When Terri's feeding tube was finally removed in March 2005, Rae told the *Los Angeles Times* he felt it was appropriate to discontinue her ANH if that clearly would have been her wish. He, too, compared feeding tubes to medical treatment. He also said that he personally would not want to be kept alive in Terri's condition: "As a Christian, I don't want anybody to delay my homecoming."

In the eyes of the law, however, the word of God doesn't matter—unless there is evidence that the patient would have heeded that word. Personal autonomy may play second fiddle to God in the Judeo-Christian traditions, but in America it is the law of the land.

There is a wild card in all this: the morality of withholding or withdrawing life-sustaining treatment from disabled persons. Rabbi Dorff has written that the Jewish tradition's prohibition of judgments based on quality-of-life assessments "serves the crucial role of reminding us that people handicapped in some way must be treated with the full respect which their divine image warrants, that, indeed, we must bless God for such variations among creatures, even if (or, especially if) we would much prefer not to be like them."

Do judges, or bioethicists, or religious moralists treat the disabled with something less than "full respect" by sanctioning the removal of their feeding tubes? Is this a quality-of-life judgment? Is it murder?

6

The Slippery Slope

When I met Diane Coleman in September 2004, she refused to shake my hand.

The occasion was a public debate on the *Schiavo* case at Florida State University in Tallahassee, on the eve of the Florida Supreme Court hearing on Michael Schiavo's challenge to the constitutionality of "Terri's Law," which had authorized Governor Jeb Bush to order the reinsertion of Terri Schiavo's feeding tube in October 2003. I was at the debate to speak for the bioethicists. Diane was there to speak for her coalition of disability rights groups. There were eight other panelists, including antieuthanasia activists Rita Marker and Wesley Smith, and the Schindlers' attorney Pat Anderson.

I had admired Diane for the tenacity and quality of her advocacy in both the *Wendland* and *Schiavo* cases, and I looked forward to meeting her. I was therefore startled by her rebuff. It spoke volumes for the passion that some disability rights activists bring to this issue.

Diane Coleman, a fifty-three-year-old lawyer, was disabled at birth and has used a wheelchair since age eleven. She has held many positions in disability advocacy groups and currently heads the Progress Center for Independent Living in Oak Park, Illinois. In 1996, she founded Not Dead Yet to advocate against euthanasia and the legalization of assisted suicide. NDY's Internet web site describes itself as being opposed to "a public policy that singles out individuals for legalized killing based on their health status."

Diane is not a member of the religious Right. In a 1999 article in the online edition of *Ragged Edge* magazine, she called herself a "progressive" and characterized the battle over removal of life-sustaining treatment as "a class struggle." According to the article, she knows quite well how much of the support for her position comes from the religious Right, and "she warns NDY supporters 'it's important we don't get too close to our allies on the topic.'" Not Dead Yet's bylaws expressly forbid it from taking "pro-life organization money."

Diane and her colleagues fear the so-called slippery slope—a drift from the "right" to die to a "duty" to die and ultimately to forced euthanasia. As a precedent for this fear, they point to Nazi Germany, where physicians euthanized the disabled as part of a eugenics-based plan to rid the nation of "undesirables" and "unworthy" lives. The disability activists worry about a perceived push by doctors and health maintenance organizations to rid the health-care system of high-cost disabled patients.

In the weeks after I met Diane, we had an extensive e-mail correspondence in which she more graciously took the time to explain herself to me—and I to her. Here is a summary of five points she made in our correspondence and has made in various publications, and how I responded to her and would respond to her colleagues:

Diane: People with cognitive disabilities, like Terri Schiavo, cannot be fully and fairly represented by surrogates because of a conflict of interest inherent in the surrogacy relationship. Surrogates often value the lives of their wards far less than the wards value their own lives. Elder abuse is just one example of this. Some surrogates have a financial or other interest in hastening the ward's death. Insensitive public guardians are also a problem, and court-appointed legal guardians are abysmally trained in understanding cognitive disabilities.

Jon: If a surrogate is not to be trusted to make decisions on behalf of cognitively impaired people who lack the competency to do so, then who is to exercise their constitutional right of personal autonomy for them? Surrogate decision-making is essential if the right of autonomy is to survive incompetency. How else can the incompetent patient be represented? Where the surrogate is a relative or friend, there is always a potential for conflict of interest, such as where the surrogate stands to inherit money. And where the surrogate is a public guardian, there is always the lure of institutional convenience. But does that mean we must discard the concept of surrogacy altogether? The result would be to keep comatose and PVS patients alive even if it is clear—despite the absence of a written advance directive—that they would not want it. Isn't it better to retain surrogate decision-making but make sure there are legal safeguards in place to prevent abuse?

Diane: Most surrogates do whatever the doctors tell them, and the doctors have a conflict of interest because of cost-cutting pressures. The medical profession generally devalues people with disabilities. Doctors too often induce families to give up on the severely disabled. The bioethicists in particular have warped the end-of-life care movement into a life-ending movement. They want to be able to kill behind the closed doors of a room in a hospital or nursing home. The disabled could end up being killed because of financial considerations if nobody is willing to fight for them in court.

Jon: The way you see it, doctors put pressure on families to kill the severely disabled, but aren't you overstating your case? If some doctors urge families to forgo tube-feeding, isn't it mostly for comatose or PVS patients? I personally respect and support the right of people to insist on life-sustaining treatment even if they become completely and irreversibly noncognitive, but I also think it is absurd to keep the heart beating and the lungs breathing under such circumstances. Many people agree with me. Do you really want to keep the permanently comatose "alive" because of the danger that doctors might abuse their positions of authority in cases where the patient is somewhere short of PVS? I don't want to see good end-of-life decision-making put beyond people's reach in order to prevent bad end-of-life decision-making. "All or nothing" doesn't work for me in these cases—on either end of the spectrum. But that would be the result of the position you advocate.

Diane: Casual, nonspecific comments to friends and family during the time preceding incompetency shouldn't be enough to justify withholding life-sustaining treatment. Such comments might not lead to actions that are consistent with the person's true wishes. People sometimes change their minds about what treatment they would want and what level of disability they would accept, particularly as they actually go through the experience of being disabled and as their fear of disability dissipates. A written advance directive should suffice, but only if it makes clear that the person would refuse life-sustaining treatment in the circumstances presented.

Jon: In the real world, "casual, nonspecific" comments to family and friends about end-of-life wishes are usually all we have to go by. That's what I had from my cousin Ros, but it surely was enough, even without her nonspecific advance directive. You know the statistics—advance written directives are relatively uncommon. Your repudiation of "casual, nonspecific" comments would put surrogate decision-making beyond the reach of all but the wealthy and informed—those who can afford a lawyer or who know how to get their hands on and fill out a form advance directive. That's elitist. And how are we to make clear in an advance directive that we would not want life-sustaining treatment in, as you put it, "the circumstances presented"? It is impossible to anticipate each and every "circumstance" that might be "presented." An infinite variety of maladies can cause incompetency, which can lie anywhere on a vast spectrum between comatose and fully competent. Few of us would ever anticipate, for example, an unusual condition like Robert Wendland's. Aren't you raising the bar impossibly high for surrogate and advance directive decision-making?

Diane: The "clear and convincing evidence" standard of proof is adequate in theory, but there can be a chasm between theory and practice. In practice, hospitals often withhold or withdraw life-sustaining treatment from the disabled even without clear and convincing evidence. Courts are complicit in this. For example, in the *Schiavo* case, Judge Greer found the evidence of Terri's wishes to be clear and convincing, but it really wasn't. If the courts won't insist on a genuine application of the clear and convincing evidence standard, then the judicial branch of government is wholly lost.

Jon: Indeed you are right that there can be a "chasm" between what the law requires in theory and what actually happens in the real world. As a lawyer, I deal with this problem more often than I would like. Judges themselves occasionally see a "chasm" between what the law technically requires and what they believe to be the fair and just result in a particular case—and so they sometimes ignore the law. That phenomenon is one of the things that has the Schindlers' advocates so angry—they think Judge Greer merely paid lip service to the "clear and convincing evidence" standard of proof, finding that the evidence met this standard when it really did not. Result-oriented judging drives the lawyer in me nuts, but I have to live with it. As lawyers, we can only combat it through strong advocacy. Usually that works; sometimes it doesn't. But would you rather have evidentiary disputes resolved in the political arena, where there are no rules of evidence and the players are motivated above all else by their own self-interest?

Diane: The evidence in the *Schiavo* case didn't pass the smell test. Terri wasn't really in PVS, and Michael's testimony regarding her previous comments about her end-of-life wishes was not sufficiently credible to constitute clear and convincing evidence supporting Judge Greer's decision to remove her feeding tube. Michael had a conflict of interest, and the Florida appellate courts should have reversed Judge Greer's decision because of Michael's lack of credibility.

Jon: Do you really think you know Terri's condition and wishes better than Judge Greer did? Like the politicians, you are relying on newspaper and television accounts. You weren't in court, and you didn't see and hear the witnesses testify, as did the judge.

In September 2004 I asked the Schindlers, through their lawyer Pat Anderson, for me to be allowed to accompany them—just the three of us—on one of their visits with Terri, so that I could see her for myself, just as I had seen Robert Wendland. I got nowhere with them. They seemed not to want me to see Terri as she truly was. Nor would Pat Anderson send me copies of the four hours of videotape of Terri from 2002. She claimed that a court order prohibited dissemination of the videotapes—yet the Schindlers had publicly posted snippets from the videotapes on their Internet web site.

How fairly were those snippets edited? Take, for example, the brief segment that seemed to show Terri responding to her name being called by opening her eyes: Did this happen, say, after many minutes of repeatedly calling her name and getting no response? Perhaps it was inevitable that sooner or later she would open her eyes, and that's what you saw in the snippet. Judge Greer knew. He saw the whole four hours. We did not.

Who was better positioned to determine Terri's condition and wishes—the judge who actually heard and saw the witnesses and medical evidence, or self-interested politicos?

And, Diane, as a lawyer you know better than to claim that the Florida appellate courts should have reversed Judge Greer's decision because of Michael's "lack of credibility." No appellate court in the land could ever legitimately do that. Don't you remember the rule of review for "substantial evidence"—the one that says an appellate court won't attempt to second-guess a trial judge's credibility determinations? Under that rule, the Florida appellate courts *had* to affirm Judge Greer, because the evidence he chose to believe was legally "substantial"—and, as such, it supported the judgment. That's the way our judicial system works.

Diane Coleman and her colleagues claim to speak for all disabled people. But do they really? Some disabled people think differently.

One was the late Andrew Batavia, a lawyer with quadriplegia who cofounded Autonomy Inc., a disability advocacy group. Autonomy Inc.'s mission statement promoted "the interests of people with disabilities who wish to be able to exercise choices concerning all aspects of our lives, including choices at the end of life." On its Internet web site, Autonomy Inc. urged that "medical treatment must never be denied or withdrawn solely because a patient has a disability, and may only be denied or withdrawn as a result of the express desire of the individual (or someone appropriately authorized to decide on the individual's behalf)." In a 1997 article in the *New England Journal of Medicine*, Andrew Batavia explained: "We believe that competent persons with disabilities, even in the oppressive circumstances of many institutions, are capable of autonomy. Most disabled persons do not consider themselves vulnerable or oppressed and want to make the decisions that fundamentally affect their lives."

Batavia thus championed the right of disabled persons to refuse medical treatment, including ANH. He even favored physician-assisted suicide. In his 1997 article, he cited a recent Harris poll showing that "66 percent of people with disabilities who were surveyed support a right to assisted suicide, as compared with 70 percent of the general population." (A 2002 Harris poll yielded virtually the same numbers.) He acknowledged the risks of abuse by a flawed health-care system but said he believed in regulatory safeguards, and "if we do not accept this risk, we will face a much greater risk: loss of our autonomy and freedom from state intrusion in our lives." He dismissed the analogy to forced euthanasia in Nazi Germany as "way off the mark," the distinction being who is in control of the decision: "In one case, the state has all the power, and in the other case, the individual has all the power."

Batavia is gone—he died in 2003—but his point of view on the withdrawal of ANH from PVS patients remains very much alive. It is echoed in a comment by a thirty-seven-year-old quadriplegic in New Jersey who, after Terri Schiavo's death, told the *Washington Post*: "For some people, the big fear is being kept alive in this persistent vegetative state. I'm one of them."

So who is right, Diane Coleman or Andrew Batavia?

Both make good points. Coleman may be justified in fearing the slippery slope. The era of managed health care has not been kind to high-cost patients, for whom it can be a constant battle to obtain proper care. And, as Batavia acknowledged in 1997, "people with disabilities have been devalued in our society throughout its history." But I think Batavia is right that America today is not Nazi Germany, where forced euthanasia was driven by a pernicious dogma that targeted so-called "inferior" and "unworthy" people such as Jews, Gypsies, homosexuals, and the disabled. Affording disabled persons the right to personal autonomy in health-care decision-making acknowledges their equality. They, too, should enjoy this peculiarly American right.

Slippery slope arguments are legion—smoking marijuana will lead to heroin addiction, gay civil unions will lead to polygamy and bestiality, the registration of firearms will lead to their wholesale confiscation, legal restrictions on cross-burning will lead to suppression of free speech. Few of these alarmist arguments are ever borne out. The columnist Molly Ivins offers this pearl of wisdom: "All of law is a process of drawing lines on slippery slopes. The difference between misdemeanor theft and felony theft is one penny. The difference between misdemeanor and felony drug possession is one gram. For that matter, the difference between a pig and a hog is one pound. We're always drawing distinctions, and it is necessary to do so—hunting rifles, OK; .50 caliber rifles, don't be a fool."

So I cast my lot with Andrew Batavia on the issue of withdrawing ANH from PVS patients. Diane Coleman and her colleagues are right to be concerned but wrong in their conclusions. Most disabled people—not the vocal activists but their constituency—seem to want personal autonomy, even including physician-assisted suicide.

On one point, however, Diane Coleman is absolutely right. Shortly after Terri Schiavo's death, Diane told the *Washington Post* that she and her colleagues "do not identify with the spouse or the parents. We identify with her." Diane put her finger on the proper focus of surrogate decision-making in the *Schiavo* case: the issue is not what Terri's spouse would want or what her parents would want, but what *she* would want. That's the essence of autonomy.

And autonomy is what I thought about when, during the Tallahassee debate in September 2004, a woman in a wheelchair asked the panelists: "Where does it stop?" My answer to her was: "Substituted-judgment decision-making stops when I don't know what you want."

The truth is, most people with disabilities want what nearly all the rest of us want.

The Voice of the People

Tom's sixty-five-year-old father, Charles, lay comatose in a Texas hospital. Charles had been putting the finishing touches on a small trolley that he and his brother had designed and installed in his backyard to carry people down a hill to a nearby lake. On a test run, the trolley crashed, throwing Charles headfirst into a tree. He sustained irreversible brain damage and was being kept alive with intravenous lines, a tracheostomy, and oxygen equipment. The only signs of cognition occurred when Tom's brother, Randy, would walk into the hospital room—Charles's pulse rate would increase—and when Charles occasionally moaned.

There was no hope for any recovery. The doctors told the family that Charles would "basically be a vegetable."

Charles had not left a written advance directive specifying his end-of-life wishes, but his wife, Maxine, and their son Tom knew what Charles would have wanted. Maxine later said: "There was no way he wanted to live like that. Tom knew, we all knew, his father wouldn't have wanted to live that way." Another relative agreed that Charles "did not want to be a vegetable. There was no decision for the family to make. He made it for them."

When Charles went into kidney failure, the doctors said he would need dialysis to survive. That's when the family called it quits. Maxine and Tom's two siblings, Randy and Tena, decided to withhold dialysis

and other life-sustaining treatment. Tom went along with the decision. Shortly thereafter, Charles died, with his family at his bedside.

What Charles had said about his end-of-life wishes, and what his wife,
Maxine, and his children, Tom, Randy, and Tena, did about it, is
hardly unusual. In a 2005 ABC News poll, a third of those polled said
they'd had relatives or friends who had died after a decision to remove
life support, and almost 20 percent said they'd been personally involved in the decision. It happens every day in America.

What makes Charles unusual is who Tom is. He is Tom DeLay, the
Republican majority leader of the U.S. House of Representatives. The
year was 1988, and DeLay had joined in his mother's decision to remove life support from his father.

In March 2005, Tom DeLay helped lead the Congressional effort to
keep Terri Schiavo on life support. He said that "the sanctity of life
overshadows the sanctity of marriage," and "unless she had specifically
written instructions in her hand and with her signature, I don't care
what her husband says." Yet, in 1988, the desire of DeLay's own father
not to live like a "vegetable"—the sort of wish Robert Wendland and
Terri Schiavo had expressed—was enough for DeLay to agree to the
removal of his father's life support, without any "specifically written instructions."

The Tom DeLay of 1988 acted like a typical American. The Tom
DeLay of 2005 did not.

What is typically American conduct? On some things it's impossible
to say. Our country is deeply divided today on many political and social issues. But on the right to refuse medical treatment, there is very
much a consensus.

Five major polls were conducted on the *Schiavo* case after Governor
Jeb Bush ordered the reinsertion of Terri's feeding tube in October
2003. The first, done that same month, was by CNN, *USA Today*, and
the Gallup Organization. The second was by two Florida newspapers,
the *St. Petersburg Times* and the *Miami Herald*, in December 2003. The

third was by the Fox News Channel in June 2004. All of these three polls were prompted by Governor Bush's intervention in the *Schiavo* case. Two more polls, one by CBS News and the other by ABC News, came in March 2005, in the wake of Congress's intervention in the case.

Cumulatively, these polls asked five questions:

- Should Terri Schiavo's feeding tube be removed?

- Was Congress wrong to intervene?

- Was Governor Bush wrong to intervene?

- Would you personally want life-sustaining treatment to be removed under Terri Schiavo's circumstances?

- Should a patient's spouse be entrusted with the decision?

The polls specified how particular groups of persons had responded to these questions, according to the following classifications:

- People overall

- Religion

- Political party

- Political/social outlook

- Gender

- Age

Thus the five polls cumulatively canvassed a broad cross section of Americans on a comprehensive set of questions about the *Schiavo* case in particular and the right to refuse medical treatment in general. A powerful consensus emerged: the people overwhelmingly want and support the constitutional right of personal autonomy, and they resent government meddling in their exercise of that right.

On whether *Terri Schiavo's feeding tube should be removed*, the people overall said yes—by margins approaching three-to-one. Here are the numbers:

- ABC News: 63% to 28%
- CBS News: 68% to 27%
- Fox News Channel: 61% to 22%
- CNN/USA Today/Gallup: 80% to 17%

By *religion*, the ABC News poll had Catholics favoring the removal of Terri's feeding tube by 63% to 26%, Protestants by 77% to 18%, and evangelical Christians by 46% to 44%.

By *political party*, ABC News had Democrats favoring removal by 65% to 25% and Republicans by 61% to 34%. The Fox News Channel had Democrats favoring removal by 68% to 20% and Republicans by 56% to 26%.

By *political and social outlook*, ABC News had liberals favoring removal by 68% to 24%, moderates by 69% to 22%, and conservatives by 54% to 40%. The Fox News Channel had liberals favoring removal by 70% to 18%, moderates by 61% to 24%, and conservatives by 56% to 26%.

By *gender*, the Fox News Channel had women favoring removal by 62% to 20% and men by 60% to 25%.

By *age*, the Fox News channel had all age groups favoring the removal of Terri Schiavo's feeding tube: 64% to 25% in the 18–34 group, 57% to 26% in the 35–50 group, 66% to 17% in the 51–59 group, 67% to 18% in the 60–70 group, and 60% to 17% in the over–70 group.

Thus a decisive majority of people from all walks of life—Catholic, Protestant, and evangelical Christian; Democrat and Republican; liberal, moderate, and conservative; men and women; the young, middle-aged, and elderly—agreed with Judge Greer's decision to remove Terri Schiavo's life support. Not one subgroup thought she should be prevented from dying.

On whether *Congress was wrong to intervene* in March of 2005, the people overall said yes. Here are the numbers:

- ABC News: 70% yes

- CBS News: 82% yes

By *religion*, the ABC News poll had Catholics opposing Congressional intervention by 56% to 38%, Protestants by 71% to 26%, and evangelical Christians by 50% to 44%. By *political party*, ABC News had Democrats opposing Congressional intervention by 63% to 34%, Republicans by 58% to 39%. And by *political and social outlook*, ABC News had liberals opposing Congressional intervention by 62% to 34%, moderates by 67% to 29%, and conservatives by 49% to 48%. (A Harris Poll taken three weeks after Terri Schiavo's death put Congress's disapproval rate at 58% to 35%.)

On whether *Governor Bush was wrong to intervene*, the St. Petersburg Times/Miami Herald poll had 65% of the people overall saying he was wrong; 57% of Catholics, 64% of Protestants, and 85% of Jews; 63% of those in the 18–34 age group, and 68% of those over 65. (The Harris Poll taken after Terri's death had Governor Bush's disapproval rate at 51% to 41%.)

On whether they *would personally want life-sustaining treatment to be removed* under Terri Schiavo's circumstances, ABC News had 80% of the people saying yes, and the Fox News Channel had 74% saying yes.

Finally, on whether *a patient's spouse should be entrusted with the decision*, the people overwhelmingly said yes. Here are the numbers:

- CNN/USA Today/Gallup: 80% yes

- *St. Petersburg Times/Miami Herald*: 75% yes

- Fox News Channel: 50% chose the spouse; 31% chose the parents or other relatives; 4% chose the doctors; 2% chose the government.

There was one other poll, announced in an August 2004 press release by the antiabortion National Right to Life Committee. The poll purported to show, contrary to all the major polls on the *Schiavo* case, that 46% opposed the removal of Terri Schiavo's feeding tube and 32% favored it. This poll was done by a private marketing firm, Wilson Research Strategies, which specializes in developing marketing strategies for political campaigns. Its president, Chris Wilson, was executive director of the Republican Party of Texas under then-governor George W. Bush.

Studies in medical journals have yielded results similar to the major *Schiavo* polls. In a 1992 survey published in the *Journal of the American Medical Association*, 76 percent of Americans said they favored legislation permitting the withdrawal of life support, including food and water, from "hopelessly ill" or "irreversibly comatose" patients if they or their families request it. Even nursing home residents feel the same; a 2000 study in the *New England Journal of Medicine* showed that only a third of them would want a feeding tube if they were unable to eat because of permanent brain damage, and a quarter of those changed their minds when told that they might have to be physically restrained to keep the tube in.

The numbers tell the story: public support for surrogate exercise of the right to refuse medical treatment is wide and deep. But enough with the statistics! Let's hear from the people themselves.

During the week before Terri Schiavo died, my daily newspaper, the *San Francisco Chronicle*, ran two pieces—the sort of "person in the street" thing we see so often—asking whether "you ever participated in the decision to remove life support" and whether the *Schiavo* case "affected your views on life support." The *Chronicle* published sixty-two responses. The voices were touching, eloquent, and unanimous. Here are a few of them:

- "Every person should have their dying wishes respected."

- "It is the most gut-wrenching, devastating, and emotional decision one can make. The right decision must be for the person it's made about, not yourself. And pray!"

- "Families need to examine whether they want to keep someone alive for that person's sake or for their own sake. The decision must be made for the person in the bed, not for the personal comfort of the family or to assuage any guilt feelings."

- "Listen to your heart when considering the person and what they would want you to do."

- "When God has called a person home, we should not interfere, no matter how difficult it is to let a loved one go. It is an affront to God to prevent a person leaving when it is their time to go."

- "If I'm confronted with the harsh reality of my loved ones stuck in a vegetative state or hooked on a respirator indefinitely with no possibility of ever getting better, then I'll opt to pull the plug and let my loved one die rather than prolonging the agony of being trapped in his or her body."

- "The moment of death is on God's clock, not ours. To interfere with the process by extraordinary artificial means, no matter how imaginative the science, is the ultimate arrogance."

- "I cannot imagine anyone would choose to persist in a vegetative state. I expect they would rather see the face of God."

- "I want the right to die on my own terms!"

- "My mother had terminal kidney failure. The only thing I'm happy about is Tom DeLay was not at her side."

What is a life without cognition—without any awareness of yourself or your surroundings? Father Kevin O'Rourke says cognition is essential "to pursue the spiritual purpose of life." A secularist might see the purpose of life as being something other than spiritual. But if life has any purpose at all—other than to sustain a beating heart and breathing lungs—one must have cognition to pursue it. Life is the world within and around us. With neither, in my opinion, there is nothingness—no life at all. Most Americans agree.

If Terri Schiavo's doctors are to be believed—and they were adjudged credible by the best legal system for adjudication of facts that Western civilization has to offer—then Terri had no cognition, no awareness whatsoever. Who among us would want to live that way? A few, perhaps, but not most. The polls and statistics confirm this.

Ask yourself. That's what the Enlightenment philosopher René Descartes did. He reassured himself of his corporeal existence with his revelation "cogito ergo sum": I think, therefore I am. He knew he was alive because he had cognition.

The End of Life

In a 2000 article on death and dying published in *Modern Maturity* magazine by the American Association of Retired Persons (AARP), the journalist Bill Moyers commented, "None of us want to die a death we deplore in a place we despise." But what about death by dehydration? That's what happens when a feeding tube is withdrawn. Is that itself a deplorable death?

The doctors call it terminal dehydration—the process of dying that occurs when a feeding tube is removed and the intake of nutrition and hydration ceases. They say it is painless. Antieuthanasia activist Wesley J. Smith thinks otherwise.

Smith is a leading voice of the right-wing assault on surrogate exercise of the right to refuse medical treatment. He calls the bioethicists a "medical intelligentsia" who are a part of the "culture of death," warning people of "the monster they did not know was lurking in the shadows." As a senior fellow with the Discovery Institute, an ultraconservative think tank, he writes prolifically on bioethical issues—euthanasia, stem cell research, cloning, even animal rights—in books and in right-wing periodicals such as the *National Review* and the *Weekly Standard*. He frequently speaks on these issues on radio and television, nationally and abroad. It's what he does for a living.

Smith calls terminal dehydration "an extremely agonizing death." He says a doctor once told him, "A conscious person would feel it [dehydration], just as you or I would. They will go into seizures. Their

skin cracks, their tongue cracks, their lips crack. They may have nosebleeds because of the drying of the mucus membranes, and heaving
and vomiting might ensue because of the drying out of the stomach
lining. They feel the pangs of hunger and thirst."

The religious Right took up this cry as Terri Schiavo lay dying in
March 2005. Dr. David Stevens of the Christian Medical Association
called terminal dehydration "a cruel, inhumane and often agonizing
death." He said he had seen people starving in Africa, and he described the process as follows: "As dehydration begins, there is extreme
thirst, dry mouth and thick saliva. . . . In misery, the patient tries to cry
but there are no tears. The patient experiences severe abdominal
cramps, nausea and dry-heaving as the stomach and intestines dry
out. . . . The skin and lips are cracking and the tongue is swollen. The
nose may bleed as the mucous membranes dry out and break down."

It sounds terrible.

These horror stories, however, are not true. None of this happens in
terminal dehydration under a physician's care, because of two things—
ketonemia and palliation.

Ketonemia is a long-term physiological adaptation to fasting, where
the human body deprived of food increasingly metabolizes fat, which
causes an increase in the production of organic compounds called ke-
tones, which in turn has the effect of suppressing hunger. The onset of
ketonemia begins within twenty-four hours after the cessation of nutrition and hydration, making complete starvation relatively tolerable.
Ketonemia is what enabled our distant ancestors to go out hunting in
times of no food, unhindered by hunger pangs.

Other physiological adaptations to fasting include substantial re-
ductions in respiratory secretions, nausea, vomiting, and diarrhea. All
are suppressed. The reduction in secretions means less coughing and
choking—which would have been a respite for Robert Wendland,
whom I watched gag on his own saliva.

It's a different story, however, when starvation is partial and gradual.
Periodic ingestion of small amounts of carbohydrates interferes with a

starving person's ketone production and results in intense and over-whelming hunger. That explains why people subsisting on occasional scraps during times of war and famine will do just about anything to get their hands on food, while hunger strikers can placidly persist until death.

So much for Smith's claim that terminal dehydration causes "pangs of hunger." Perhaps he doesn't know about ketonemia. And the ketone-suppressing effects of partial starvation would seem to explain the "nausea and dry-heaving" that Dr. Stevens says he saw in Africa—evidently the victims were eating just enough to prevent the physiological adaptation to complete starvation.

What about the nightmarish visions of dry mouths, cracked skin, and nosebleeds? That's where palliative care comes in.

The National Hospice and Palliative Care Organization defines palliative care as "treatment that enhances comfort and improves the quality of an individual's life during the last phase of life," including "relief from distressing symptoms" and "the easing of pain." Conventional palliation includes pain relief through use of drugs, symptom control through proper medical care, and emotional and spiritual support.

Nobody dying from terminal dehydration need suffer from dry mouth, cracked skin, or nosebleeds. Those symptoms are easily alleviated by application of ice chips and moistening lubricants—standard features of palliative care for the dying.

Another standard feature of palliative care is pain relief through drug therapy—for those who are sufficiently cognitive to feel pain—with the administration of narcotics carefully adjusted to relieve pain while avoiding sedation. And as a last resort, where pain cannot be relieved without complete sedation, there is another option, terminal sedation: the use of high doses of sedatives to render patients unconscious and thus unable to feel any pain until they die.

Wesley Smith is wrong. Terminal dehydration under a physician's palliative care is not "an extremely agonizing death." As the coauthor of a book on palliative care called *Power over Pain: How to Get the Pain Control You Need*, Smith should know better.

But how can we really know whether a PVS patient like Terri Schiavo feels pain from terminal dehydration?

Why not ask conscious and competent patients what *they* feel as they undergo terminal dehydration? A 1994 study in the *Journal of the American Medical Association* did just that. The study monitored thirty-two terminally ill patients in a long-term health-care facility in Rochester, New York. All the patients were mentally aware and competent. Most had diagnoses of cancer or stroke. None was expected to live more than three months.

Each of the thirty-two patients had chosen to cease nutrition and hydration and die with palliative care. Their mouths were kept clean and were moistened with small sips of water. Narcotics were administered when necessary to treat pain and shortness of breath. Meanwhile, a multidisciplinary team—consisting of a nurse, a physician, a social worker, a dietician, a recreational therapist, and a chaplain—studied the patients as they gradually died. Several times a day, the team asked each patient a series of questions about sensations of hunger, thirst, and dry mouth. The team also posed questions to the patients and their relatives about pain, shortness of breath, nausea, fears, and anxiety—that is, each patient's level of physical and emotional comfort. Here are the results.

On the *absence of hunger*:

- 63% said they experienced no hunger at all.

- 34% experienced hunger "initially but eventually lost their appetites."

On the *palliation of dry mouth and thirst*:

- 34% said they had no symptoms of dry mouth or thirst.

- 28% experienced these symptoms only initially.

- 38% experienced these symptoms until death.

- Most important, 100% of those who experienced these symptoms had them relieved by palliative care.

On the *level of comfort*:

- 84% were rated "comfortable."

- 13% were thought to have experienced "some discomfort."

- One patient was comfortable initially, but a few days before death he became so delusional that his level of comfort could no longer be determined.

The study concluded that conscious terminally ill patients undergoing terminal dehydration can die comfortably with proper palliative care: "Those patients able to communicate consistently reaffirmed our hypothesis that lack of food and fluids sufficient to replete losses did not cause them suffering, as long as mouth care was provided and thirst alleviated with sips of water." The study attributed the absence of hunger or thirst to the appetite-suppressing effects of ketonemia, if not the underlying disease itself. Ketonemia explains why 34 percent of the patients experienced hunger "initially but eventually lost their appetites."

This isn't the only study showing the effectiveness of palliative care in cases of terminal dehydration. A 2003 study published in the *New England Journal of Medicine* surveyed those on the front lines of health care—the nurses—asking 102 of them how *they* perceived death by voluntary terminal dehydration in conscious hospice patients. The nurses were asked to rate four variables—suffering, pain, peacefulness, and overall "quality of death"—on a scale of 0 to 9. A "0" rating was the lowest for suffering and pain; "9"was the highest. "0" denoted "very much at peace"; "9" meant "not at all peaceful." "0" indicated "a very bad death"; "9" was "a very good death." Here are the median results:

- Suffering: 3

- Pain: 2

- Peacefulness: 2

- Overall quality of death: 8

Thus suffering and pain were perceived as low, while peacefulness and overall quality of death were perceived as high. The study concluded, "On the basis of reports by nurses, patients in hospice care who voluntarily choose to refuse food and fluids are elderly, no longer find meaning in living, and usually die a 'good' death within two weeks after stopping food and fluids."

The 1994 report in the *Journal of the American Medical Association* was a landmark for hospice care. Within six months of the report's publication, Dr. Ira Byock, past president of the American Academy of Hospice and Palliative Medicine, speculated in the *American Journal of Hospice and Palliative Care* on the conclusion that "starvation and dehydration do not contribute to suffering among the dying and might actually contribute to a comfortable passage from life." Dr. Byock said that "at least within the context of adequate palliative care, the refusal of food and fluids does not contribute to suffering among the terminally ill. The literature is consistent on two points: (a) rarely does fasting cause any discomfort beyond occasional and transient hunger, and (b) symptoms referable to dehydration are few—mostly dry oral and pharyngeal mucous membranes—and are readily relieved by simple measures." He, too, attributed the absence of hunger to ketonemia, referring to studies indicating that "total fasting causes hunger for less than twenty-four hours."

Wesley Smith should be familiar with Dr. Byock's conclusions. The back cover of Smith's book on palliative care bears an endorsement by Dr. Byock.

Now let's extrapolate. We know that, given the appetite-suppressing effects of ketonemia and proper palliative care, conscious patients do not suffer from the process of voluntary terminal dehydration. It is painless. From that knowledge, we can reasonably infer what the unconscious patient can't tell us—that properly palliated PVS and comatose patients likewise do not suffer when terminally dehydrated. And if the patient is truly unconscious—as Terri Schiavo was, according to her doctors—then the patient would feel no pain even without ketonemia and palliation.

Wesley Smith insists that a conscious patient's refusal of food and water cannot fairly be compared with withholding ANH from an unconscious patient. In an article he published in the *Weekly Standard* in November 2003, he claimed (without citing any support in the medical literature) that when patients suffering from terminal diseases such as cancer stop eating and drinking, it is "because the disease has distorted their senses of hunger and thirst," and "the disease makes the food and water repulsive to them." Here again, he overlooks the appetite-suppressing effects of ketonemia. It's not just the underlying disease that suppresses appetite. It's also the fasting itself—independent of the underlying disease, which may or may not distort hunger and thirst.

Should we have faith in what the doctors say? I didn't at first. In 1998, when a hospital ethics committee okayed the cessation of ANH for my cousin Ros and assured me that she needed no pain relief, I couldn't quite believe it. I wondered, "How can that be? Why take a chance? Why not just sedate her heavily until it's over?" Well, now I know the answer to the last two questions: Doctors worry about being accused of euthanasia.

But what about my first question? Could it really be true that Ros would feel no pain or discomfort as she slowly died?

Now I know the medical explanation: the total lack of food caused a metabolic change in her that would have suppressed any hunger pangs if she were conscious enough to feel them.

If the specter of an agonizing death incites our worst fears, then the facts should allay those fears. That's a benefit of the human advantage over animals—higher reasoning.

I also had something else to reassure me—my own personal observations of Ros as she went through the ten-day process of dying.

During the first week, there were no discernable changes in Ros's condition. She just lay there as before, an empty shell of her former self. The nurses attended to her frequently and with obvious compassion—which was a great comfort to me, if not to Ros. They turned her. They moistened her mouth. Sometimes they talked to her. They kept her bedding clean and fresh. But I think it was more for us than for Ros. She seemed totally unaware of it all. She never made a sound.

After a week, the changes began. Her urine output slowed, darkened, and then stopped entirely. Her hands got cold and mottled. She did not get thin, but I suppose that's because she was overweight to begin with. Toward the end, her pulse became weak and her breathing shallow.

Ros died while I was home eating lunch. I wished I had been with her. But that saddened only me, not her. From the day of her stroke until the day of her death, I don't think she ever knew I was there.

Ros's death wasn't gruesome. It was nothing like what Smith, Dr. Stevens, and all the rest of the alarmists in the *Schiavo* case would have you believe. She was well cared for until the end. There was no cracked skin, lips, or tongue; no nosebleed; no seizure; no vomiting; no heart-wrenching attempt to cry. It was, as they often say, rather peaceful.

But it wasn't pretty. I suppose death never is. After I got the telephone call informing me of Ros's death and I rushed to the hospital, I saw that she had died with her eyes closed but her mouth wide open—something I wasn't prepared for. I gently tried to raise her lower jaw. It wouldn't budge.

Dr. Byock has written, "Medicine cannot sanitize dying." It's true.

So why are Wesley Smith and Dr. David Stevens—operatives of the Discovery Institute and the Christian Medical Society—telling us that the doctors are all wrong about terminal dehydration? And, more intriguingly, who is behind them? How is it that Smith can make a career out of his advocacy? How about his colleagues in the right-wing assault on the bioethicists?

After my debate with Smith, Rita Marker, and the Schindlers' attorney Pat Anderson in Tallahassee on the eve of the Florida Supreme Court hearing. I began to wonder who was funding them all.

The Think-Tank Machinery

I n early September 2004, a few days after I returned home to Oakland from Tallahassee, wondering who was funding the Schindlers' advocates, I asked my law firm's librarian, Alexis Wright, to hit the computer and see if she could find anything on funding for Rita Marker or Wesley Smith. A few hours later, she produced something baffling—an Internet reference indicating that Marker's organization, the International Task Force on Euthanasia and Assisted Suicide, had received a grant of $110,390 in 2001 from the Randolph Foundation.

"What," I wondered, "is the Randolph Foundation, and why did it give money to Rita Marker?"

Alexis explained that she found this reference on a web site called mediatransparency.com, which tracks funding by right-wing organizations. She told me to check out the web site, saying it would show me "one big web of donations and grants."

Once I visited the web site, I began to understand the think-tank machinery and its critical role in the *Schiavo* case. There is a money trail leading to virtually all of the lawyers for the Schindlers and Governor Jeb Bush, through more than a dozen religious Right organizations, from a handful of foundations that are quietly funding just about every ultraconservative cause on the political map.

This money trail shows that the exploitation of the *Schiavo* case by leaders of the religious Right is part of a broader scheme to change

America into a theocracy where the Constitution is subservient to the Bible and religious fundamentalists across the Judeo-Christian spectrum would intrude on our lives from conception to death by taking away our rights of personal autonomy. One of their ultrarich funders, Howard Ahmanson Jr., put it succinctly: "My purpose is total integration of biblical law into our lives."

It goes back to 1964, when the Republican Party chose ultraconservative Barry Goldwater to run for president. It was a heady time for the religious Right, which had been in cultural eclipse starting with the 1925 "Monkey Trial" of John Scopes for teaching Darwinism in a Tennessee public school, followed by decades of national political leadership by Democrats and moderate Republicans. With Goldwater's nomination, the ultraconservatives came out of hibernation. But Goldwater lost the 1964 election in a landslide to President Lyndon Johnson. It was a debacle for the religious Right.

In the wake of that defeat, a small group of ultraconservatives conceived a plan for revitalizing the Republican Party. They were to create a network of private think tanks—entities that employ researchers, writers, and publicists to develop and disseminate political and social thought, thereby shaping public policy—on such conservative causes as free-market economics, tax reduction, and increased spending on national defense, plus evangelical Christian causes such as the elimination of abortion rights, creationism, and prayer in public schools.

It would take a lot of money to do this, but money was not a problem. Backers of the plan included some extremely wealthy men— Richard Mellon Scaife (heir to the Mellon industrial, oil, and banking fortune), Lynde and Harry Bradley (electronics), the Smith Richardson Family (pharmaceuticals), Richard DeVos (the Amway line of household products), and Joseph Coors (beer).

The plan started to come together with the creation of the Heritage Foundation in 1973, funded by Joseph Coors. Later came the Lynde and Harry Bradley Foundation, several Scaife-funded foundations, the Richard and Helen DeVos Foundation, the Smith Richardson

Foundation, the Randolph Foundation, and many others. By the end of the twentieth century, there were more than six hundred conservative foundations and think tanks, with assets exceeding $2 billion, loosely organized under the umbrella of the Philanthropy Roundtable, a national association of like-minded groups and individuals.

That's who was giving money to Rita Marker.

I heeded the advice given by Mark "Deep Throat" Felt to *Washington Post* reporters Bob Woodward and Carl Bernstein during the Watergate scandal: "Follow the money." I began to study the right-wing think-tank machinery and trace its funding of advocates for Bob and Mary Schindler and Governor Jeb Bush. I was increasingly amazed as I learned that nearly everyone on the Schindler-Bush team was somehow connected—mostly financially, sometimes in other ways—with one or more right-wing foundations and think tanks. Alexis was right. It was, as she put it, "one big web of donations and grants"—and the *Schiavo* case was smack in the middle of the web.

I discovered a three-tiered structure. In the top tier are the funders—the foundations themselves. Given the "culture wars" banner of the ultraconservatives, I came to think of the foundations involved in the *Schiavo* case as the *high command.*

The middle tier consists of the think tanks and other organizations that get money from the foundations to pursue their litigation, publication, activism, education, and lobbying strategies. In the *Schiavo* case, these groups are consistently members of the religious Right. I came to think of them as the *officer corps.*

The bottom tier consists of the people who do the work of the funded organizations—the lawyers, activists, and politicians who represented and supported Bob and Mary Schindler and Governor Jeb Bush in their efforts to keep Terri Schiavo's PEG tube attached. I came to think of them as the *foot soldiers.*

Eventually, I was able to identify seven foundations in the high command, fourteen think tanks and other religious Right members of the officer corps, and eighteen foot soldiers behind the Schindlers and Governor Bush in the *Schiavo* case.

First, I focused on the foot soldiers—the most visible people working on the front lines of the *Schiavo* litigation. As the case proceeded to its denouement in March 2005, my list grew to include the following eighteen lawyers and politicians:

- *David Gibbs III* and *Barbara Weller*, attorneys with the Tampa-area Gibbs Law Firm, which provides legal services to evangelical Christian churches, ministers, and schools. David Gibbs III and his family control the Christian Law Association, which styles itself as dedicated to providing "legal assistance to Bible-believing churches and Christians who are experiencing legal difficulty in practicing their religious faith because of governmental regulation, intrusion, or prohibition of one form or another." Gibbs was involved in the *Schiavo* litigation starting in 2003 and became the lead attorney for Bob and Mary Schindler in September 2004.

- *Pat Anderson*, a St. Petersburg lawyer who was the Schindlers' lead counsel before September 2004.

- *Robert Destro*, a law professor at Catholic University of America in Washington, D.C. Destro has been active in groups opposing abortion and gay marriage, recently serving as principal investigator for the antigay "Marriage Law Project." He represented Governor Jeb Bush in litigation arising from the passage of "Terri's Law" in 2003, and he joined David Gibbs III in representing the Schindlers in March 2005.

- *Jay Sekulow*, chief counsel for the evangelical American Center for Law and Justice and one of the Schindlers' attorneys in the "Terri's Law" litigation. Sekulow was recently in the news for opposing Michael Newdow in his unsuccessful Supreme Court challenge to the recitation of the Pledge of Allegiance in public schools.

- *Deborah Berliner* and *Brett Wood,* attorneys who represented the Schindlers in arguing to Judge Greer that the pope's allocution on ANH required that Terri be kept alive. Berliner and Wood were formally affiliated with the right-wing group Judicial Watch, through which they participated in the Paula Jones litigation against President Bill Clinton.

- *Wesley J. Smith,* the antieuthanasia activist and author of numerous books and articles on bioethical issues. In addition to writing frequently about the *Schiavo* case for the conservative magazine the *Weekly Standard,* Smith—who is a lawyer—served as a behind-the-scenes "informal advisor" to the Schindlers.

- *Rita Marker,* executive director of the antieuthanasia International Task Force on Euthanasia and Assisted Suicide, who spoke in support of the Schindlers at the Tallahassee debate. Marker—also an attorney—writes and speaks frequently on euthanasia and right-to-die issues. Wesley Smith has served as the group's legal advisor.

- *Kenneth Connor,* a highly successful Florida trial lawyer who, with Robert Destro, represented Governor Jeb Bush in the "Terri's Law" litigation. In 2000–2003, Connor was president of the Family Research Council, a spin-off of James Dobson's evangelical Christian organization, Focus on the Family.

- *William Saunders* and *Jan Halisky,* lawyers for the Family Research Council's Center for Human Life and Bioethics.

- *Max Lapertosa, Kenneth Walden,* and *George Rahdert,* disability rights lawyers.

- *Tom DeLay,* Texas Republican and majority leader of the U.S. House of Representatives, who helped spearhead the congressional intervention into the *Schiavo* case.

- *Mel Martinez*, Republican U.S. senator from Florida, who sponsored a version of the congressional bill that threw the *Schiavo* case into the federal courts.

- *Governor Jeb Bush*, a constant presence in the *Schiavo* case on behalf of the Schindlers.

Next, the officer corps—the organizations on the religious Right that do the hands-on work. There are hundreds of these groups nationwide. I was able to identify fourteen with links to the *Schiavo* case:

- *Alliance Defense Fund*, a Christian legal firm founded by, among others, James Dobson of Focus on the Family. Alliance Defense Fund is very active in antiabortion and antigay rights litigation. Its 2003 assets were $19,530,630.

- *Family Research Council*, a Christian lobbying group that styles itself as an advocate for "public policy that values human life and upholds the institutions of marriage and the family"—including prayer in public schools, the right to discriminate against homosexuals, and antiabortion policies. Family Research Council's revenue in 2003 was $10,110,397. Its current president, Tony Perkins (who replaced Kenneth Connor), once bought a mailing list from former Ku Klux Klan grand wizard David Duke for $82,500.

- *American Center for Law and Justice*, the legal advocacy group whose chief counsel, Jay Sekulow, represented the Schindlers in the "Terri's Law" litigation and was later involved in the federal litigation generated by the congressional *Schiavo* bill. American Center for Law and Justice was founded by Christian evangelist Pat Robertson to litigate against abortion rights and gay marriage, and for other causes of the religious Right. Its 2003 budget was $15,900,000.

- *Life Legal Defense Foundation*, an antiabortion group that provides legal representation for persons arrested at demonstrations against abortion clinics. Between 1996 and 2002, Life Legal Defense Foundation received grants totaling $2,492,522. Its administrator, Mary Riley, has served jail time for trespassing at abortion clinics.

- *National Right to Life Committee*, a national antiabortion group founded in 1973 to fight the U.S. Supreme Court's decision in *Roe v. Wade.*

- *Christian Law Association*, which is controlled by the Gibbs family and funds the Gibbs Law Firm.

- *Discovery Institute for Public Policy*, which promotes the teaching of the neocreationist "intelligent design" theory in public schools. Discovery also has a "bioethics program" spearheaded by Wesley Smith, a paid senior fellow there. Between 1997 and 2003, Discovery received grants totaling $14,095,092.

- *Encounter Books*, whose publisher, Peter Collier, teams with neoconservative David Horowitz, head of the right-wing Center for the Study of Popular Culture. Encounter Books publishes Wesley Smith.

- *International Task Force on Euthanasia and Assisted Suicide*, the group run by Rita Marker. This group is the operating name for Family Living Council, which was incorporated in 1986 by Franciscan University of Steubenville, Ohio, for whom Marker and her husband directed a "pro-life" library. Between 1999 and 2003, the Family Living Council received grants totaling $2,074,371.

- *National Organization on Disability* and *World Institute on Disability*, two organizations that joined in the disability rights amicus curiae brief filed in the "Terri's Law" litigation.

- *Judicial Watch,* Bill Clinton's nemesis. Between 1997 and 2002, Judicial Watch received think-tank grants totaling $7,069,500.

- *Values Action Team,* a coalition of Republican members of Congress and groups on the religious Right, organized by House majority leader Tom DeLay and other House conservatives at the request of the Family Research Council. The Values Action Team is chaired by Pennsylvania Republican representative Joe Pitts, who was hand-picked by DeLay to lead the group.

- *Alexander Strategy Group,* a lobbying business founded by two former aides to Tom DeLay, one of whom was DeLay's former pastor.

Finally, the high command—the foundations that fund the whole enterprise. A recent study of thirty-seven conservative foundations showed grants to Christian evangelical groups totaling $168 million during the period 1999–2002. My list of foundations with links to the *Schiavo* case reached seven:

- *Lynde and Harry Bradley Foundation,* founded by two brothers who made a vast amount of money in the electronics industry. The Bradley Foundation's 2001 assets were $584 million.

- *Scaife family foundations,* funded by the Mellon industrial, oil, and banking fortune. Their combined 2001 assets were $478 million.

- *Richard and Helen DeVos Foundation,* an offshoot of the Amway empire, with 2003 assets of $96 million.

- *Randolph Foundation,* a spin-off of the Smith Richardson Foundation, with 2002 assets of $49 million.

- *JM Foundation,* with 2002 assets of $21 million.

- *Koch family foundations*, funded by two brothers who control an energy industry empire and have a combined net worth of $4 billion.

- *Heritage Foundation*, with 2003 assets of $129 million and grants totaling $57 million between 1985 and 2003.

In following this money trail, I mostly used two sources. The first is an archive of records on conservative think-tank funding, maintained by a handful of watchdog groups and generally available on the Internet. The second is the so-called 990 forms (Form 990: Return of Organization Exempt from Income Tax) that the Internal Revenue Service requires of tax-exempt organizations, which are open to public inspection. (See Appendix, fig. 1)

Through these and other sources, I tracked the flow of money from the foundations in the high command, to the think tanks and other members of the officer corps on the religious Right, to the foot soldiers for the Schindlers and Governor Jeb Bush in the *Schiavo* case. In some instances, I was able to trace payments directly to a foot soldier for work on the *Schiavo* case. In other instances, I discovered broader financial connections, where there was a constant flow of money to the foot soldiers, not discernibly earmarked for the *Schiavo* case in particular but generally financing the foot soldiers' work in the trenches of the culture wars, thus facilitating their work in the *Schiavo* battle. As noted by the watchdog National Committee for Responsive Philanthropy, "Conservative grant making has focused on building strong institutions by providing general operating support, rather than project-specific grants." Some connections were business related, as where a group published a foot soldier's books or articles. Other links were political.

My challenge was to manage the volume of information. Between September 2004 and June 2005, I spent dozens of hours wading through a sea of Internet references, 990 forms, and news reports, reviewing financial data through 2003 (more recent data not yet being available). Sometimes I ran into dead ends. Some of the players are extremely secretive and strive mightily to hide the amount and sources of their funding. Often, however, I found what I was looking for: connections between the Schindler/Bush advocates and groups on the religious Right, and then to the right-wing foundations that are funding the culture wars.

Eventually, I was able to chart a dizzying map of the religious Right's financial and political links to the *Schiavo* case—some links direct and well documented, others just a glimpse of what is undoubtedly a much larger but hidden picture.

Now let's connect the dots:

David Gibbs III, Barbara Weller, and the Gibbs Law Firm → Christian Law Association and Life Legal Defense Foundation. The Christian Law Association—which the Gibbs family controls—funneled $12,772,869 to the Gibbs Law Firm and another Gibbs-related firm during the years 1997–2003. (See Appendix, fig. 2)

Financial contributions to the Christian Law Association between 1993 and 2003 totaled $29,246,873. Just where all that money came from is a secret I couldn't penetrate. However, I did discover a link between Christian Law Association and a right-wing think tank. Christian Law Association's former president, Earl Little, was affiliated with a think tank called the Council for National Policy, which in August 2004 bestowed its Thomas Jefferson Award on Senate majority leader Bill Frist.

On April 27, 2004, when David Gibbs III appeared on CNN's *Larry King Live*, King asked Gibbs whether he was working on the *Schiavo* case "for nothing." Gibbs replied, "That's correct." Almost a year later, on March 16, 2005, Gibbs told a reporter for the Associated Press that he was working on the *Schiavo* case "for free," although Life Legal Defense Foundation was paying "some of his expenses." Gibbs seems to have a rather self-serving view of what it means to work "for nothing." If it means that Bob and Mary Schindler never paid him directly for his efforts, that's probably true. But his law firm thrives on a massive influx of income from his Christian Law Association, which enables him to work for nonpaying clients. Receiving $12,772,869 is not working "for nothing."

Pat Anderson → Life Legal Defense Foundation, Alliance Defense Fund, and American Center for Law and Justice → Lynde and Harry Bradley Foundation, Richard and Helen DeVos Foundation, and Bill and Bernice Grewcock Foundation. Life Legal Defense Foundation paid Pat Anderson at least $300,000 for her work on the *Schiavo* case. Alliance Defense Fund admits to paying Anderson a sum "in the six figures." In addition to representing the Schindlers in the guardianship proceeding, Anderson joined with American Center for Law and Justice as its local counsel in the Florida Supreme Court proceedings on "Terri's Law." In 2002, Alliance Defense Fund paid about $275,000 to American Center for Law and Justice and $90,000 to Life Legal Defense Foundation.

The combined assets of Alliance Defense Fund and American Center for Law and Justice, along with the much smaller Life Legal Defense Foundation, are vast—about $36 million in 2003. I managed to trace a trickle of this money to the DeVos Foundation ($75,000 to Alliance Defense Fund in 1998–2001 and $50,000 in 2003), the Grewcock Foundation ($80,000 to Alliance Defense Fund in 1998–2003), and the Bradley Foundation ($2,000 to Alliance Defense Fund in 1994).

Robert Destro → Alliance Defense Fund and American Center for Law and Justice → Bradley, DeVos, and Grewcock Foundations. Destro's anti-gay Marriage Law Project will receive $260,000 between 2004 and 2006 from Alliance Defense Fund, a recipient of funds from the Bradley, DeVos, and Grewcock Foundations. In fiscal year 2002–2003, Destro's employer, the law school at Catholic University of America, received grants from Alliance Defense Fund totaling some $270,000.

Destro, who frequently writes book chapters and articles on religious Right issues, has been published by two right-wing think tanks—the Ethics and Public Policy Center (recipient of $11 million from various foundations between 1992 and 2003, including $5,331,700 from the Bradley Foundation) and the Center for Economic and Policy Education (recipient of $30,000 from JM and Randolph Foundations between 1995 and 2002).

Deborah Berliner and Brett Wood → Judicial Watch → Scaife foundations. Berliner and Wood, the Schindlers' lawyers in their attempt to keep Terri's PEG tube attached because of the pope's 2004 allocution on ANH for PVS patients, are formerly of Judicial Watch, which received $7 million from the Scaife foundations between 1997 and 2002.

Wesley Smith → Discovery Institute for Public Policy, Encounter Books, and Life Legal Defense Foundation → Bradley, Scaife, and Randolph foundations. Wesley Smith is paid by Discovery Institute, which received $14,095,092 in grants between 1997 and 2003. I was able to spot, among these grants, $175,000 from the Bradley Foundation and $40,000 from one of the Scaife foundations.

Smith's publisher, Peter Collier's Encounter Books, and its institutional sibling, David Horowitz's Center for the Study of Popular Culture, have together received at least $5 million from the Bradley foundation, $3.7 million from the Scaife foundations, and $245,000 from the Randolph Foundation.

Some of Smith's articles have been published in the newsletter for Life Legal Defense Foundation, which gave away copies of Smith's most recent book in exchange for donations to help pay the group's *Schiavo* expenses. Smith's wife, Debra J. Saunders, who is a columnist with the *San Francisco Chronicle*, wrote a 2001 column for another publication professing to "admire" how Life Legal Defense Foundation's administrator Mary Riley and her family "lived its beliefs" by doing jail time for the antiabortion cause (although Saunders added, "I disagree with their cause"). Saunders has written frequently in the *San Francisco Chronicle* about the *Schiavo* case without disclosing her husband's paid employment by Discovery, saying only occasionally that he "served at one time as an unpaid formal advisor to the Schindlers." I wrote to the *Chronicle*'s editor, Philip Bronstein, suggesting that, as a matter of good journalistic ethics, Saunders ought to disclose in her *Schiavo* columns that her husband is a paid operative of Discovery. Bronstein never responded.

Rita Marker → International Task Force on Euthanasia and Assisted Suicide → Randolph Foundation. Between 1999 and 2003, Marker and her husband were paid $331,790 from the International Task Force on Euthanasia and Assisted Suicide (via the Family Living Council), which received $100,390 from Randolph Foundation.

Kenneth Connor → Family Research Council → Bradley Foundation and others. In 2001 and 2002, when Ken Connor was head of Family Research Council, it paid him $357,024 in salary and benefits. Between 1999 and 2002, Family Research Council received a total of $1,748,450 from several right-wing foundations, including the Bradley Foundation ($215,000 between 1992 and 1999).

Connor's law school roommate was Senator Mel Martinez, sponsor of congressional legislation in the *Schiavo* case.

William Saunders and Jan Halisky → Family Research Council → Bradley Foundation and others. These two lawyers filed an amicus curiae brief in support of Governor Jeb Bush in the "Terri's Law" litigation for the Family Research Council's Center for Human Life and Bioethics.

Max Lapertosa, Kenneth Walden, and George Rahdert → National Organization on Disability and World Institute on Disability → Scaife, DeVos, and JM foundations. These three lawyers filed an amicus curiae brief supporting Governor Bush in the "Terri's Law" litigation on behalf of seventeen disability rights organizations, with Diane Coleman's Not Dead Yet at the helm. Two of those organizations have received ultra-conservative foundation money—National Organization on Disability ($340,000 from Scaife in 1994–1999, $200,000 from DeVos in 1998–2002, and $90,000 from JM in 1995–2002) and World Institute on

Disability (I was able to spot only $20,000 from JM Foundation in 1997).

Representative Tom DeLay → Family Research Council, Values Action Team, and Alexander Strategy Group → Bradley and Koch foundations and others. Republican House majority leader Tom DeLay's Values Action Team was organized at the request of the Family Research Council, beneficiary of grants from Bradley and other foundations. Alexander Strategy Group set up an entity that in 2001 funded a $106,921 DeLay junket to South Korea—leading to calls for an investigation of DeLay by a House ethics panel. Alexander Strategy Group, which also employed DeLay's wife, was itself funded by Americans for a Republican Majority, one of whose major contributors was the Koch foundations.

Senator Mel Martinez → Alexander Strategy Group → Koch foundations. Senator Martinez's legal counsel during the congressional intervention in the *Schiavo* case, Brian H. Darling, was a former lobbyist for Alexander Strategy Group, a recipient of funds from the Koch foundations.

Governor Jeb Bush → Heritage Foundation. Jeb Bush served on Heritage Foundation's board of trustees before his election as Florida governor.

Finally, the Schindler family:

Bob, Mary, and Bobby Schindler → National Right to Life Committee and Response Unlimited. I never found evidence of a large flow of money directly to the Schindler family, but there was some. Bob and Mary Schindler set up their own foundation to solicit donations, garnering $38,567 in 2003. Records for the crucial 2004–2005 period are not yet available.

The Schindlers also authorized Response Unlimited, a conservative direct-mailing firm, to sell their donor list to buyers at $150 per month for six thousand names and $500 per month for four thousand e-mail addresses. The firm withdrew the list after the *New York Times* exposed the arrangement on March 29, 2005, two days before Terri died. A few days earlier, on March 24, 2005, the *Washington Post* reported that the National Right to Life Committee had escorted the Schindlers' son, Bobby, and paid his travel expenses on a trip to Washington, D.C., to lobby for congressional intervention.

In September 2004, the state of Florida notified the Schindlers that they had failed to comply with Florida law mandating that they register their foundation as a professional fundraising organization. Eventually, the Schindlers registered and were fined $1,000. They were assisted by the Tampa law firm Carlton Fields, one of whose lobbyists is former Florida Republican governor Bob Martinez, who as "drug czar" under the first President Bush employed as one of his deputies John Walters, the 1996–2001 president of the Philanthropy Roundtable.

In the *Schiavo* case, it seems like all roads lead to the conservative foundations and think tanks.

To be fair, let's also follow the money for Michael Schiavo's attorneys:

- *George Felos*, lead litigation counsel: $358,434 paid from Terri Schiavo's trust fund between 1998 and 2002; no payment from 2002 to 2005.

- *Deborah Bushnell*, guardianship counsel: $80,309 paid from Terri Schiavo's trust fund between 1993 and 2002; no payment from 2002 to 2005.

- *Team of lawyers at Jenner & Block*, the law firm that joined in the litigation following "Terri's Law" in 2002 and the congressional intervention in 2005: no payment.

- *Jon B. Eisenberg*: no payment.

- *ACLU of Florida*, also involved in the "Terri's Law" and congressional litigation: assets of $1,923,269 in 2004; two staff attorneys (Randall Marshall and Becky Steele) working on the case; no payment to ACLU for its *Schiavo* work.

The playing field is hardly level. The truth is that moderates and leftists on the national political scene are vastly outfunded by ultraconservatives. The few wealthy funders of moderate and liberal causes, such as financier George Soros, are no match for the six-hundred-member Philanthropy Roundtable. This money-laden network of conservative foundations, think tanks, and evangelicals was the juggernaut behind the advocates for the Schindlers and Governor Jeb Bush in the *Schiavo* case.

"So," you might ask, "what's the big deal? What's wrong with conservatives spending money on a cause they believe in?"

It's wrong when it is designed to subvert the American way of government by making the Constitution subservient to scripture. It's wrong when it is done by lawyers who publicly claim to be working "for nothing" but in truth are rolling in right-wing money. It's wrong when religious leaders exploit a family tragedy for political gain, turning what should have remained a private matter into a national spectacle. And it's truly frightening when seen in the broader context of a forty-year ultraconservative quest to control the most private aspects of our lives and take away our most basic of personal rights—the right of autonomy.

If you care about preserving your rights, you need to understand the money machine that you're up against.

The dictionary defines "conspiracy" as "a group plan to commit an evil act." If you believe it was evil that a group of lawyers, politicians, and think tanks used Terri Schiavo to mount an assault on the U.S. Constitution, then it is no exaggeration to call their plan a conspiracy to take away your rights. It's what made possible the debacle that the *Schiavo* case became when Governor Jeb Bush ordered the reinsertion of Terri's PEG tube in October 2003.

PART TWO

Where It Went

Jeb Strikes Out

To reflect on the amazing and sometimes bizarre twists and turns of the *Schiavo* case in its final eighteen months is to understand the lengths that the religious Right, backed by its vast funding, will go to subvert the right of personal autonomy and tilt the constitutional balance of American government. The battle lines were drawn by an antiabortionist in eclipse and a governor on the rise.

In October 2003, four days before the date Judge Greer had scheduled for removing Terri Schiavo's feeding tube, opportunity knocked at Randall Terry's door. Terry, the founder of the radical antiabortion group Operation Rescue, had been in the media spotlight throughout the 1980s and early 1990s, notorious for his harassment of abortion clinics and his public pronouncements that abortion doctors should be executed. By the late 1990s, however, Terry had retreated from the public eye. As the subject of an antiracketeering lawsuit, he had been forced to submit to a court injunction against future harassment of abortion clinics.

Everything changed on October 11, 2003, when Terry received a telephone call from conservative political activist Phil Sheldon, the son of Reverend Lou Sheldon of the religious Right's Traditional Values Coalition. Joining Sheldon on the call was the chief of staff for Alan Keyes, the conservative talk show host and fringe Republican presidential candidate. Sheldon had decided to begin a public rela-tions campaign to oppose the removal of Terri Schiavo's feeding tube, and he wanted Randall Terry's help.

Terry did not miss a beat. He immediately got on the telephone with Terri Schiavo's father, Bob Schindler, who gave Terry the green light. As Bob Schindler described it, "We gave him carte blanche to put Terri's fight in front of the American people."

Within two days, on October 13, a press release announced that Terri Schiavo's parents had invited Randall Terry to come "help save her life." Terry and a few demonstrators showed up at Hospice House Woodside in Pinellas Park, Florida, where Terri Schiavo was being cared for, beginning a noisy twenty-four-hour vigil that soon grew to one hundred. The minions sang hymns, shouted slogans, and waved signs quoting the Bible. One sign read, "Michael Schiavo is a mur-derer," another, "God numbers your days—not man." Priests prayed through bullhorns. Reporters scurried for interviews. Terry got the Schindlers to park a motor home nearby, which they used as a com-mand center to coordinate their public relations efforts.

Conservative radio talk show hosts warned that if Terri died, Florida governor Jeb Bush and the Florida legislature would be held accountable.

The media circus had begun.

Meanwhile, Phil Sheldon started a widely publicized e-mail cam-paign. The Florida legislature was bombarded with more than one hundred thousand e-mails urging passage of a law that would compel the retention of Terri's feeding tube, scheduled for removal on October 15. The e-mail barrage caused the legislature's Internet server to crash.

The October 13 press release said that the duty to "rescue" Terri "begins with Gov. Bush." Randall Terry sent protestors to Jeb Bush's public appearances and to the governor's mansion. On the morning of October 15, just hours before the feeding tube was to be removed, Terry arranged for himself and the Schindlers to meet personally with the governor. They begged for his help.

Bush must have known that he had no power to interfere with

Judge Greer's ruling. His spokesman told the press, "The simple fact is that there is a separation of powers here, and the governor does not have the power to overrule a court order."

But what's a presidential aspirant to do? The pressure was on. The Schindlers' lawyer, Pat Anderson, said publicly that the governor was "the last hope." Terry told the press, "We will hold Jeb Bush's feet to the fire relentlessly."

Bush promised Terry and the Schindlers that he would try somehow to prevent Terri's death. After meeting with them, he announced that he would "seek whatever legal alternatives are available and seek the best minds to find another avenue to submit to the courts to see if there can be a change in this ruling." The result was "Terri's Law"—or what one journalist called "*Terry's* Law"—authorizing Governor Bush to keep Terri Schiavo on ANH. "Terri's Law" passed in the Republican-controlled Florida legislature with remarkable speed. It took about a day.

Florida politics of the time had a lot to do with it. Florida House speaker Johnnie Byrd was a Republican candidate for the U.S. Senate, running on an extreme right-wing platform. He expected to face Florida state senator Daniel Webster in the upcoming Republican primary election, and the antiabortionists were crucial to Byrd's success. He was eager to get their votes.

Over the weekend of October 18–19, a small group of Republican legislators and staff put together a bill that would have imposed throughout Florida a six-month general moratorium on withdrawing ANH. That Sunday evening, they arranged for Byrd to put the bill before the legislature the next day, when the legislature was scheduled to go into special session to discuss a proposal to lure a biomedical research institute to the state. Byrd solicited the support of Republican senate president Jim King. Byrd's campaign organization sent e-mail to supporters saying he would appear Monday evening on Fox News Channel's *Hannity & Colmes* to announce a "bill to save Terri Schiavo." Byrd's rallying cry was "Every life is precious!" A colleague warned, "No one should take God's power in their hands. We need to step in here. We need to do this. It's the right thing." The fence-sitters were running scared—Republican and Democrat alike.

By the evening of October 20, with Randall Terry on hand to watch, the House was presented with a freshly minted "Terri's Law." But it wasn't the six-month moratorium crafted over the weekend. Senate president King had something else in mind—a bill that would apply only to Terri Schiavo, drafted earlier that day by members of King's staff and one of Governor Bush's lawyers after King had pitched the idea to the governor personally. To sponsor the rival bill, King selected Senator Webster—Byrd's expected opponent in the upcoming U.S. Senate race.

"Terri's Law" went before the House on Monday, October 20, at 7:44 P.M. There was no committee debate and no legal staff analysis. None of the representatives had yet seen the bill, and some didn't even read it before voting. The proponents gave the legislators a prepared script of statements they could make if asked any questions about the law—for example, "Someone needs to be a voice for the voiceless like Terri Schiavo."

By 10:10 P.M., the bill had passed by a vote of 68 to 23 with 28 members absent. The next morning, October 21, promptly at 8:00 A.M., a Senate committee heard the bill. At 3:30 P.M, the full Senate approved a slightly revised version by a vote of 23 to 15. The bill returned to the House for final approval by 4:00 P.M. A half-hour later, Governor Bush signed the bill into law—just twenty-one hours after its introduction.

The public pressure behind "Terri's Law" had been, as Randall Terry promised, unrelenting. It even came from Republican members of Congress. Pennsylvania representative Joe Pitts, chair of the Values Action Team organized at the behest of the religious Right's Family Research Council, cried out on the floor of the U.S. House of Representatives, "Death by dehydration is a painful, agonizing, and arduous process!" Evidently he, too, is ignorant of ketonemia and palliation. Florida representative Dave Weldon insisted that "Terri is not unconscious." Florida representative Tom Feeney parroted Byrd, saying, "All life is precious." Arizona representative Rick Renzi e-mailed Governor Bush, telling him that "saving" Terri's life "is a top priority in our quest to save and protect the innocent."

A week after Jeb Bush signed "Terri's Law," President George W. Bush said at a press conference, "I believe my brother made the right decision." Antieuthanasia activist Wesley Smith agreed—he told the *Washington Post* that "Terri's Law" was "an important first step in revisiting this issue of dehydrating people to death."

The bioethicists and law professors were appalled. Bill Allen, director of bioethics at the University of Florida, said, "Things are going a little crazy. This has been legally settled for over a decade." University of Florida law professor Joseph Little said, "In my view the bill is plainly unconstitutional." The renowned Harvard constitutional law professor Laurence Tribe said, "I've never seen a case in which the state legislature treats someone's life as a political football in quite the way this is being done."

Some of the Florida legislators who caved in seemed to know in their hearts that they were making a mistake. Republican senator Tom Lee commented, "I have never had a worse day as a senator. You could feel how rotten people felt having to vote on this." Senator King worried, "I keep on thinking, 'What if Terri Schiavo really didn't want this at all?' May God have mercy on us all." A few Democrats stood their ground. Dan Gelber of Miami Beach made a prescient statement: "This is a patently unconstitutional bill. It would be an awful stain on this chamber."

Oddly enough, the political maneuvering by Byrd and Webster didn't catapult either of them into the U.S. Senate. Webster later withdrew from the race—choosing instead to run for reelection to the Florida senate—after Mel Martinez, former secretary of housing and urban development under President George W. Bush, announced his candidacy. Martinez won the Republican primary, with Byrd coming in a distant fourth. Martinez also won the general election. He went on to play an embarrassing role in the endgame of the *Schiavo* case.

"Terri's Law" was a remarkable piece of legislation—perhaps equaled only by the progeny it spawned in the U.S. Congress a year and a half later. It read sort of like a law of general application, but as a practical matter it applied to only one person—Terri Schiavo.

The law gave Governor Bush the authority "to issue a one-time stay to prevent the withholding of nutrition and hydration from a patient if, as of October 15, 2003," four conditions were met:

- The patient "has no written advance directive";
- "the court has found that patient to be in a persistent vegetative state";
- "that patient has had nutrition and hydration withheld"; and
- "a member of that patient's family has challenged the withholding of nutrition and hydration."

There was only one such person in Florida—Terri Schiavo.

And just to make sure that the law could never apply to anyone else, it was written to provide specifically that it would expire fifteen days after the governor signed it. It was indeed "Terri's" law—and nobody else's.

Why did this law upset the law professors so much? It's because of a constitutional doctrine called "separation of powers."

The U.S. Constitution created three branches of federal government: legislative, executive, and judicial. The legislative branch is the U.S. Congress, of which there are two houses—the Senate and the House of Representatives. The executive branch is the presidency. The judicial branch is the federal judiciary—the U.S. Supreme Court, the intermediate federal appellate courts (called the Circuit Courts of Appeals), and the federal trial courts (called the district courts). Each branch functions independently in a system of checks and balances in-tended to prevent any single branch from abusing its power.

Like all the states, Florida likewise has three branches of state gov-ernment—legislative (the Florida legislature), executive (the gover-nor), and judicial (the Florida state courts). The Florida Constitution, like the U.S. Constitution, prescribes a separation of powers, stating, "No person belonging to one branch shall exercise any powers apper-taining to either of the other branches unless expressly provided herein." That provision imposes two distinct restraints on each branch: it may not encroach on the powers of another branch, and it may not delegate its own power to another branch.

The constitutional separation of powers forbids any legislation that would overturn a judicial ruling in a particular case, which is subject to review only by a higher court. The role of Congress and state legisla-tures is to make laws of general application, while the role of the judi-ciary is to apply those laws to specific cases. "Terri's Law" was crafted solely for a specific case. Through it, the Florida legislature purported to give Governor Bush a power of review over the decisions of Judge Greer and the appellate courts in the *Schiavo* litigation. This makes "Terri's Law" unconstitutional. And that's what Governor Bush's spokes-man meant when he told the press that the separation of powers pro-hibited the governor from overruling a court order. He knew.

Promptly after signing "Terri's Law" on the afternoon of October 21, Governor Bush ordered the reinsertion of Terri's feeding tube. Two hours later, an ambulance took her to Morton Plant Hospital in Clear-water, where the feeding tube was surgically reattached—six days after its removal.

Michael Schiavo vowed to fight back. He told CNN's Larry King that it was "Terri's wish" to have her feeding tube removed, and "I am going to follow that if this is the last thing I can do for Terri."

Michael sued Governor Bush. Michael's attorney, George J. Felos of Dunedin, Florida (who had litigated the 1990 Florida right-to-die case *Guardianship of Browning*), filed a lawsuit in the general civil division of the Pinellas County Circuit Court, requesting a judicial determination that "Terri's Law" was unconstitutional. This lawsuit went before a new judge, W. Douglas Baird.

Felos had some help with this lawsuit. The American Civil Liberties Union of Florida joined in it, along with a group of attorneys at the Washington D.C. office of a highly regarded Chicago-based law firm, Jenner & Block, headed by partner Thomas J. Perrelli. On October 29, 2003, the new team filed a forty-three-page brief asserting multiple constitutional infirmities in "Terri's Law."

Meanwhile, a disability rights organization called Advocacy Center for Persons with Disabilities filed a federal lawsuit claiming that the removal of Terri's PEG tube would constitute unlawful physical abuse and neglect. But the federal judge refused to intervene, citing another constitutional doctrine, federalism, which prohibits federal courts other than the U.S. Supreme Court from reviewing a state court judgment. Federalism is a function of states' rights. It would become a major issue when Congress intervened in the *Schiavo* case in March 2005. For now, at least, the federal courts were not in play. The Florida state courts would decide whether Terri's feeding tube should stay attached.

With the stakes thus raised, the Schindlers' advocates pursued a multifaceted public relations campaign. They did a very good job of it.

It began even before "Terri's Law," with a clever use of the four hours of videotape taken of Terri in 2002. Judge Greer had ordered Michael Schiavo, the Schindlers, and their lawyers not to "disseminate" the tapes to the public "in any way." But that didn't stop the Schindlers. They ignored the court order and posted excerpts from the videotapes—totaling four minutes and twenty seconds—on their Internet web site. Michael's lawyers complained in vain. Those snippets became the most powerful visual images of the *Schiavo* case, broadcasted endlessly on cable television channels.

Eventually, the tapes were made available for public viewing at the Pinellas County Courthouse. A reporter for the *St. Petersburg Times*, Stephen Nohlgren, watched the entire four hours, and then described the tapes in an article published on November 10, 2003. Nohlgren told the whole story—including what the Schindlers had omitted to show the public.

About those snippets, Nohlgren said, "Such moments that suggest awareness—culled from four hours of medical examinations that were videotaped in the summer of 2002—are rare compared to the times when Schiavo lies in bed, slack-jawed and seemingly unresponsive, her limbs stiff, her eyes vacant, her hands curled in tight contractions. . . . Over and over, Robert and Mary Schindler beg their daughter to demonstrate any sign of consciousness. . . . Here and there, their daughter's glances and moans seem to coincide with what's being asked of her and might lead one to conclude that she responds. But more often than not, the parents' entreaties fall flat." Terri would occasionally seem to track a balloon with her eyes, and sometimes she seemed to smile or laugh—once spontaneously, another time forty-five seconds after her mother started playing some music. At one point, Nohlgren said, she "makes a sound a lay person might interpret as a laugh," but "her noises get louder and louder until they exceed any other sound she makes during all four hours."

It seems that someone had done a very good job of editing the four hours of videotape into a few minutes of misleading images—precisely what I had suggested to disability rights activist Diane Coleman in our e-mail exchange about the case. The editors had selected the few times when Terri's actions—which the neurologists had said were merely reflexive, not cognitive—coincided with the constantly repeated entreaties to her. Judge Greer had addressed this very point in his written opinion after the 2002 hearing, saying he had counted 111 commands to Terri and seventy-two questions to her and had concluded there were "few actions that could be considered responsive to either those commands or those questions."

As misleading as the video snippets were, however, there was no denying their power. The Schindlers' advocates fully exploited them.

And the Schindlers thoroughly demonized Michael. Although in 1993 they had urged Michael to go out with other women and had even met his dates, they now bitterly decried what they had previously encouraged. By this time, Michael was living with another woman, with whom he had two children. Wesley Smith, who advised the Schindlers, concocted the notion that this meant Michael was "estranged" from Terri. In an article published on October 31, 2003, Smith said, "By siring two children with another woman, Michael effectively estranged himself from his marriage." Never mind that Terri might have wanted what her parents had wanted in 1993—for Michael to make a new life for himself. Smith's concoction became another mantra in the case: "Terri's estranged husband Michael."

Smith went even further as the months passed. In the *Weekly Standard* of April 30, 2004, he called Michael's behavior "utterly despicable," saying that Michael "had been romancing other women since shortly after the time of Terri's collapse," had "abandoned his marriage," and now "wants Terri dead," suggesting that Michael was motivated by the fact that "he would have inherited her $700,000," the trust-encumbered money from the medical malpractice lawsuit. In fact, by 2004 the trust fund was nearly depleted, the money having been spent on medical and legal bills.

That's about the time I got involved in the case.

When I heard about "Terri's Law," my first thought was: "Hey, they can't do that!" It didn't take a constitutional scholar—and I'm not one—to figure out there was a separation of powers problem.

I was more interested, however, in the bioethical aspects of the case—a subject I knew something about, given my prior representation of the forty-three amicus curiae bioethicists in *Wendland*. Thinking it could be helpful to file an amicus curiae brief in *Schiavo* explaining the bioethical aspects of the case, much as I had done in *Wendland*, I decided to see whether the bioethicists might want a reprise.

Through the wonders of e-mail, I managed to reach most of my former bioethicist clients very quickly. Some of them contacted others. In short order we assembled fifty-five bioethicists from across the country, along with the disability rights organization Autonomy Inc., to file a bioethicists' brief in *Schiavo*. All I had to do was wait for the case to make its way up on appeal, at which point I would file the brief.

It took quite a long time for Judge Baird to rule on Michael's challenge to "Terri's Law." Felos and company were now facing a new clutch of lawyers—the team representing Governor Bush, led by Ken Connor, the veteran attorney who had previously headed the religious Right's Family Research Council. Connor's game was delay—he tried to stall Judge Baird at every opportunity. After all, for Governor Bush and the Schindlers, each day of delay was a day of victory, with Terri's PEG tube remaining in place.

Connor peppered Judge Baird with motions: to dismiss Michael's lawsuit on the ground it was filed in the wrong venue; to disqualify Judge Baird because he supposedly was biased; to subject seven witnesses, including Michael, to depositions (interviews of witnesses conducted by lawyers and officially transcribed); and for a full jury retrial of the issues that Judge Greer had already decided—Terri's medical condition and wishes. The Schindlers' attorney, Pat Anderson, joined in, filing a motion to allow the Schindlers to intervene in the lawsuit.

Whenever Connor lost, he appealed to the Court of Appeal. And all during that time, because of stays resulting from the pending litigation, Terri Schiavo's PEG tube remained attached.

Meanwhile, Judge Baird said he would not decide the constitutionality of "Terri's Law" until the Court of Appeal had decided the venue issue. That didn't happen until April 23, 2004, when the appellate court held that Michael's lawsuit was properly venued. The door was finally open for Judge Baird to issue his constitutionality ruling.

At the outset of all this legal maneuvering, in late October 2003, an independent legal guardian was appointed to prepare a report on Terri Schiavo. This was mandated by "Terri's Law," which required the circuit court to "appoint a guardian ad litem for the patient to make recommendations to the Governor and the court." The court selected Jay Wolfson, a professor of law at central Florida's Stetson University College of Law and professor of public health and medicine at the University of South Florida in Tampa.

Wolfson reviewed all the legal and medical records for the case, including nearly thirty thousand pages of court filings. He interviewed family members, lawyers, doctors, bioethicists, clergy, and scholars. He conducted his own independent medical research. He frequently visited Terri. He even met with Governor Bush. On December 1, 2003, Wolfson announced his conclusions and recommendations in a thirty-eight-page report.

Wolfson reported that Terri was indeed in PVS: "Highly competent, scientifically based physicians using recognized measures and standards have deduced, within a high degree of medical certainty, that Theresa is in a persistent vegetative state. This evidence is compelling." Neurological tests and CT scans, he said, "indicate that Theresa's cerebral cortex is principally liquid." He noted that Terri "sometimes groans, makes noises that emulate laughter or crying, and may appear to track movement," but "the scientific medical literature and the reports obtained from highly respected neuro-science researchers indicate that these activities are common and characteristic of persons in a persistent vegetative state." In all his visits with Terri—"sometimes daily, and sometimes, more than once each day"—he saw no signs of cognition. He was "not able to independently determine that there were consistent, repetitive, intentional, reproducible interactive and aware activities." He concluded that "the behavior that Theresa manifests is attributable to brain stem and forebrain functions that are reflexive, rather than cognitive."

Wolfson addressed the question of whether Terri's condition could ever improve. He concluded the answer was no: "In recent months, individuals have come forward indicating that there are therapies and treatments and interventions that can literally re-grow Theresa's functional, cerebral cortex brain tissue, restoring part or all of her functions. There is no scientifically valid, medically recognized evidence that this has been done or is possible, even in rats, according to the president of the American Society for Neuro-Transplantation."

Wolfson also addressed whether Terri might ever be able to take nutrition and hydration orally, without a feeding tube. Swallowing tests performed in 1991, 1992, and 1993 had indicated that Terri was unable to swallow food and liquid without risk of aspiration and infection. Wolfson thought that further tests might shed more light on her ability to swallow and whether it might be restored to any extent by therapy, but the Schindlers and Michael Schiavo were unable to agree on a process for conducting such tests.

The report's conclusion was that Terri "is in a persistent vegetative state with no likelihood of improvement" and "the neurological and speech pathology evidence in the file support the contention that she cannot take oral nutrition and hydration and cannot consciously interact with her environment." In other words, Judge Greer had correctly determined her medical condition.

Some of the Florida legislators became contrite. In an interview with the *St. Petersburg Times* reported on February 10, 2004, Senate president Jim King conceded, "The Terri Schiavo vote that I made was probably one of the worst votes that I've ever done." He said other senators had told him "they also regret it, but the pressure of tens of thousands of phone calls and e-mails—and physical and political threats—was enormous." They subsequently realized their political blunder: "After the vote there were far more people critical of what we had done and very vehemently angry at what we had done than there were people supporting it."

King made clear that he wouldn't make the same mistake again. He said that "if it comes up again I will not do it." Then why not repeal the law? Because, the article said, "he expects it will be overturned in court."

King told the *St. Petersburg Times* that he would "block any bills aimed at making it harder to remove feeding tubes from comatose or mentally incompetent patients without living wills." And that's just what happened. In April 2004, a proposed bill in the Florida Senate to require ANH for PVS patients in virtually all circumstances faced fatal opposition and was withdrawn from consideration.

Senator King was right about the fate of "Terri's Law." On May 5, 2004, Judge Baird held it unconstitutional. He ruled that the law violated the constitutional separation of powers in two ways: first, by allowing the executive branch (Governor Bush) to encroach on the powers of the judicial branch; and second, by delegating legislative power to the governor.

Governor Bush's appeal of the ruling went straight to the Florida Supreme Court, via a rarely invoked procedure for bypassing the Court of Appeal in extremely important and urgent cases. The time had come for me and all the other "friends of the court" to file our amicus curiae briefs.

Three amicus curiae briefs were filed in support of Governor Bush: by a group of disability rights organizations headed by Diane Coleman's Not Dead Yet; by the right-wing Family Research Council's Center for Human Life and Bioethics; and by Pat Anderson on behalf of the Schindlers, now joined by Jay Sekulow, chief counsel for Christian evangelist Pat Robertson's American Center for Law and Justice. Three amicus curiae briefs were filed in support of Michael Schiavo: by the Elder Law Section of the Florida Bar Association; by the Academy of Florida Elder Law Attorneys; and by my fifty-five bioethicists and Autonomy Inc.

In the bioethicists' brief, I explained how the Florida right-to-die laws embody the bioethical value of personal autonomy and the three bioethical models for surrogate exercise of an incompetent patient's right to refuse medical treatment. I argued that "Terri's Law" violated these core principles of bioethics by "placing the authority to make a substituted judgment decision for Terri in the hands of a stranger who knows nothing of her preferences and values." I argued that the legislation "violates bioethics by usurping a substituted judgment decision with a political decision in disregard of Terri Schiavo's wishes." And I argued, "The constitutional separation of powers puts case-specific decision-making, such as proxy exercise of Terri Schiavo's right of personal autonomy, in the hands of judges, who are guided by time-tested rules of evidence and procedure and thus, unlike policy-making legislators and governors, are properly equipped to adjudicate."

The bioethical principles were important to understand, but it was really, ultimately, about the Constitution.

The Florida Supreme Court heard oral arguments in *Bush v. Schiavo* on August 31, 2004. I flew to Tallahassee a couple of days beforehand to join Wesley Smith, Rita Marker, Pat Anderson, and the others in the public debate at Florida State University that started me on the money trail. I then attended the Florida Supreme Court hearing. The court heard argument from George Felos on behalf of Michael Schiavo and from a new attorney—Robert Destro, Catholic University of America law professor and opponent of gay marriage—on behalf of Governor Bush.

When the court ruled, just three weeks later, on September 23, 2004, that "Terri's Law" was indeed unconstitutional, few were surprised. The opinion was unanimous. All seven justices agreed that "Terri's Law" violated the constitutional separation of powers—which the court called "the cornerstone of American democracy"—in both ways Michael's lawyers had asserted.

First, the law encroached on judicial power by authorizing the executive—Governor Bush—to overturn a Florida state court judgment. Second, the law wrongly delegated legislative power to Governor Bush by giving him "absolute, unfettered discretion" to interfere with the judicial determination to remove Terri's feeding tube, in a manner that "failed to provide any standards" of conduct and "makes the Governor's decision virtually unreviewable." The court said "Terri's Law" "does not even require that the governor consider the patient's wishes" —the bioethical and legal underpinning of substituted-judgment decision-making.

The court said it would not reexamine Judge Greer's factual determinations regarding Terri's medical condition and wishes. No appellate court properly could have, given the restrictive rules against appellate second-guessing of trial court credibility determinations. The issue here was not factual, but legal—whether "Terri's Law" violated the constitutional separation of powers. Plainly it did.

Within a week of the Florida Supreme Court's ruling, Pat Anderson—a passionate advocate who had once told Michael Schiavo's guardianship attorney, Deborah Bushnell, that "you're going to burn in hell, lady"—withdrew from representing the Schindlers. She was replaced by David Gibbs III of the Gibbs Law Firm and the Christian Law Association.

Four months later, on January 24, 2005, the U.S. Supreme Court denied Governor Bush's request that the court take up *Bush v. Schiavo*. The case was over. "Terri's Law" had been struck down. Jeb Bush—and Randall Terry—had struck out. The governor's lawyer, Ken Connor, told the *New York Times* that "this matter is now at an end for the governor."

Connor was dissembling. He began working with Governor Bush's legal staff to coordinate new efforts by the governor and the Florida legislature to keep Terri's PEG tube attached. On January 26, 2005, Connor e-mailed Governor Bush's lawyers Raquel Rodriguez and Christa Calamas a proposed newspaper op-ed article that Connor had drafted. The article argued that Terri Schiavo had "been issued a death sentence by the courts," invoked the governor's "ability, in a criminal death sentence, to grant clemency," and advocated for the effort "to extend the same protection to Terri Schiavo."

Connor's op-ed piece was subsequently published in *USA Today*—but not under his name. The newspaper identified the author as Florida state senator Daniel Webster—the sponsor of "Terri's Law." The article's true author is revealed in Connor's January 26 e-mail to Calamas and Rodriguez, which says: "Here is an op-ed I drafted for Dan Webster." (See Appendix, fig. 3)

It would take a bit of time, however, before Connor, Bush, Webster, and their cohorts could gear up for a run at another "Terri's Law." Meanwhile, the battle lines shifted back to Judge Greer.

Judge Greer Toughs It Out

F or the religious Right, Terri Schiavo was a tool to be used. For Judge George W. Greer, Terri was part of his job.

When Michael Schiavo filed his 1998 petition asking the Pinellas County Circuit Court to authorize the removal of Terri's PEG tube, Judge Greer, then fifty-six years old, had been a member of the court for six years. Brooklyn-born but raised in Florida, he attended St. Petersburg Junior College and Florida State University. One of his former college roommates later recalled him as "stable, mature, and structured ... an organized guy with a sort of balanced personality, very even-headed, not controversial, very solid." He was the polar opposite of one of their other roommates, future rock star Jim Morrison, who aggravated his housemates by helping himself to their food and beer and playing Elvis Presley records at full blast.

Greer became a lawyer and hung his shingle in Clearwater, where he practiced law for twenty-three years, specializing in zoning and land use. He married, had twins boys, divorced, and remarried. A Southern Baptist, he regularly attended church. He was a conservative Republican, unseating a Democrat on the Pinellas County Commission in 1984. A friend later said of him, "George *is* the religious right."

In 1992, Greer ran unopposed for a seat on the circuit court. By 1998, he was sitting in the court's probate division and had settled into a steady diet of wills, estates, trusts, and guardianships.

Probate judging is not often the stuff of newspaper headlines, public prayer vigils, and the wrath of politicians. But the *Schiavo* case was unlike any other. From the moment Judge Greer ruled in February 2000 that Terri Schiavo's ANH should be discontinued, he was attacked vehemently and relentlessly.

Greer received hate mail accusing him of murder and comparing him to the Nazis. He got occasional death threats. His courthouse was picketed. He felt compelled to stop attending his church, Calvary Baptist, after it sent members of the congregation a publication criticizing him. Toward the end of the case, he withdrew entirely from the church after its pastor asked him to "reconsider" his membership, and he required armed police protection whenever he traveled.

When Greer ran for reelection in 2004, he drew an opponent who seized on the *Schiavo* case as a campaign issue. The rival sent mailers to voters who drove cars with "Choose Life" license plates, asking, "Do you believe that God created life? Do you believe that each of us has the right to enjoy and defend life?"

After Greer handily won reelection, his contributors received mailers that said, "Please help stop a judicial murderer!" Religious groups circulated a petition to impeach him that garnered some seven thousand signatures. Even antieuthanasia activist Wesley Smith went on the attack, writing in the *Weekly Standard* that "Judge Greer's performance" in the *Schiavo* case "has been so deficient that he should be removed from the case forthwith, if not impeached." A former campaign worker for Greer told the *New York Times*: "People threatening to kill him and claiming it has something to do with the right to life—explain that, will you?"

Greer himself might well have lamented, in the immortal words of the late Chicago mayor Richard J. Daley, "They have vilified me, they have crucified me; yes, they have even criticized me!"

None of these assaults affected the quality of Greer's judging. The former campaign worker told the *New York Times*, "He always voted the way he sincerely believed to be right, regardless of how many people were standing in front of him screaming and carrying on." An article in the *St. Petersburg Times* quoted Greer: "My oath is to follow the law, and if I can't follow the law, I need to step down." In that article, he also addressed his critics on the religious Right, saying they "have nothing to do with my relationship with God. They can't affect it." Greer added, "My faith is based on forgiveness because that's what God did."

This was a tough and thoughtful judge.

Greer needed both those qualities to handle the litigation barrage that came his way in early 2005, after the U.S. Supreme Court let stand the Florida Supreme Court decision overturning "Terri's Law," and Randall Terry, the radical antiabortionist, announced in a February 16 press release that "we will fight tooth and nail to keep Terri from being starved to death."

After the U.S. Supreme Court's ruling, Michael Schiavo's litigation attorney, George Felos, and his guardianship attorney, Deborah Bushnell, faced a tag team of lawyers for the Schindlers and Governor Bush: David Gibbs III of the Christian Law Association, who took over from Pat Anderson; Brett Wood and Deborah Berliner, veterans of the Paula Jones litigation against former president Bill Clinton, who filed written arguments before Judge Greer for a new trial in light of the pope's allocution on ANH; and Florida state government lawyers for the Department of Children and Families, which did Governor Bush's bidding as a proposed participant in the guardianship proceeding.

Gibbs's first move was to resume efforts to forestall Judge Greer's order to remove Terri's PEG tube, issued back in November 2002 but legally "stayed" (put on hold) by appeals and other legal maneuvering during the "Terri's Law" period:

- *February 11, 2005.* After an initial flurry of procedural efforts to keep the stay in place, Judge Greer rules that the removal order is again effective but will remain stayed pending further appellate review.

- *February 15.* Gibbs asks Judge Greer for a further "indefinite stay" based on the Schindlers' appeal of the February 11 order.

- *February 22.* The Court of Appeal paves the way for the stay to be lifted. Judge Greer extends the stay until February 23, and then February 25, to permit further consideration of pending issues.

- *February 25.* In a written order, Judge Greer denies a further stay and schedules the removal of Terri Schiavo's feeding tube to occur three weeks hence, on March 18, 2005.

In the February 25 order, Judge Greer explained, "Five years have passed since the issuance of the February 2000 Order authorizing the removal of Theresa Schiavo's nutrition and hydration and there appears to be no finality in sight to this process. The Court, therefore, is no longer comfortable in continuing to grant stays pending appeal of Orders denying Respondents' various motions and petitions. The process does not work when the trial court finds a motion to be without merit but then stays the effect of such denial for months pending appellate review. Also, the Court is no longer comfortable granting stays simply upon the filing of new motions and petitions since there will always be 'new' issues that can be pled."

Judge Greer had had enough.

Gibbs, however, was anything but through. He didn't just appeal the order of February 25—he struck back at Judge Greer with a vengeance.

The opening salvo came immediately on February 25, with two filings:

- A petition asking Judge Greer to issue an order requiring "experimental treatment" to determine whether Terri really was in PVS—the Schindlers continued to insist she was not—and whether she might be trained to swallow through "electrical charge" therapy.

- A motion asking the judge to order a completely new "medi-cal/psychiatric/rehabilitative evaluation" of Terri to determine whether she had been misdiagnosed as being in a persistent vegetative state or might have moved into a minimally con-scious state.

The next blast came three days later, on February 28, when Gibbs filed a huge pile of additional motions—a blizzard of paper—asking Judge Greer to do the following:

- Allow a priest to give Terri the last rites of the Catholic Church after her PEG tube was removed, and allow the Schindlers to visit her while she was dying. That's about as sensible as the motions got.

- Forbid Terri's cremation—an echo of my cousin Ros and her brother Alex's adamant opposition to cremation. According to Gibbs, "To a Catholic such as Mrs. Schiavo, cremation is unacceptable from the historic context of pagan rituals and Gnostic heresy that hold to a dualistic nature of man.... De-struction of the body flies in the face of the Christian belief that the body we die in will be resurrected in the future." The problem with Gibbs's argument was that, since 1963, the Catholic Church has allowed cremation. The catechism of the church states that it "permits cremation, provided that it does not demonstrate a denial of faith in the resurrection of the body." Most Catholic cemeteries offer crypt spaces for cre-mated remains.

- Initiate proceedings for Terri to divorce Michael because he "has engaged in open adultery." Never mind that Florida is a "no fault" divorce state where adultery is irrelevant to the legal question of whether a marriage should be dissolved.

- Allow "limited media access to Mrs. Schiavo and visits with her family," permit "a limited number of specified legal and religious counselors" (perhaps Randall Terry?) to visit her "on a daily basis," and allow a "one-time visit" by two media representatives of the Schindlers' choosing. Plainly this motion was designed to exploit the media circus that the case had engendered.

- Allow the Schindlers to photograph and videotape Terri, and to retain control over the photos and tapes—perhaps as ammunition for another media blitz?

- Authorize depositions of Michael and his girlfriend.

- Allow the Schindlers to try to get Terri to take nutrition and hydration orally.

- Transport Terri to the Schindlers' home for her to die there.

- Clamp instead of remove her PEG tube (so that it wouldn't have to be reattached by surgery if ANH was later ordered restored).

- Appoint a "neutral medical witness" to observe the procedure by which the PEG tube was removed or clamped.

Gibbs asked for forty-eight hours of court time for hearings on the various motions. Ironically, he also asked that the "neutral medical witness" be allowed to "assure that Terri is given appropriate palliative care to relieve her from the painful effects of starvation and hydration." Even Gibbs knew that palliation can alleviate any pain from terminal dehydration.

All these motions were added to an existing pile of pending court filings by the Schindlers, which included a new petition asking Judge Greer to remove Michael as Terri's legal guardian, a request that Judge Greer declare his original judgment void on the ground Terri had lacked independent legal counsel, and renewed efforts to obtain a new trial based on the pope's allocution. All told, there were now fifteen pending motions and petitions before Judge Greer.

The motions and petitions were largely unsuccessful, with most of them going down to defeat in early March.

Perhaps most important, in an order filed on March 9, Judge Greer addressed the Schindlers' requests for experimental treatment and a new medical evaluation to determine whether Terri was truly in PVS or might possibly be trained to swallow. The Schindlers had presented thirty-three supporting medical affidavits, but Judge Greer discounted most of them as being "based on [the doctors'] understanding of Terri's condition from news reports or video clips they have seen." The Schindlers' doctors had relied on those edited video snippets and the television news to make their claims—a phenomenon that would soon be repeated by U.S. Senate majority leader Bill Frist.

Further, Judge Greer explained, upon examination of the affidavits, it became obvious that the Schindlers' doctors had not even been aware of the medical tests that had been given to Terri for the October 2002 evidentiary hearing. The doctors "suggest the very tests that were given at that time or appear to be unaware that batteries of tests have been given at all." And, the judge said, "Although all of the affiants urge that new tests be given, most are vague as to the course of treatment that should be given, while others suggest treatment that has already been considered."

As for the suggestion that Terri might be trained to swallow, Judge Greer explained that she already had undergone swallowing tests and there was no evidence that the swallowing therapy the Schindlers proposed could be performed on patients in PVS.

Meanwhile, Governor Bush attacked on another front by using a state agency under his control, the Department of Children and Families, or DCF—which, among other things, investigates reports of child or spousal abuse.

On February 23, DCF, represented by state government lawyers, filed a motion to "intervene" in the *Schiavo* guardianship proceeding—that is, to enter the guardianship case formally as a new litigant. According to the motion, on two previous days that week, DCF had received, from unnamed sources on a telephone hotline, approximately thirty "detailed allegations of abuse, neglect or exploitation" of Terri Schiavo.

The motion gave few details of the allegations, saying only that they involved things like "failure to file [a] proper guardianship plan or report," unspecified "confinement issues at the ward's residence," improper performance of experimental procedures, and two claims the Schindlers had already made—that Terri had been deprived of independent legal counsel and potentially beneficial new experimental treatments. The motion conceded that DCF had investigated earlier allegations of abuse and had found them to be "unfounded."

What Governor Bush's attorneys were really seeking was more delays. The motion said DCF wanted to intervene "for the limited purpose" of forestalling the court order for termination of Terri's life support until DCF could complete a sixty-day "investigation" of the allegations. Once again, the executive branch, of which DCF is a part, was attempting to interfere with the final judgment of a state court—an unlawful encroachment on the judicial branch.

Judge Greer was unfazed. On March 10, he denied DCF's motion. His written order was meticulous. First he pointed out a fundamental technical flaw in the motion: the legislation prescribing DCF's powers and duties did not authorize the agency to become a party to a guardianship proceeding. DCF had no power to intervene here.

Next, Judge Greer noted that the order to discontinue Terri's ANH "does not interfere with DCF's statutorily mandated duty to investigate." In other words, if DCF was really concerned about allegations of abuse, it could go ahead and investigate them. And, the judge noted, DCF had already investigated reports of abuse in 2001 and 2003, had concluded they were unfounded, and had not attempted to intervene in the guardianship proceedings at those times.

The judge described as "particularly unsettling" a comment by the state's attorney at the hearing on the motion: When Judge Greer asked the attorney "whether DCF believed that part of its mandated duty was to review orders of this court," the attorney replied, "Yes." Counsel was amazingly candid in admitting that this was another instance of the executive branch attempting to review a court's judgment—which violated the constitutional separation of powers. Evidently, the governor needed to be reminded yet again of what Justice Antonin Scalia said in the 1995 U.S. Supreme Court case *Plaut v. Spendthrift Farm, Inc.*—that a court's judgment is subject to review only by higher appellate courts. Judge Greer did just that.

Ultimately, Judge Greer said, DCF's motion was merely a subterfuge "brought for the purpose of circumventing the Court's final judgment and order setting the removal date, in violation of the separation of powers doctrine."

Hadn't Jeb Bush learned anything from *Bush v. Schiavo?*

DCF appealed, of course, but got nowhere. The Court of Appeal refused to issue another stay, as did the Florida Supreme Court.

And what about the allegations that Terri Schiavo had been abused? They turned out to be bogus. Two weeks after Terri's death, Judge Greer ordered the public disclosure of nine reports that DCF had compiled on eighty-nine complaints of abuse between 2001 and 2004 (with the names of the complainants blacked out). There were unsubstantiated allegations of beatings and strangling by Michael, bed sores, suspicious needle marks, insulin injections, broken bones, and an infection where Terri's feeding tube was attached to her stomach. All of the complaints proved to be unfounded. The DCF investigators, whose efforts had included unannounced visits to Terri's bedside, concluded that there were "no indicators of medical neglect or exploitation," that Terri was in good condition, and that all her imminent medical needs were "being met." There were no broken bones, no needle marks, no insulin injections. A skin ulcer appeared to have been treated and healed. The claim of infection at the site of the feeding tube turned out to have been made by someone who had gotten her "information" from an Internet chat room.

In fact, most of the reports of abuse read suspiciously like the public relations campaign against Michael Schiavo: "The husband wants to

starve Ms. Schiavo to death." "Mrs. Schiavo is not in a persistent vegetative state." "The husband wants Mrs. Schiavo to die so that he can
inherit a million dollars." "Ms. Schiavo is not getting the therapy she
needs to get better." "Mr. Schiavo wants to kill her by having her feeding tube removed." It was just more of the same rhetoric.

The thirty additional "detailed allegations" of abuse reported in
2005 were publicly disclosed in June of that year, and they were no different, except for one—a complaint on March 7, 2005, that in July
2004 a nurse's aide had put air freshener in Terri's bath water, causing a
rash. The DCF investigator learned that the aide had put aromather-
apy oil in an air freshener spray bottle, not in Terri's bathwater.

On March 16, 2005, the Court of Appeal issued its last opinion in
the *Schiavo* case. After reviewing the case's "extensive legal history"
and the applicable legal principles, the appellate court said that the issues "have long been resolved" upon a "full and independent inquiry"
under "a heightened standard of proof." The court observed that
Judge Greer's decision "has been subject to appeals and postjudgment
scrutiny of all varieties, and it remains a valid judgment pursuant to
the laws and the constitution of this state. Not only has Mrs. Schiavo's
case been given due process, but few, if any, similar cases have ever
been afforded this heightened level of process."

The appellate court had this to say about the public clamor against
Judge Greer: "We are well aware that many people around the world
disagree with the trial court's decision. However, when he became a
judge, the trial court judge took an oath, required by the Florida Constitution, to obey the rule of law and the constitution of this state. The
trial judge followed and obeyed the law as set out by the precedent of
the Supreme Court of Florida and by the general laws adopted by the
Legislature. The trial judge made this most difficult decision after fully
considering the evidence and applying a heightened standard of proof
that is designed to protect society's interest in sustaining life.... No
one who considers the dismal history of countries in which courts and
judges have abandoned the rule of law would ask us to abandon the
rule of law even in this case."

The appellate court fully vindicated Judge Greer and denied any further stay. Terri's PEG tube was to come out on schedule, two days later, on March 18.

Once again, the Schindlers went to the U.S. Supreme Court—and, once again, on March 17, the court refused to step in, denying a request for an immediate stay. The Florida state court battle had reached a dead end. The war had to be taken to another front.

After the battle over "Terri's Law" ended in February 2003, I watched the next round of litigation madness from the sidelines. My role as counsel for the amicus curiae bioethicists was over. But when the Court of Appeal ruled on March 16 and the removal of Terri's PEG tube seemed imminent, I knew that George Felos and Deborah Bushnell were about to be deluged even further by the Schindler and Bush attorneys and could use some help. I volunteered to join them on Michael Schiavo's legal team, figuring I could assist with crafting legal arguments and with whatever else George and Debbie might think of. Tom Perrelli at Jenner & Block took the lead on legal writing and research.

None of us was being paid. George and Debbie had previously been compensated for their legal fees out of Terri's trust, but that money was long since depleted. The folks at Jenner & Block were, as always, working entirely on a pro bono basis, as was I.

What could be left in the Schindlers' war chest of litigation tactics? Why . . . how about suing Judge Greer?

Incredibly, that's just what Gibbs did, with the assistance of Robert Destro—law professor at the Catholic University of America, opponent of gay marriage, and one of Governor Jeb Bush's attorneys in *Bush v. Schiavo.*

On March 18, 2005, Destro and Gibbs filed a lawsuit in the local federal district court—the Middle District of Florida, Tampa Division—entitled *Theresa Marie Schindler Schiavo v. The Honorable George Greer.* The Schindlers, suing on Terri's behalf—and recycling the same arguments they had presented in state court—asked the federal judge to

issue two orders: a writ of habeas corpus (a written court order prohibiting an unlawful custodial detention) requiring Terri's release from
state "custody," and an injunction prohibiting Judge Greer and
Michael Schiavo from "taking any action to cause Mrs. Schiavo to die
while this action is pending."

This was certainly creative litigation, but there were two major
problems with it.

First, to get a writ of habeas corpus in *Schiavo v. Greer*, the
Schindlers had to show that Terri was truly in the "custody" of the
state. She was not, of course—she was a patient at Hospice House
Woodside. The Schindlers' theory was that being "confined to a hospice" was no different under Terri's circumstances than confinement
"in a state correctional facility." But a similar argument had gone
down to defeat more than two decades earlier in *Lehman v. Lycoming
County Children's Services Agency*, where the U.S. Supreme Court rejected a theory that children in foster homes under court order were in
"custody" for purposes of habeas corpus relief. The Supreme Court explained that "custody" means a "restraint on liberty," and to extend
that notion to foster care would be "an unprecedented expansion of
the jurisdiction of the lower federal courts." That's what Destro and
Gibbs were asking for—which was ironic indeed, given the right
wing's aversion to expanding judicial power. And in a more recent
guardianship case, *Hemon v. Office of Public Guardian*, a federal appeals
court had concluded that a nursing home patient is no more in "custody" than a foster child. Thus there was no way that a hospice patient
such as Terri Schiavo could logically be treated as being in "custody."

The other problem with *Schiavo v. Greer* was the rule of federalism—
the constitutional doctrine that prohibits federal courts other than the
U.S. Supreme Court from reviewing a state court judgment. In America,
we have two legal systems—the federal courts and the state courts—
which function separately, with the federal courts deciding only cases
that involve issues of federal law or disputes between residents of different states. A state court judgment such as Judge Greer's decision in
the *Schiavo* guardianship proceeding cannot be reviewed by the federal
district court or Circuit Court of Appeals. This rule is necessary to pre-

serve the integrity of state court judgments. Without it, the constitutional balance between the federal and state judicial systems would be disrupted. The Schindlers' lawsuit against Judge Greer was a not-so-subtle attempt to achieve what federalism prohibits—a review in federal district court of a state court judgment. The lawsuit expressly requested a retrial "to determine Terri's present physical and mental condition, as well as her wishes regarding both medical treatment and rehabilitation"—issues Judge Greer had already decided.

I'm no expert on habeas corpus and federalism. My specialty is appellate procedure. When I was pegged to help draft the legal arguments on these points in *Schiavo v. Greer*, I knew that I needed some fast tutoring—and I was fortunate to get it from Harvard constitutional law professor Laurence Tribe.

I telephoned Jim Braden, the San Francisco lawyer who had brought me into the *Wendland* case. I knew that Jim had been one of Tribe's students at Harvard in the 1970s and they had stayed in touch. Could Jim somehow connect me with Tribe? Within an hour of calling Jim, I was on the phone with Tribe himself.

That was the beginning of what was, for me, a remarkable two-week e-mail correspondence with Professor Tribe, in which he educated me on a mass of constitutional issues arising from the *Schiavo* case. Whenever I called on him—which was almost daily—he responded with detailed written analyses that could have been published "as is" in a law journal, complete with citations to pertinent cases and to his own treatise on constitutional law. I would read his e-mail, ruminate, research his sources, think some more, bounce a few questions off him . . . and then write. A lot of Professor Tribe ended up in my work product. He would prove an invaluable resource to me in the days to come.

As for the federal lawsuit against Judge Greer, the district court judge instantly denied the Schindlers' petition—the same day it was filed— saying, "This court is not an appellate court for state courts' decisions." Judge Greer had weathered another attack.

Now what?

The Florida Legislature Bows Out

In February 2005, as Judge Greer was on the verge of reinstating his 2000 order to remove Terri Schiavo's PEG tube, the Florida legislature—still licking its wounds from the Florida Supreme Court's stinging rebuke of "Terri's Law"—went at it again. It was time for "Terri's Law II."

David Baxley, a Republican member of the Florida House, resurrected the proposed bill that had died in the legislature in April 2004—Senate Bill 692. SB 692 was now reincarnated as House Bill 701, which Baxley introduced on February 4, 2005. HB 701 became the new battlefront as the assault on Judge Greer approached its dead end.

If there is any doubt about the antiabortion roots of Baxley's bill, it is dispelled by tracing HB 701 to its source—the National Right to Life Committee. NRLC was formed in 1973 to combat the U.S. Supreme Court's decision in *Roe v. Wade* to legalize abortion. NRLC's mission statement describes its "ultimate goal" as being "to restore legal protection to innocent human life," which mostly means opposing abortion but also extends to "the right to life issues of euthanasia and infanticide." NRLC is large, active, and well funded.

In October 2003, NRLC decided to do something about the *Schiavo* case by promoting a piece of "model" legislation—an all-purpose law that can be adopted by any state legislature in the United States—to forbid withholding or withdrawing ANH in cases like Terri's. NRLC called its brainchild the "Model Starvation and Dehydration of Persons with Disabilities Prevention Act."

NRLC's model act is a bioethicist's nightmare. It almost entirely does away with surrogate exercise of an incompetent patient's right to refuse ANH by creating a legally binding "presumption" that the patient would want ANH: "It shall be presumed that every person legally incapable of making health care decisions has directed his or her health care providers to provide him or her with nutrition and hydration to a degree that is sufficient to sustain life."

The act further prohibits any surrogate, guardian, or court from making a decision to withhold or withdraw ANH except in the following three circumstances—none of which is ever likely to arise:

- The provision of ANH is not medically possible or would hasten death or if the patient is incapable of digesting or absorbing ANH.

- The patient previously made an advance directive authorizing the withholding or withdrawing of ANH. This clause might seem reasonable enough—at least for the 10 to 20 percent of Americans who actually make an advance directive—until you get to the fine print. The act says that the advance directive must contain a provision that specifically authorizes refusal of ANH, and that any such provision is effective only "to the extent the authorization applies." This is a lawyer's trick. It leaves the door wide open for arguments that a particular advance directive is not specific enough or that its authorization does not apply to the patient's particular physical condition—for example, the advance directive doesn't say that ANH should be withheld even if the patient is diagnosed as being in PVS but can make noises that sound like laughter.

- There is clear and convincing evidence that the patient, when competent, ruled out ANH with an expression of informed consent given "in the applicable circumstances." The act defines informed consent as knowledge of the procedure and any risks and alternatives, so as to enable the patient "to make an understanding and enlightened decision." But it is virtually impossible for anyone—except perhaps an oracle—to foresee what medical conditions and potential treatments might lie in one's future. And what does "enlightened" mean? This is another lawyer's trick, opening the door to all sorts of arguments that a patient's pre-incompetency statements about end-of-life decision-making might not apply to the current circumstances or why the patient's decision was not sufficiently enlightened— for example, the patient was never told the canard that death by terminal dehydration is agonizing.

NRLC's model act should be subtitled "How to Make It Virtually Impossible to Withhold or Withdraw ANH From a PVS Patient."

A month after NRLC announced the model legislation, it found its first forum—the Florida legislature—when a Republican member of the Florida state Senate introduced Senate Bill 692 on November 21, 2003. All the salient portions of NRLC's model law were transplanted wholesale into SB 692, which even had the same title—"Starvation and Dehydration of Persons with Disabilities Prevention Act." Thus, yet again, as with so much in the *Schiavo* case, efforts to keep Terri Schiavo's feeding tube attached trace back to well-funded antiabortion groups.

SB 692 was the 2004 bill that Senate president Jim King had vowed to kill after having second thoughts about "Terri's Law." It was referred to a Senate committee for "further consideration," where it quietly died in April 2004.

SB 692 returned on February 4, 2005—this time in the Florida House, as House Bill 701. HB 701 was identical to the former SB 692—same title, same provisions, same antiabortion roots. On February 18, it was referred to three House committees for consideration.

The Florida bioethicists were in an uproar. A group of nine bioethicists from the state's leading medical and law schools and universities gave the House a detailed written analysis of HB 701, explaining all the ways in which it violated various principles of bioethics developed over the past quarter-century.

The Florida bioethicists voiced their concern that the definition of "informed consent" in HB 701—taken verbatim from NRLC's model act—required an "impossible level of conversational specificity" in people's discussions about end-of-life choices. The bioethicists argued, "HB 701 requires too much evidence of a patient's wishes—so much evidence that most people who would want to have medically supplied nutrition and hydration withheld or withdrawn would end up receiving it against their wishes." They worried that HB 701 would "impose impossible burdens on physicians and patient surrogates, proxies and guardians" and would "establish insurmountable barriers to Floridians' exercise of uncontroversial rights to refuse burdensome medical treatment."

The bioethicists also debunked the notion that Terri Schiavo was "disabled," saying "it is widely and accurately agreed that a person who is permanently unconscious is most certainly not disabled in either the ordinary or the medical use of the term. To be disabled is to be in some way physiologically harmed or different such that the patient is unable in varying degrees to do or experience things that other people do or experience. If someone is unable to do or experience *anything*, it is incoherent to suggest that such a person is *disabled* in the sense of having less or different-than-customary capacity."

The proponents of HB 701 were undeterred. The bill went forward. And on March 9 it received some startling amendments. One amendment added a requirement that, in the unlikely event someone actually managed to satisfy the bill's convoluted requirements for withholding or withdrawing ANH, the surrogate first had to sit with the patient for either twenty-four hours at two hours per week or thirty hours at ten hours per month over a three-month period. Another amendment took away the circuit court's authority to act as a surrogate, as Judge Greer had done for Terri Schiavo. Yet another amendment said that "any interested party"—not just a relative or friend, but someone like, for example, the radical antiabortionist Randall Terry or the antieuthanasia activist Wesley Smith—could sue to prevent someone's refusal of ANH. Finally, the bill was expressly made retroactive so that it would apply to Terri. It was truly "Terri's Law II."

Representative Baxley proclaimed, "I have an intimate respect for human life, for the special gift that it is, and I hope that this is a defining moment for our culture. Let it be that we let somebody live." He repeated the now-familiar mantra: "I certainly hope that whatever error I make is on the side of allowing someone to live rather than to die."

Other legislators didn't seem to be as thrilled. Republican House speaker Allan Bense commented, "I just don't think we're doing a service to Terri by ginning up a bill and getting it out quickly in helter-skelter fashion." The Senate's new president—Tom Lee, who had lamented in 2003 when the legislature passed "Terri's Law" that "I have never had a worse day as a senator"—cautioned that he wanted to be "fair to all the people who have feelings about end-of-life issues."

Public reaction was more frank. A hospice doctor warned that HB 701 would require thousands of patients near death to have feeding tubes attached. Baxley responded, "That's thousands of people you can't kill now." The chair of the Florida Bar Association's elder law section lamented the provision requiring a surrogate to sit with the patient for twenty-four to thirty hours over a three-month period, calling it "an extremely cruel punishment" for the patient. Representative John Stargell responded, "If you are going to withdraw hydration or starve them to death, you should spend some time with them."

The most poignant comments came from Representative Charlie Justice, who issued a public statement describing his mother's death the previous week: "Around her bedside were her children, her brother and her good friend. There was no room at her bedside for politicians." As for HB 701, Justice opined, "I do not know all the facts of the Schiavo family tragedy. But we cannot honestly debate this bill without acknowledging that this legislation is centered on this one family. Without the omniscience of God, it is impossible to determine who is right and who is wrong. For me, after what my family has gone through in recent months, I cannot support having politicians in Tallahassee make that decision for another family when I wouldn't want them making it for mine."

Cracks appeared in the edifice of HB 701. It continued to go forward, but in a substantially truncated version. By March 14, when the bill went to a vote before the House Judiciary Committee, large portions had been gutted. Gone were the legally binding "presumption" against ANH, the impossibly ambiguous definition of "informed consent," the clause requiring the surrogate to sit with the patient for twenty-four to thirty hours over a three-month period, and the deprivation of judicial authority to act as a surrogate.

But the revised bill still would have done what Baxley wanted— prevented the removal of Terri Schiavo's PEG tube. It passed in the House Judiciary Committee on March 14 by a vote of 8 to 2.

That's when HB 701 began to crumble. A rival bill was proposed in the state Senate—Senate Bill 804—sponsored by Daniel Webster, sponsor of the first "Terri's Law," in 2003, and ostensible author of Ken Connor's February op-ed article. Senator Webster vowed to get SB 804, rather than HR 701, passed and signed by Governor Bush before 1:00 P.M. on March 18, when Terri Schiavo's feeding tube was scheduled to be removed. SB 804 quickly went to the Senate Judiciary Committee, where it passed on March 15 by a vote of 6 to 2. There were now dueling bills.

SB 804 was very different from HB 701. It merely provided that if "a conflict exists" between family members or friends as to whether a PVS patient's ANH should be suspended, and the patient has not made an advance written directive authorizing the suspension of life-prolonging procedures, then the objector may petition a court to prevent the suspension of ANH.

SB 804 had the political advantage of functioning as a "Terri's Law II" without wreaking havoc with the existing Florida right-to-die laws and underlying principles of bioethics. But it also risked the fatal flaw of the first "Terri's Law"—violation of the constitutional separation of powers doctrine, which prohibits the legislative branch from overruling a court's judgment in a specific case. The bill had a clause saying it would apply not just to Terri but also to persons in PVS "after" its effective date—meaning to any other case like *Schiavo* that might arise in the future. But SB 804's proponents were fooling no one. There was only one *Schiavo* case in Florida, and it is unlikely there will be another Florida case like it in the foreseeable future. This was plainly just another attempt to overrule Judge Greer—and an invitation for another constitutional rebuke from the Florida Supreme Court.

Some of the senators understood this. Democrat Steve Geller complained, "We are once again substituting our judgment for that of the courts." Senator King said that to apply SB 804 to Terri Schiavo "is to do exactly what everyone said they didn't want to do. They said they didn't want to make a carve-out for Terri and that's exactly what they are doing." Senator Lee was equivocal, saying: "We should move slowly and cautiously. I don't want to repeat the problems we had last time."

In the end, both bills failed. A group of nine Senate Republicans, led by Senator King, bolted from the pack and opposed SB 804. King commented, "As far as we're concerned we don't want anything to change the existing law." Senator Dennis Jones remarked, "The last time I voted yes and it was the wrong vote." Senator Charlie Dean, who had also voted for the 2003 "Terri's Law," said that "after reflection" he had decided "this was a family matter." Senator David Russell explained, "I received a number of communications from my constituents, many of them conservative Republicans, asking that we not intervene. And I listen to my constituents."

The bills went to a vote on March 17. HB 701 passed in the House with a vote of 78 to 37. But SB 804 failed in the Senate with a vote of 21 to 18. The legislators couldn't reach a compromise agreement, so the Senate never voted on HB 701. "Terri's Law II" was dead. Governor Jeb Bush, who had lobbied hard for legislative action, called the outcome a "huge disappointment." An editorial in the *St. Petersburg Times* praised the "fortitude" of the nine Republican senators who had caused the defeat of SB 804, saying that "their independence is commendable and refreshing."

Others, however, were vengeful. A few days after the vote, posters appeared at the state capitol building picturing the nine Republican senators who had voted against the bill and bearing the warning "Wanted: The Republican 9." Security measures had to be boosted. An agent of the Florida Department of Law Enforcement was posted outside Senator King's office. Senator Nancy Argenziano reported that she was getting vicious voicemail messages: "One person told me they hoped I died from cancer, another said my family members should rot in hell. They are the most awful, venomous, un-Christian things you have ever heard." She accused Governor Bush of inciting the nastiness, saying, "I feel like my political party has been hijacked."

Senator King was puzzled by the outcry from the religious Right: "I'm really saddened by the fact that people don't understand [that] for some of us, heaven is a place where we think Terri will go. And we think, as good ardent Christians, that heaven is a better thing than anything we have experienced here on earth. We can't understand why anybody would try—particularly staunch Christian advocates—would try to deny Terri the opportunity to have what has always been described to us as the promised land."

The Florida legislature had bowed out, and time had run out. The March 18 deadline had arrived.

13

The Tube Comes Out

Terri Schiavo's feeding tube was removed at 1:45 P.M. on March 18, 2005. It had been fifteen years since Terri's collapse; twelve years since Bob and Mary Schindler urged Michael Schiavo to date other women and get on with his life; seven years since Michael filed his petition in the Pinellas County Circuit Court asking for judicial authorization to remove Terri's PEG tube; five years since Judge Greer ruled that Terri was in a persistent vegetative state and would have wanted to die; four years since the ruling was upheld by the Court of Appeal, the Florida Supreme Court, and the U.S. Supreme Court; two and a half years since Judge Greer held a further evidentiary hearing and again ruled that Terri was in PVS and had no hope of improvement; a year and a half since the federal district court refused to intervene for lack of federal jurisdiction; and five months since the Florida Supreme Court overturned "Terri's Law."

Even after the U.S. Supreme Court refused on January 25, 2005, to review the decision on "Terri's Law," Judge Greer had given the Schindlers another seven and a half weeks to make a final attempt to show good cause for keeping Terri's PEG tube attached. The Schindlers tried, and they failed. The delay game was over.

On Friday afternoon of March 18, George Felos announced at a press conference that Terri's PEG tube had come out. He said, "It was an emotional occasion, prayers were said at that time and the feeding tube was removed without incident." He later added, "Let her go in peace."

Meanwhile, the radical antiabortionist Randall Terry was back at Hospice House Woodside with another twenty-four-hour vigil. Protestors stood behind police barriers holding signs that read, "She wants to live!!" "What part of thou shalt not kill don't you understand?" "It's murder not mercy," "Stop playing God!" "The leftist media won't tell you that Terri was beaten by Michael Schiavo," "Jews for Terri." They sang, "What can wash away our sins? Nothing but the blood of Jesus." Pickup trucks and trailers hauled around a huge crucified Jesus figure, a ten-foot-high Ten Commandments tablet, and a working replica of the Liberty Bell. Bob and Mary Schindler held on-site media interviews.

President George W. Bush spoke out, issuing a press release in which he said that "in instances like this one, where there are serious questions and substantial doubts, our society, our laws, and our courts should have a presumption in favor of life.... It should be our goal as a nation to build a culture of life." So did his brother, Governor Jeb Bush, who lamented, "It is frustrating for people to think that I have power that I don't, and not be able to act. I don't have embedded special powers. I wish I did in this particular case."

Echoing the sentiments of bioethicists across the country, Dr. Arthur Caplan, director of bioethics at the University of Pennsylvania, said on MSNBC, "The time has come to let Terri Schiavo die." A pseudonymous Internet blogger had a different take: "Terri died a long time ago."

The religious Right was quick to speak out. Richard Land, an appointee of President Bush to a federal commission on religious freedom and president of the public policy arm of the Southern Baptist Convention, said, "The depth, breadth and height of Judge Greer's chutzpah really beggars the imagination." Troy Newman, current head of the antiabortion group Operation Rescue West, wrote: "We will not stand idly by while an innocent woman is starved. Operation Rescue vows to peacefully intervene to offer Terri Schiavo bread and water. It is our duty as Christians to rescue those unjustly sentenced to death. That is a higher law from a Higher Judge than Judge Greer, and if that means we must spend time in jail, then it is the least we can do for this helpless young lady." The antieuthanasia activist Wesley Smith complained that "if only she were a convicted murderer, her life would be seen as worthy of greater respect."

Some began to warn of darker consequences. The editors of *The New Pantagruel*, a conservative Christian political journal, issued a statement saying that "those closest to Terri—her family, friends, and members of their communities of care—are morally free to contemplate and take extra-legal action as they deem it necessary to save Terri's life, up to and including forcible resistance to the State's coercive and unjust implementation of Terri's death by starvation."

The Internet bloggers were more frank—and more frightening. Cyberspace was cluttered with pseudonymous postings like this: "Will someone please kill Michael Schiavo before it is too late? My only comfort is that if Terri dies someone will avenge her by spilling Michael's blood. Perhaps they will kill his mistress and the two fowl [sic] offspring he had by her while thier [sic] at it!" And: "If we kill Michael Schiavo, the parents will be her closest relatives. Florida gun owners, it's in your hands."

Some of the bloggers called for insurrection: "If our laws permit Terri to be starved to death then we need to burn down EVERY courthouse in this country and start our justice system anew!" One warned of a new Civil War: "50 years from now historians will look back and note that the second US Civil War, the war to Restore National Values, was set off by a young woman who had been in a coma since 1992."

Even former Green Beret colonel Bo Gritz got in on the action. He and his wife drove to Florida from their home in Nevada, bearing a notarized "Citizen's Arrest Notice" which was executed by Colonel Gritz and purported to authorize him to arrest Judge Greer and Michael Schiavo for a "felony conspiracy" to kill Terri Schiavo. Colonel Gritz announced in a press release: "Amer-I-cans will always fight for freedom."

There were demands for congressional intervention—and warnings of dire consequences for the Republicans if Congress didn't act. Peggy Noonan, speechwriter for former presidents Ronald Reagan and George H. W. Bush, threw down the gauntlet in the *Wall Street Journal,* saying: "The Republican Party controls the Senate, the House and the White House. The Republicans are in charge. They have the power. If they can't save this woman's life, they will face a reckoning from a sizable portion of their own base. And they will of course deserve it. . . . *Politicians, please think of yourselves!* Move to help Terri Schiavo, and no one will be mad at you, and you'll keep a human being alive. . . . You have to pull out all the stops. . . . You have to win on this. If you don't, you can't imagine how much you're going to lose."

Robert Destro, attorney for Governor Jeb Bush in *Bush v. Schiavo* and now representing the Schindlers, wrote to House representative James Sensenbrenner asking for a congressional "Terri's Law," pleading: "She is a person with a severe brain injury whose only 'crime' is that she is incapacitated. . . . We need this law . . . before she dies from starvation and dehydration." Ken Conner said, "I would urge the House to consider sending agents to gain control of Terri and to reinsert her feeding tube in order to preserve the evidence and to preserve Terri as a potential witness."

The Republican leadership acted quickly. Senate majority leader Bill Frist and House Speaker Dennis Hastert issued a joint statement: "The House and Senate leadership are committed to reaching an agreement on legislation that provides an opportunity to save Mrs. Schiavo's life." House majority leader Tom DeLay, speaking to a meeting of the Family Research Council, said, "I tell you, ladies and gentlemen, one thing God has brought to us is Terri Schiavo to elevate the visibility of what's going on in America. That Americans would be so barbaric as to pull a feeding tube out of a person that is lucid and starve them to death for two weeks. I mean, in America that's going to happen if we don't win this fight. . . . This is a huge nationwide concerted effort to destroy everything we believe in."

Randall Terry warned that the Republicans had better mean what they said: "This is the biggest test for DeLay and Hastert. We will hold the House leadership accountable if this thing fails. We didn't get here so they could pour this down the drain. They owe us a political debt of honor. We are about to find out what the United States House of Representatives is made of."

Democratic representative Henry Waxman worried about "turning the Schiavo family's personal tragedy into a national political farce" if Congress were to intervene.

On the *News Hour with Jim Lehrer*, Florida bioethicist Bill Allen debated with House representative Dave Weldon:

Weldon: "You look at the videos of her. She follows commands; she smiles. This is not a persistent vegetative state."

Allen: "You can't tell from a videotape; even a physician can't watch a short snippet of videotape and make this diagnosis. The leading neurologists have examined her personally and they've concluded that she is in a persistent vegetative state."

Weldon: "It's unprecedented for a state court judge to order from the bench the withdrawal of food and water. That's never been done before."

Allen: "This has happened many times not only in Florida but around the nation.... [T]his law has been well settled in Florida and Florida statute allows this. It allows people to testify as to what the patient's wishes were when they were capacitated; and the courts found that to be the case with Ms. Schiavo, that she had testified to meet their burden of clear and convincing evidence."

Weldon: "The real issue here is not whether it comports with Florida law or not; it's really whether it's right or wrong. And sometimes laws are wrong."

As if to chime in, a protestor outside Hospice House Woodside held a sign that read: "Jesus is the standard."

Even some officials of the Catholic Church—revisionists opposed to the church's four-hundred-year tradition on end-of-life issues—spoke out. Cardinal Renato Martin, head of the Pontifical Council for Justice and Peace, said on Vatican Radio: "[If Michael Schiavo] legally succeeded in provoking the death of his wife, this would not only be tragic in itself, but it would be a serious step toward legally approving euthanasia in the United States."

Bishop Thomas G. Wenski of the Diocese of Orlando, Florida— who had been appointed by Governor Jeb Bush to a state commission on Haiti—issued a written statement saying: "Terri's agony has already begun and barring some miracle the denouement of Terri's drama will be her death. . . . From the cross Jesus cried out and his cry is echoed today by all those held captive to a world of pain and sin. . . . Like Jesus did, Terri Schiavo cries out, though with muted voice: 'I thirst!'"

Did Terri cry out anything? One of the attorneys for the Schindlers, Barbara Weller of the Gibbs Law Firm, said that when she visited Terri's bedside on the morning of March 18, she took Terri's arms in her hands and "begged her to try very hard to say, 'I want to live.'" According to Weller, Terri cried out: "Ahhhhhhh!" "Waaaaaaaa!" Weller announced to the world that Terri had tried to say "I want to live." The doctors, however, would call it just more noncognitive moaning.

Republican leaders took very seriously the warnings and threats from the likes of Peggy Noonan and Randall Terry. The next battleground was the U.S. Congress.

The Democrats Bail Out

The Congressional effort to keep Terri Schiavo's PEG tube attached was spearheaded by a handful of politicians and their lawyers and staff—including House majority leader Tom DeLay, Senate majority leader Bill Frist, Senator Mel Martinez, and Schindler attorney Robert Destro—who collaborated in an effort to draft federal legislation that might not be as blatantly unconstitutional as "Terri's Law." They left a paper trail consisting of e-mail messages (obtained by reporter Dara Kam of the *Palm Beach Post*) that circulated between them and to Governor Jeb Bush—who was constantly kept in the loop—throughout March 2005.

Robert Destro made his demands clear in an e-mail message he sent to lawyers for Frist, Martinez, the House Judiciary Committee, and the National Right to Life Committee: "We need a statute!!!"

It would prove to be a tricky business, however, to craft a federal version of "Terri's Law" that wouldn't risk unintended consequences in other areas of the law—say, for example, by creating a procedure for the *Schiavo* case that death row inmates might also try to use. That was the modus operandi of the first proposed House bill, HR 1151, sponsored by Representative Weldon and introduced in the House on March 8.

HR 1151 would have changed the law of habeas corpus—which presented an obstacle to the Schindlers' soon-to-be-filed federal lawsuit against Judge Greer because Terri was not in state "custody," as required for habeas relief. The bill would have created a legal fiction of "custody" for Terri and others like her by providing that "an incapacitated person shall be deemed to be in custody" whenever a court order "authorizes or directs the withholding or withdrawal of food, fluids or medical treatment necessary to sustain the person's life."

Robert Destro had suggested HR 1151's habeas corpus approach. He feared that a bill directed only at Terri Schiavo would suffer the same fate as "Terri's Law" and be overturned as violating the constitutional separation of powers.

Around this time, an anonymous memo began to circulate in the halls of Congress, boasting of the political hay to be made from HR 1151. (See Appendix, fig. 4) Noting that Terri Schiavo's feeding tube was scheduled to be removed on March 18, the memo said that "the pro-life base will be excited that the Senate is debating this important moral issue.... This is a great political issue, because Senator Nelson of Florida has already refused to become a cosponsor and this is a tough issue for Democrats." (Senator Bill Nelson, a Democrat, would be up for reelection in 2006.)

The memo dispelled any doubt that HR 1151's proponents intended to exploit Terri Schiavo for political advantage. Who was the author? That remained a mystery for weeks. The memo was leaked to ABC News on March 18 and to the *Washington Post* on March 19, but nobody would own up to writing it. Some people even claimed it was phony—a dirty trick by the Democrats. Wesley Smith's wife, Debra J. Saunders, joined the naysayers, writing in her *San Francisco Chronicle* column that the "alleged" memo "said things only a moron would be dumb enough to put on paper" and "the memo that was supposed to show how craven the GOP is instead shows how gullible the media is."

Saunders was wrong—the memo was no phony, and it really did "show how craven" some Republicans were. On April 7, 2005, a week after Terri Schiavo's death, Brian H. Darling, legal counsel to Senator Martinez, publicly admitted that he was the author. Then he resigned.

Before going to work for Senator Martinez, Darling had been a lobbyist with the Alexander Strategy Group, which had been founded by two former aides to Tom DeLay (one of whom was also DeLay's pastor), had employed DeLay's wife, and had set up the entity that funded the DeLay junket to South Korea in 2001. Alexander Strategy Group was funded by Americans for a Republican Majority, one of whose major contributors was the Koch foundations. Just about every attempt to keep Terri Schiavo's PEG tube attached traces back to those right-wing think tanks and foundations.

There was a big problem with HR 1151. For proponents of the death penalty, tinkering with the law of habeas corpus was dangerous stuff. There was no telling whether or how some clever criminal defense attorney might be able to use the hastily written law in an unforeseen way.

The Republicans had to regroup. On March 14 Senator Martinez sent e-mail directly to Governor Bush: "Just spoke with Frist and am encouraged. We are prepared go forward here but it won't be easy." They abandoned HR 1151 and tried a new idea—HR 1331, introduced on March 16 and sponsored by Wisconsin Republican representative F. James Sensenbrenner. HR 1332 would have allowed a "next friend of an incapacitated person" to obtain federal district court review of a state court judgment that had authorized the withholding or withdrawal of ANH—not just in the *Schiavo* case but as a law of general application. HR 1332 passed in the House by a voice vote on March 16, the same day it was introduced, with just a few Democrats opposing it. It went to the Senate on March 17.

There were plenty of problems with HR 1332, too. For one thing, it was vulnerable to the challenge of being unconstitutional as a violation of the doctrine of federalism, which prohibits federal courts other than the U.S. Supreme Court from reviewing a state court judgment. Other potential arguments were that it violated the constitutional separation of powers as well as Terri's Schiavo's constitutional right to refuse medical treatment. HR 1332 stalled in the Senate.

Time was running out.

The next scheme was probably the most bizarre and grotesque episode in the history of congressional subpoenas. Congress has the power to conduct investigations to help it decide whether and how to legislate. As part of this investigatory power, a congressional committee can issue a subpoena—a written order requiring a person to appear before the committee and bring any documents or other things the subpoena might specify. People who fail to comply with a congressional subpoena can be held in contempt of Congress and be punished by a fine or incarceration, or both.

On the morning of March 18—just hours before Terri Schiavo's PEG tube was to come out—Tom DeLay and Speaker Dennis Hastert issued a press release announcing that the House Committee on Government Reform would be issuing subpoenas "which will require hospice administrators and attending physicians to preserve nutrition and hydration for Terri Schiavo to allow Congress to fully understand the procedures and practices that are currently keeping her alive." The press release added, "This fight is not over."

The committee then subpoenaed Terri Schiavo.

Tom Davis, a Virginia Republican who chaired the committee, wrote a letter addressed to Terri at her hospice residence, telling her she had to appear at a committee meeting a week later, to be held at the hospice, where the committee would conduct "an inquiry into the long term care of incapacitated adults." The letter concluded, "Thank you in advance for your participation in this important hearing." The subpoena itself, attached to the letter, commanded Terri to appear at the meeting to "testify." (See Appendix, figs. 5, 6)

The committee also subpoenaed Michael Schiavo, ordering him to bring Terri's PEG tube to the meeting "in its current and continuing state of operations"—that is, with Terri still attached to it—"subject only to such routine and necessary maintenance as is necessary to ensure its continued proper functioning to provide such nutrition and hydration to Theresa Schiavo." Similar subpoenas were sent to Terri's doctors and the hospice director.

For good measure, Senator Frist issued a press release stating that federal law prohibits obstruction of a congressional investigation and warning that "anyone who violates this law is subject to criminal fines and imprisonment." Meanwhile, another congressional committee— the Senate Health, Education, Labor and Pensions Committee— scheduled a hearing in Washington, D.C., for March 28 and wrote to Terri and Michael Schiavo asking "both of you" to attend.

Never before in American history had Congress attempted to use its subpoena power to obtain testimony from someone in a persistent vegetative state and compel the production of a functioning PEG tube. The ploy was obvious. The purpose of the subpoenas was not to investigate anything but simply to prevent the implementation of Judge Greer's order. A *New York Times* editorial called it a "ghoulish gimmick."

The constitutional scholars were outraged once again. Harvard professor Charles Fried fumed, "It is abusive and disgraceful. Even a senator has an obligation to use his power honestly and not to engage in subterfuge and pretense." Professor Laurence Tribe said, "I can't think of any parallels." Referring to Senator Joseph McCarthy's abuses of congressional investigatory power in the 1950s, Tribe noted that "McCarthy, for all his abuses, did not reach out and try to undo the processes of a state court."

There it was again—the constitutional "separation of powers" doctrine, which prohibits Congress from interfering with a court's judgment in a specific case. In the 1959 case *Barenblatt v. United States*, the U.S. Supreme Court held that Congress may not use its investigatory power to inquire into matters that are within the exclusive province of the judiciary—for example, whether a judgment in a specific case should be implemented. The Schiavo subpoenas were an abuse of the investigatory power—not to mention the likelihood that they violated Terri's constitutional right to refuse medical treatment, as established by the *Cruzan* case.

But that didn't stop the House lawyers. They immediately went to Judge Greer with a motion to "intervene" in the guardianship proceeding—just as the Florida Department of Children and Families had tried unsuccessfully to do during the previous month. The House lawyers asked Judge Greer to postpone removal of Terri's PEG tube for eleven days, until March 29, in order to ensure compliance with the committee's subpoenas. Meanwhile, Elliot Berke, the general counsel for Tom DeLay, e-mailed Governor Bush's staff a list of "Terri Schiavo Talking Points" to be used for putting pressure on Judge Greer by pointing out how the subpoenas created a "grave constitutional dilemma" for the recipients—either violate the subpoenas or violate Judge Greer's February 25 removal order—which Greer could "resolve" by "modifying" the removal order.

Judge Greer promptly denied the House request, saying: "I find no cogent reason why the committee should be able to intervene in a case involving the decision whether or not to remain on life support. I must remind you that this order is over five years old." By the end of the day, the committee's appeals to both the Court of Appeal and Florida Supreme Court had been rejected—and Terri's PEG tube was out. With the feeding tube removed, the subpoena game was over. There was no point in compelling Terri's "testimony" or requiring her doctors and Michael to produce the PEG tube once it was no longer attached to her.

The House and Senate committees quietly abandoned their "investigations." The baton was passed to the full U.S. Senate, where a new proposed bill had been introduced on March 17, the same day the Senate received HR 1332 from the House. The Senate bill, S 653, avoided the House bills' dangers of unintended consequences by applying only to Terri Schiavo. Sponsored by Mel Martinez—of subsequent notoriety for his legal counsel's anonymous memo—S 653 was candidly titled an act for "the relief of the parents of Theresa Marie Schiavo." It purported to create jurisdiction in the U.S. District Court for the Middle District of Florida to determine "de novo"—that is, anew—"any claim of a violation of any right of Theresa Marie Schiavo" under the Constitution and laws of the United States "notwithstanding any prior State court determination." The bill also said it would not change any "substantive rights" under federal law or create any "precedent with respect to future legislation." In other words, S 653 called for a new trial in the *Schiavo* case, and in no others. The proposed bill also included a provision for the federal district court to "stay"—that is, to suspend—Judge Greer's order for removal of Terri's PEG tube.

There were still all sorts of constitutional challenges that could be mounted to this bill, but at least the problems were limited to Terri Schiavo. On March 17, in the middle of a Senate debate on the federal budget, majority leader Bill Frist interrupted debate to present S 653. Senator Martinez proceeded to describe the bill as "very narrowly tailored to provide relief to this young woman." Senator Frist, who is a physician, chimed in with his own personal diagnosis—based on the 2002 videotapes—that Terri Schiavo was not really in a persistent vegetative state. He said, "I have had the opportunity to look at the video footage upon which the initial facts of this case were based. And from my standpoint as a physician ... the facts upon which the case were [sic] based are inadequate to be able to make a diagnosis of persistent vegetative state."

It didn't matter to Frist that physicians who had actually examined Terri Schiavo—and who had no political agenda—thought otherwise.

S 653 passed by voice vote in the Senate on the same day it was introduced. Now, however, there was a new problem. It was time for Congress's Easter recess. By the time S 653 was sent to the House, most of its members had left town. And by the time the House was scheduled to reconvene, two weeks hence, Terri Schiavo would certainly be dead.

On March 19—a pleasant Saturday morning in Oakland, California—I was at home, taking a breather from drafting legal arguments in opposition to the Schindlers' federal lawsuit seeking a writ of habeas corpus against Judge Greer, when I received an urgent call from Debbie Bushnell, Michael Schiavo's guardianship attorney. Debbie told me that Michael's lead counsel, George Felos, had just gotten a desperate call from an Oregon congressman, David Wu, in which Wu warned Felos that Senator Frist and Representative DeLay were concocting a scheme to get a Schiavo bill passed by unanimous consent. I asked Debbie, "What's unanimous consent?"

She had to explain it to me: it's a procedure by which a bill can be passed instantly in either house of Congress on a voice vote, without any debate, so long as no member objects. Unanimous consent can be prevented by a single objection from any member, which was why Wu had telephoned Felos. Wu needed help finding members of Congress to oppose the unanimous consent plan. Nearly everyone was out of town because of the Easter recess.

Debbie asked whether I had any ideas whom we might call. I had one. Within an hour, I managed to get my hands on a telephone number for an aide to Senate minority leader Harry Reid—head of the Senate Democrats. I telephoned the aide, introduced myself as one of Michael Schiavo's attorneys, and described the Frist-DeLay scheme we'd heard about. Her response was, "They can't do that." I responded, "But they're apparently trying." She replied, "That just can't happen. The House is in recess. Congress can't do anything for two weeks."

I told the aide that Frist and DeLay were planning to call the House back into session immediately, with just a few Republicans present, and get a bill passed by unanimous consent without any Democrats there to object. She repeated, "That's not possible."

I was getting nowhere with her, so I asked, "Well, could you at least tell me whom I might call for help in rounding up someone to run over to the Capitol to stop the unanimous consent?" She said, "No, I can't." I asked, "Then can you at least call Senator Reid and warn him what's happening?" Her reply was, "The senator knows everything that goes on in Washington."

Sensing that something was amiss, I thanked her and hung up.

An hour later, the Reuters news agency reported that Senators Reid and Frist had "reached an agreement" that would allow the House to reconvene in order to pass a Schiavo bill. The agreement was announced by Jim Manley, a spokesman for Senator Reid. No wonder the aide wouldn't help me. At the very moment I was asking her to call Harry Reid to get his help in opposing the Frist-DeLay scheme, Senator Reid was colluding in it!

At the same time I was getting nowhere with Reid's aide, Robert Destro was telling House Judiciary Committee general counsel Philip Kiko why S 653 was vulnerable to constitutional attack. At 8:50 A.M. on March 19, Bill Wichterman, a policy advisor for Senator Frist, asked Destro to address concerns Destro had expressed about the efficacy of S 653. At 10:50 A.M., Destro e-mailed Kiko, explaining that he had suggested the habeas-based approach of HR 1151 because a bill directed at only Terri Schiavo "will inevitably be viewed as an attempt by Congress to overturn the judgment of a state court," thus violating the constitutional separation of powers just like "Terri's Law" did. Destro said, "Unless the House and Senate conferees can agree on language that makes it clear that Congress is simply trying to afford Terri her existing remedies under federal law, it is going to look like it is creating new ones just for her. That, in my view, would be a disaster of immense proportions, and would complicate the lives of her now-extremely-tired legal team enormously." Destro warned that the U.S. Supreme Court "is in no mood to brook dissent from its views that Congress may not overturn a settled judgment of any court." (See Appendix, fig. 7)

That afternoon, Frist and Hastert issued a statement announcing that Congress had "reached an agreement on legislation which provides an opportunity to save Mrs. Schiavo's life"—a compromise between the competing House and Senate bills. The statement added, "We want to thank Senate Minority Leader Harry Reid for working with us toward a legislative solution." The compromise was approved that evening, during an eight-minute senate session attended by just four senators, including Iowa Democrat Tom Harkin. Evidently, the Republican leadership heeded Destro's warning to House Judiciary Committee counsel Philip Kiko about S 653 creating remedies for just one person. S 653 was modified and reintroduced in the Senate as S 686, with a new clause adding that it would create no precedent for future legislation "including the provision of private relief bills" directed at a single person. Also, the bill no longer included the provision for the federal district court to stay Judge Greer's removal order.

So it came to pass that Robert Destro—a private attorney for Bob and Mary Schindler and former counsel for Governor Jeb Bush—had a hand in drafting the Congressional bill on which the Republican leadership pinned its hopes for keeping Terri Schiavo alive. It isn't often that a lawyer can tell members of Congress how to craft legislation designed to benefit that lawyer's clients—and nobody else—in such fashion that the bill might not "look like" what it really is and thus might evade settled U.S. Supreme Court authority on the constitutional separation of powers. Such was the leverage of the religious Right in the *Schiavo* case.

Emergency sessions were scheduled for the next day, Sunday—at 1:00 P.M. in the House and 2:00 P.M. in the Senate—for the Senate bill to be passed by unanimous consent. Late Saturday evening, the White House announced that President Bush, who was at his ranch in Crawford, Texas, would return to Washington on Sunday to sign the bill. On Sunday afternoon, the bill passed in the Senate by unanimous consent, with just a few members present. Not a single Democrat bothered to object.

Something happened, however, that proved to be critical in the federal court litigation to come. During the Senate session, Democratic senator Carl Levin of Michigan said he wanted clarification regarding the disappearance of the bill's provision for the federal district court to stay Judge Greer's order. He said his understanding was that the absence of the stay provision meant that the general law governing stays would apply, under which a judge may decide whether to grant a stay— meaning that the judge's decision is entirely discretionary. Levin asked majority leader Bill Frist: "Does the majority leader share my understanding of the bill?" Frist replied: "I share the understanding of the Senator from Michigan, as does [Senator Martinez] who is the chief sponsor of this bill. Nothing in the current bill or its legislative history mandates a stay." In other words, S 653 did not require the federal court to suspend Judge Greer's order while reviewing the state court guardianship proceedings. This turned out to be a huge blunder by the Republicans.

At the close of this brief Senate session, Senator Frist expressed his gratitude for Senator Reid's collaboration, saying: "I thank Senate Minority Leader Harry Reid for his leadership on this issue. He and I have been in close contact throughout this process."

In the House, however, things didn't go as smoothly. Representative Wu came through, along with Representatives Debbie Wasserman Schultz, Barney Frank, James Davis, Earl Blumenauer, and Robert Wexler—all Democrats. They objected to unanimous consent, thereby thwarting the scheme. The bill would have to be put to a formal vote. Under the rules of the House, that couldn't happen until the next day, Monday, at 12:01 A.M.

The stage was set for an extraordinary political event—a frenzied roundup of the vacationing representatives to begin debate on S 686 at 9:00 P.M. that evening and vote on the bill as soon as the clock struck midnight. The Republican leadership did its job well, corralling all but sixty-two of the Republican representatives—about three-quarters of the total number of House Republicans—to vote on S 686. The Democrats were another story. They stayed away in droves. A hundred of them—half of the House Democrats—were absent.

The House debate that night was gripping. Republicans spoke of the Passion of Christ (it was Palm Sunday) and a "culture of life." The few Democrats who entered the fray spoke of the U.S. Constitution and notions of family privacy. Here are some highlights:

- *Debbie Wasserman Schultz, D-Florida*: "Heartbreaking decisions like this are deeply intimate, personal, and private matters; and the federal government and this body, in particular, should not inject itself into the middle of this private family matter.... If we do this, we will end up throwing end-of-life decisions into utter and complete chaos; and we cannot and should not do that. We are members of Congress. We are not doctors. We are not medical experts. We are not bioethicists."

- *F. James Sensenbrenner, R-Wisconsin:* "To starve someone to death or have them die of dehydration slowly is one of the most cruel and inhumane ways to die."

- *Barney Frank, D-Massachusetts:* "Separation of powers. When they wrote the Constitution, they were not kidding around.... The caption tonight ought to be 'We are not doctors. We just play them on C-SPAN.'"

- *Trent Franks, R-Arizona:* "If we as a nation subject her to the torture and agony of starving and thirsting to death while her brother, her mother and her father are forced to watch, we will scar our own souls. And we will be allowing those judges who have lost their way to drag us all one more ominous step into a darkness where the light of human compassion has gone out and the predatory survival of the fittest prevails over humanity."

- *David Wu, D-Oregon:* "By forcing this vote through Congress, the Republican leadership is demonstrating that no bedroom in America and no hospital room in this land is beyond the reach and power of the federal government. This is wrong."

- *Jeff Miller, R-Florida:* "Two thousand years ago Jesus Christ entered Jerusalem on Palm Sunday, marking the beginning of a week that throughout history and the world over has signified the sanctity of human life. Tonight we are here on Palm Sunday to afford the greatest presumption of life possible under our United States Constitution to a woman who has never truly been afforded representation and whose wishes are truly unknown."

- *James Davis, D-Florida*: "Tonight, congressional leaders are poised to appoint this Congress as a judge and a jury. These actions are a threat to our democracy.... This Congress is about to overturn the separation of powers by disregarding the laws of Florida and the decision of a judge that have never been reversed. This Congress is on the verge of telling states and judges and juries that their laws, their decisions, do not matter."

- *John Gingrey, R-Georgia*: "I believe we have a duty as members of Congress to uphold a culture of life and compassion. It is important that we act today to save Terri Schiavo's life and uphold the moral and legal obligation of our nation, indeed this poor woman's constitutional right to life."

- *John Lewis, D-Georgia*: "This is demagoguery. This is a step in where we have no business. This is walking where the angels fear to tread. We are playing with a young woman's life for the sake of politics."

- *Jack Kingston, R-Georgia*: "Terri is not a PVS, someone in a persistent vegetative state.... Terri is able to laugh, she is able to cry, and she apparently can hear."

- *Jerrold Nadler, D-New York*: "The doctors testified, doctors who examined her, not doctors standing up on the floor here who say, well, from the videotape we can infer ... doctors who have actually examined this patient have testified her cerebral cortex is liquified; that it is destroyed. Without a cerebral cortex there is no sensation, there is no consciousness, there is no feeling, there is no pain, there is no possibility of recovery. That is what a persistent vegetative state is."

- *Rick Renzi, R-Arizona*: "Out of Florida, there is no justice."

- *John Conyers, D-Michigan*: "By passing legislation which takes sides in an ongoing legal dispute, we will be casting aside the principle of the separation of powers. . . . By passing legislation which wrests jurisdiction away from a state judge and sends it to a single preselected federal court, we will forgo any pretense of federalism."

- *Tom DeLay, R-Texas:* "Terri Schiavo has survived her Passion weekend, and she has not been forsaken. No more words, Mr. Speaker. She is waiting. The members are here. The hour has come. Mr. Speaker, call the vote."

S 686 went to a roll call vote on Monday, March 21, at 12:45 A.M. Because of the expedited procedure by which it went before the House, the bill's passage required a two-thirds vote of the members present. That proved to be no problem, because nearly half of the one hundred Democrats who showed up—forty-seven of them—voted for the bill, joining 156 Republicans. Fifty-three Democrats and five Republicans voted against the bill. The final tally was 203 to 58.

True to his word, President Bush returned to Washington from his ranch in Texas to sign the bill—in his pajamas—at 1:08 A.M. He immediately issued a statement: "In cases like this one where there are serious questions and substantial doubts, our society, our laws, and our courts should have a presumption in favor of life." The next evening, during a speech in Arizona, he repeated the now-familiar mantra: "It is wise to always err on the side of life."

Governor Jeb Bush, whose staff had helped to craft the early versions of the congressional bill, said, "I thank the Congress for its swift action allowing Terri's parents to seek a federal review of this case. Certainly, an incapacitated person deserves at least the same protection afforded criminals sentenced to death."

Michael Schiavo retorted, "For Congress to come in and interfere in a personal family matter is outrageous. [If they] can do it to me, they'll do it to every person in this country. And they should be ashamed of themselves. Leave my wife alone. Leave me alone. Take care of your own families."

The success of S 686 was a product of collaboration by Democratic leader Harry Reid and political weakness in his followers, who feared that the Martinez memo was right—that *Schiavo* was a "great political issue" for the Republicans that the Democrats could not win. A few brave souls such as Debbie Wasserman Schultz and Barney Frank had the courage to point out the obvious—that Congress is not the place for a medical diagnosis and that the constitutional separation of powers is serious business—but most Democrats bailed out. They were running scared from a perception of public opinion that turned out to be incorrect, as demonstrated by the subsequent CBS News and ABC News polls showing that the vast majority of Americans thought Congress had been wrong to meddle. It's too bad the pollsters didn't ask the people *before* the March 20 vote whether they thought Congress ought to intervene.

Two weeks after Terri Schiavo's death, Democratic National Committee chairman Howard Dean announced that in upcoming elections the Democrats would attack the Republicans for "grandstanding" in the *Schiavo* case. Here's what antieuthanasia activist Wesley Smith said about this on his Internet blog: "If Dean and [the] Democrats try to revise history and claim that the law was exclusively a Republican venture, then they will be branding themselves cynics and demagogues, who, when the heat was on, meekly went along. But later, when some polls showed that the move was unpopular, they claim federal intervention was an attempt to impose theocracy. Talk about political cowardice and cynicism!"

For once, I agree with Wesley Smith.

Congress had thrown the *Schiavo* case into the federal courts. Would the federal courts come to the Schindlers' rescue and refuse to honor what the Florida state courts had determined were Terri's wishes? Bruce Fein, a constitutional lawyer and columnist for the right-wing *Washington Times*, made a prescient statement: "I don't think the chance is much above zero."

15

The Judges Speak Out

he Schindlers' lawyers were ready to pounce as soon as President
Bush signed the federal "Terri's Law." On March 21, 2005, they
filed a new lawsuit in the U.S. District Court for the Middle District of
Florida, formally requesting the retrial authorized by the congressional
bill—now designated Public Law 109-3.

The lawsuit was filed at 3:00 A.M. that Monday morning—just two
hours after President Bush signed Public Law 109-3. The federal courts
aren't usually open for business that early, but in this case the court
clerk made an exception, on advance request by the Schindlers'
lawyers. Just in case Schindler attorney David Gibbs III didn't know,
Tom DeLay's general counsel, Elliot Berke, had e-mailed Gibbs on
March 20 explaining that federal district courts can issue an emergency injunction at "any time of day," although the parties "need to
get before the court to get the decision made." The case was randomly
assigned to Judge James D. Whittemore, a 1999 appointee of President
Bill Clinton.

That morning, I boarded a flight for Washington, D.C.

By this time I was transfixed by the Schiavo drama. Over the previous
weekend, I had been able to work with Michael Schiavo's lawyers
long-distance from California. I knew, however, that if Congress
passed the Schiavo bill, things would get very busy at Jenner & Block

in Washington, D.C., where Tom Perrelli was coordinating the federal litigation. I wanted to be there.

I had been planning to be in Washington and Virginia that week on matters unrelated to *Schiavo*. I ended up canceling those plans and spending the next four days with Tom Perrelli's team.

The Schindlers' new lawsuit—filed by David Gibbs III, along with former Governor Bush attorney Robert Destro and another Florida lawyer—requested two things. The first was the congressionally authorized retrial to determine whether any of Terri Schiavo's federal rights had been violated in the Florida state court proceedings. The second was a court order similar to the "stay" that the Schindlers had been desperately seeking for weeks, although now that Terri's PEG tube had been removed, the order would properly be called a "temporary injunction" requiring immediate reattachment of the PEG tube. The Schindlers' request for a retrial put forward various theories as to how Terri's rights had supposedly been violated: Judge Greer acting as proxy was not impartial; Terri was unfairly deprived of independent counsel; and her rights of religious freedom were violated in light of the pope's 2004 allocution against removal of feeding tubes from PVS patients. All of these issues had already been litigated in the Florida state courts.

Of course, a retrial would be meaningless if Terri were to remain without ANH for much longer. By this time, her feeding tube had been out for three days, and the doctors had predicted that she would die within two weeks. The first order of business for Gibbs and Destro was to request a temporary injunction compelling reinsertion of the tube. Their big problem was that the congressional bill required nothing of the sort, as Senate majority leader Frist had made clear when he told Senator Levin that "nothing in the current bill or its legislative history mandates a stay" (now an injunction).

It was entirely within Judge Whittemore's discretion whether to grant the injunction. If he chose not to, then Terri would die before there could be any retrial. Thus the Schindlers had no hope without a temporary injunction. The injunction was the key battle.

On Monday afternoon, while I was still en route to Washington, Tom Perrelli's team quickly put together a written opposition to the Schindlers' injunction request. The opposition papers focused on rebutting one of the factors generally required to get a temporary injunction—a showing that it is likely the plaintiffs will eventually win the lawsuit. Perrelli attacked the Schindlers' case in two ways: by pointing out that they were trying to relitigate meritless arguments that had been rejected repeatedly by numerous state and federal courts, and by showing that the congressional bill violated the constitutional separation of powers and Terri's constitutional right to refuse medical treatment. Perrelli pointedly exploited the fact that Congress had not required a stay.

At 3:00 on Monday afternoon, Judge Whittemore held a two-hour hearing on the injunction request. He ended the hearing without issuing a ruling, and then went to work on reaching a decision.

Judge Whittemore and his staff evidently worked through the night. At the crack of dawn the next morning—6:00 A.M. Tuesday— he issued a thirteen-page written opinion denying the injunction.

In the opinion, Judge Whittemore rejected any notion that the congressional bill required him to grant an injunction, so that the "traditional requirements for temporary injunctive relief" were applicable—meaning his decision was entirely discretionary. His opinion focused on the question of whether the Schindlers were likely to win the lawsuit on its merits. He decided they were not: Judge Greer had fulfilled all "his statutory judicial responsibilities," Terri's rights had been adequately protected by three independent court-appointed legal guardians as well as by the advocacy of "her parents and their able counsel," and the religious freedom claims were without merit because the law forbids only *government* infringement on religious freedom, and neither Michael Schiavo nor Hospice House Woodside was a government entity.

It was a solid, no-nonsense opinion.

Three hours later, at 9:00 A.M., Gibbs and Destro appealed to the Eleventh Circuit Court of Appeals—the intermediate federal appellate court for the southeastern United States. Because Judge Whittemore had not ruled on the request for a retrial but only on the injunction request, the issue in this appeal would be very narrow—whether the judge had erred in denying the injunction.

As Gibbs and Destro were filing their appeal, I was poking my head into Tom Perrelli's office for the first time. This thirty-nine-year-old former Department of Justice lawyer for Attorney General Janet Reno, now cochair of Jenner & Block's entertainment and new media practice, also seemed to have worked through the night. His office was scattered with piles of paper, and he hadn't shaved for several days. But he was clearly ready for more. I said, "Put me to work."

What a wild day that turned out to be. Perrelli had a half-dozen of his firm's lawyers, plus me, working on bits and pieces of legal arguments to be assembled for the opposition to the Schindlers' briefs—which we hadn't even seen yet. Gibbs and Destro would be filing two briefs—one on the appeal from Judge Whittemore's order, the other a separate request for an injunction via a special kind of writ under federal statutory law. The Eleventh Circuit announced that we would have four hours—four hours!—to prepare and file written responses to each of the two briefs.

The wheels of justice were no longer grinding slowly. In my twenty-six years as a lawyer, I have never seen an appellate court require opposition on such short notice. The courts usually give at least a few days to respond.

Thank goodness for Laurence Tribe and e-mail. I bombarded him with inquiries; he responded with impromptu explications on all sorts of constitutional principles and U.S. Supreme Court opinions with which I was only vaguely familiar. I was forced to learn quickly.

The first of the Schindlers' briefs arrived at Jenner & Block at 1:30 P.M., the second at 2:30 P.M. Our four-hour deadlines meant we had to file responding briefs at 5:30 P.M. and 6:30 P.M.

Gibbs and Destro plainly knew they were in trouble because of

Frist's blunder in acceding to the deletion of the stay provision from the congressional bill and admitting to Senator Levin that the revised bill did not compel the reinsertion of Terri Schiavo's PEG tube. Their appeal brief tried to finesse the problem by arguing that Congress *must* have intended to require a stay because, "for the merits of the case to be reached, Terri Schiavo must remain alive long enough for her case to be heard on the merits."

The balance of their brief broke a fundamental rule of appellate advocacy. Gibbs and Destro claimed that "the real truth of the patient is in doubt." Terri, they said, had "as recently as last Friday . . . made her desire to live known"—presumably when she vocalized "Ahhhhhhh" and "Waaaaaaaa" to Barbara Weller. As to whether Terri was in PVS, they claimed that neither Michael Schiavo nor George Felos was "interested in discovering Terri's true current medical condition."

Thus Gibbs and Destro were not just arguing that Terri's federal rights had been violated—which was the only inquiry that Congress had authorized. They were arguing that Judge Greer had gotten the facts wrong regarding Terri's wishes and condition. They wanted the appellate court to second-guess factual determinations by a trial judge—and not even by the judge against whom the appeal had been filed! Appellate courts can't legitimately do that.

Our hasty response expanded on the arguments that Perrelli had previously made before Judge Whittemore. This time we directly quoted Senator Frist's comment that he understood the congressional bill *not* to require a stay. It couldn't have been clearer. The judge's ruling was discretionary. The rule on appeal was that the Schindlers had to prove Judge Whittemore had "abused his discretion" in denying the injunction—a rule of appellate review that is very difficult to overcome.

Our two opposition briefs were on file by dinnertime Tuesday. Now it was my turn to work through the night. We knew what was coming: whoever lost in the Eleventh Circuit would take the case to the U.S. Supreme Court. Given the lightning speed with which the litigation was proceeding, that would likely happen the next day, Wednesday. We had to be ready to file something in the Supreme Court—either an opposition to the Schindlers' request to the court if we won, or our own request if we lost.

We had written two Court of Appeals briefs in great haste—four hours! They had to be edited and turned into a single comprehensive brief suitable for filing in the U.S. Supreme Court. I did some of the editing overnight in my hotel room. By the next morning at 7:30 A.M., I had produced something from which Perrelli could work as a template for the Supreme Court brief.

The morning of Wednesday, March 23 brought the Eleventh Circuit's decision by a three-judge panel. On a vote of 2 to 1, the court upheld Judge Whittemore's order denying an injunction. The ten-page majority opinion was concise and incisive—impressive for a one-day product.

The opinion explained the legal standards governing Judge Whittemore's decision and appellate review of it. Quoting Senator Frist, the court said that the usual rules for an injunction request were applicable—that is, the injunction was discretionary, not mandatory. Nothing in the congressional bill required Judge Whittemore to order the reinsertion of Terri Schiavo's PEG tube; to the contrary, Congress had "deliberately removed" the stay provision from the bill "in order to clarify that pre-existing law did govern this issue." The standard of appellate review was "abuse of discretion," and the court concluded that "the district court's carefully thought-out decision to deny temporary relief in these circumstances is not an abuse of discretion." Judge Whittemore had not erred in determining that the Schindlers were unlikely to win on a retrial.

This conclusion meant that the Eleventh Circuit did not have to consider and decide the constitutional issues—that is, whether the congressional bill violated the constitutional separation of powers or Terri Schiavo's right to refuse medical treatment. The court specifically said that it "need not decide that question."

Ultimately, no court ever did. Constitutional law scholars can only speculate what the bill's fate might have been.

At the close of the majority opinion, the judges spoke from the heart: "There is no denying the absolute tragedy that has befallen Mrs. Schiavo. As the Florida Second District Court of Appeal has observed, we all have our own family, our own loved ones, and our own children. However, we are called upon to make a collective, objective decision concerning a question of law. [Citation.] In the end, and no matter how much we wish Mrs. Schiavo had never suffered such a horrible accident, we are a nation of laws, and if we are to continue to be so, the pre-existing and well-established federal law governing injunctions as well as Pub. L. No. 109-3 must be applied to her case. While the position of our dissenting colleague has emotional appeal, we as judges must decide this case on the law." The dissenter said: "Theresa Schiavo's death, which is imminent, effectively ends the litigation without a fair opportunity to fully consider the merits of Plaintiffs' constitutional claims."

The next move by Gibbs and Destro was to file a petition for a "rehearing en banc"—a request for all twelve judges on the Eleventh Circuit to rehear the appeal. The rehearing petition was on file within hours. And a new lawyer appeared on the petition—Jay Sekulow, of Christian evangelist Pat Robertson's American Center for Law and Justice, who had previously represented the Schindlers in the *Bush v. Schiavo* litigation over the Florida "Terri's Law."

Over at Jenner & Block, we frantically began preparing an opposition brief. By midafternoon, Perrelli had completed a fourteen-page draft and had given it to me to edit. I was halfway through editing when one of the firm's associates stuck his head into the office I was using and told me that the Eleventh Circuit had ruled on the rehearing request.

"What'd they say?

"Denied."

I tossed the half-edited fourteen pages into the air, and as they fluttered to the ground, the associate exclaimed, "That's the funniest thing I've ever seen in a law office!"

The en banc decision was 10 to 2. Judge Whittemore's decision had survived the Eleventh Circuit's review.

Because we had won, it was Gibbs and Destro—not us—who would
have to ask the U.S. Supreme Court to take the case. Late that day
(still Wednesday), they filed an application asking the Supreme Court
for an injunction—specifically, for "an order staying further withholding of nutrition and hydration from Theresa Marie Schiavo."

The tenor of their Supreme Court application was pure emotion:

- Terri "is dying of starvation and dehydration."

- "A miraculous event occurred . . . when Congress, in a bi-
  partisan and dramatic fashion, thundered the message through
  P.L. No. 109-3, that the United States of America must stand
  for life, accuracy, and fairness in the process afforded to an innocent, incapacitated woman."

- "Without a stay from this Court, Terri will die a horrible death
  in a matter of days."

- "If Terri Schiavo dies . . . the entire exercise of Congressional
  authority . . . was a colossal waste of both Congress' and this
  Court's time."

- Michael Schiavo "was abusive, not only to Terri, but to other
  women," and "the obligations of his new family—a girlfriend
  and two children born while he remained 'married' to Terri—
  gave him a personal interest in ending Terri's nutrition and
  hydration."

- Michael's "attorney, George Felos, is closely associated with
  the 'Right to Die' movement" and "blocked the admission and
  development of evidence that would prove Terri's current condition."

- "A tragedy of unbelievable proportions would occur if . . . this
  Court does not respond in time to save Terri Schiavo's life."

Once again, Gibbs and Destro had broken a fundamental rule of appellate advocacy. Emotional appeals are best for juries, not appellate

judges, most of whom are concerned more with deciding what the law is or should be than with lingering on the facts of a given case. Thus the Eleventh Circuit's majority opinion had chastised the dissenter for succumbing to "emotional appeal" rather than deciding the case "on the law."

Our opposition brief, filed in the Supreme Court early the next morning, March 24, was the culmination of a few days' work by a dozen attorneys working around the clock—the group at Jenner & Block, George Felos and Debbie Bushnell in Florida, the Florida ACLU attorneys, and me—and it was perfect. The brief demonstrated:

- that the Schindlers had failed to sustain the heavy burden of demonstrating that Judge Whittemore had abused his discretion in refusing to order Terri's PEG tube reattached;

- the indisputable fact that Congress had never required the tube's reattachment and in fact had rejected a stay provision;

- the correctness of Judge Whittemore's decision that the Schindlers had failed to show they were likely to win on a federal retrial of their claims;

- that the congressional bill violated the constitutional separation of powers and Terri's right to refuse medical treatment.

The brief also offered some wisdom penned by one of the Jenner & Block lawyers: "The great tragedy of Mrs. Schiavo's life is not what lies ahead; it is in what she is trying to leave behind. Her tragedy was the cessation of her heartbeat fifteen years ago, and the persistent vegetative state that has trapped her since. Ours is that we allow a fear of death to rob the dignity of her life."

Later that morning—at 10:30 A.M., Thursday, March 24—the U.S. Supreme Court ruled: "The application for stay of enforcement of judgment pending the filing and disposition of a petition for writ of certiorari presented to Justice Kennedy and by him referred to the Court is denied."

In plain English: "The tube stays out."

Incredibly, Gibbs and Destro still didn't give up on the federal case. Two days earlier, they had filed an additional pleading with Judge Whittemore, adding four legal theories to the federal action. On Thursday, the day the Supreme Court refused to intervene, Gibbs and Destro filed yet another pleading with Judge Whittemore, adding one more legal theory and again requesting an injunction requiring Terri's feeding tube to be reattached.

This time, Gibbs and Destro blundered. They argued that Terri's constitutional rights had been violated because the U.S. Supreme Court's *Cruzan* decision *required* proof of end-of-life wishes by clear and convincing evidence and the evidence before Judge Greer purportedly failed to meet that standard. Their premise, however—that *Cruzan* required the heightened standard of proof—was flat-out wrong. *Cruzan* said only that the states *may* choose to require proof by clear and convincing evidence. Nothing in the constitution mandates the heightened standard of proof. That's why the California Supreme Court was able to say in its *Wendland* opinion that the normal standard of proof by a preponderance of the evidence applies in most California right-to-die cases. The new arguments by Gibbs and Destro were destined for failure.

Judge Whittemore held a Thursday night hearing on the Schindlers' new legal theories. Gibbs argued for the Schindlers, and again his appeal was to emotion. When he called Terri Schiavo's impending death a "murder," the judge responded, "That's the emotional aspect of this case, and the rhetoric that does not influence this court. We have to follow the rule of law and that's what will be applied." The next morning—Friday, March 25—Judge Whittemore issued an opinion denying the latest request for an injunction and rejecting each of the Schindlers' new legal theories.

Back Gibbs and Destro went with another appeal to the Eleventh

Circuit—that very day, March 25. But they seemed to be running out of steam. Their brief—just six pages long—sounded resigned to the inevitable. It was nothing but emotion. And by the end of the day, the three-judge panel of the Eleventh Circuit had ruled. Again, the Schindlers had lost.

This time, the appellate court's decision was unanimous. Even the judge who had previously dissented was now on board with the majority, saying in a separate concurring opinion that the Schindlers "have been unable to come forward in their second amended complaint with any new claims palpably alleging the denial of a right secured by the Constitution or laws of the United States."

That evening, the Schindlers announced they would no longer pursue any more federal court appeals. The federal litigation had come to a halt, and my work on the *Schiavo* case seemed to be at an end. I returned to Oakland that Friday night.

But the litigation circus wasn't over yet. Not nearly. The Schindlers went back to the Florida state courts—and to Governor Jeb Bush.

Jeb Chickens Out

With the federal litigation going badly for the Schindlers, the pressure was once again on Florida governor Jeb Bush. Terri Schiavo was approaching one week without ANH, and the Schindlers and their supporters were clamoring for Bush to do something—anything— to get Terri's PEG tube reinserted. Politically, he had little choice but to get back into the game.

Bush made his first move on Wednesday, March 23—the day the Eleventh Circuit rebuffed the legal maneuvers by Schindler lawyers Gibbs and Destro and they were forced to go to the U.S. Supreme Court. Bush's Department of Children and Families (DCF), which had tried unsuccessfully the previous month to intervene before Judge Greer in the state court guardianship proceeding, gave it another try, filing a new motion to intervene.

The earlier motion by DCF had been based on allegations of physical abuse that later turned out to be bogus. The March 23 motion took a different tack, sounding the Schindlers' theme that Terri was not really in a persistent vegetative state. This time the Schindlers were armed with something new—an affidavit by a neurologist, Dr. William Cheshire, who said he found "reasonable doubt" in Terri's diagnosis of PVS and thought she might instead be in a "minimally conscious state" (MCS).

Dr. Cheshire said he had reviewed Terri's medical records and portions of the 2002 videotapes and had visited her once, although he did not conduct a medical examination. He commented, "Although Terri did not demonstrate during our 90 minute visit compelling evidence of verbalization, conscious awareness, or volitional behavior, yet the visitor has the distinct sense of the presence of a living human being who seems at some level to be aware of some things around her."

Where did the Schindlers find Dr. Cheshire? Why him, among countless other neurologists?

Dr. Cheshire is director of biotechnology ethics for the Center for Bioethics and Human Dignity, which describes itself as adhering to "Biblical values." On March 8, 2005—two weeks before the Schindlers submitted Dr. Cheshire's affidavit—the center's president, John Kilner, appeared on a nationally syndicated radio broadcast by the religious Right's Focus on the Family and called for Michael Schiavo's removal as Terri's guardian. Dr. Cheshire also happens to be a member of the Christian Medical Association's Ethics Commission, whose self-styled "Biblical principles" position on ANH is that "physicians, other health care professionals, and health care facilities should initiate and continue nutritional support and hydration when their patients cannot feed themselves." Perhaps that's why the Schindlers chose Dr. Cheshire.

And how did the Schindlers find Dr. Cheshire? He is on the Board of Directors of the Center for Bioethics and Culture, one of whose "special consultants" is none other than Wesley Smith, the anti-euthanasia activist and behind-the-scenes advisor to the Schindlers.

The DCF intervention motion wasn't Bush's only move on March 23. DCF secretary Lucy Hadi announced at a news conference that DCF was considering removing Terri Schiavo by force from Hospice House Woodside. Hadi said DCF was relying on its authority to take custody of an abused or neglected person who was at risk of death or serious physical injury—a legal argument going back to October 2003, when Gibbs and a few other lawyers wrote letters to Governor Bush at the behest of Randall Terry, asserting that the governor had the legal authority to take custody of Terri. As for Judge Greer's rulings in the

case, Hadi stated, "We're not compelled to look at prior judicial proceedings."

Jeb Bush wasn't merely thinking about taking Terri by force. He actually tried to do it. (See Appendix, fig. 8) On the afternoon of March
23, the governor's office contacted Morton Plant Hospital, which was
close to Hospice House Woodside, and said DCF was preparing to
seize Terri Schiavo at 4:00 P.M. and take her to the hospital. An attorney for the hospital alerted George Felos, who tried to reach Judge
Greer, while Debbie Bushnell hurried to Hospice House Woodside.

Debbie warned the local police who were guarding the hospice—
the Pinellas Park Police Department and the Pinellas County sheriff—
that a move was afoot to grab Terri. They had heard nothing about it.
Then Debbie learned that the Florida Department of Law Enforcement (FDLE)—a police agency under the governor's control—would
be accompanying DCF to seize Terri. Hospice authorities contacted
someone at FDLE, who said its agents were on their way.

Meanwhile, Judge Greer convened an emergency hearing and ordered DCF not to seize Terri, saying DCF "is hereby restrained from
taking possession of Theresa Marie Schiavo or removing her from the
Hospice Woodside facility, administering nutrition or hydration artificially, or otherwise interfering with this Court's final judgment." For
good measure, the judge added that "each and every and singular
Sheriff of the State of Florida" was "directed to take such actions or action as is necessary to enforce" the order.

A few minutes later, Debbie got word that the FDLE agents would
not be coming to the hospice after all. Jeb Bush's move to abduct Terri
had been narrowly averted.

The clamor from the Schindlers and the religious Right became still
more strident. The next day, Thursday, March 24—the day the U.S.
Supreme Court refused to intervene—Bob Schindler publicly begged
Governor Bush to take custody of Terri, saying, "With the stroke of his
pen, he could stop this. He's put Terri through a week of hell." Former
Republican fringe presidential candidate Allan Keyes said Bush had a
"constitutional obligation" to protect Terri and demanded that he "act

unilaterally and not wait for her to die." A protestor at the state capitol held a sign reading, "Jeb Bush, are you a man or a mouse?"

Lieutenant Kevin Riley of the Pinellas Park Police Department said his officers were under court order not to let DCF seize Terri, and "we intend to enforce that order."

Jeb Bush publicly insisted, "We have done everything that we can, and we will continue to do so, within the powers that I have." But he also lamented that "I can't go beyond what my powers are, and I'm not going to do it."

What would have happened if Bush had violated Judge Greer's order and instructed DCF to seize Terri? Judge Greer could have held DCF, and maybe even the governor himself, in contempt of court— meaning a possible fine and incarceration. Can you imagine the spectacle of Judge Greer throwing the governor in jail? Plainly Jeb Bush did not want *that* to happen.

The religious Right had put Governor Bush in an impossible position—either break the law and risk a nasty confrontation between the state and local police, not to mention his own incarceration, or follow the law and incur the wrath of the "right-to-life" political base for chickening out. Either course would damage the governor politically. I almost felt sorry for him.

At midday on that Thursday, Judge Greer denied DCF's latest intervention motion and refused to change his original judgment, saying in a written order that neither the motion nor Dr. Cheshire's affidavit had alleged "that there is any new treatment that would significantly improve the quality of [Terri's] life so that she would reverse the prior decision to withdraw life-prolonging procedures." In other words, the judge found no reason to change his determination that Terri would want to discontinue her ANH.

Meanwhile, the governor did it again: he again attempted to abduct Terri.

That Thursday morning at 8:15 A.M., DCF had filed an appeal of the previous day's order by Judge Greer forbidding DCF from seizing Terri. Under Florida law, the effect of the appeal was to automatically suspend the antiseizure order, throwing it into a temporary appellate limbo. That created a window of opportunity for Jeb to have another go at grabbing Terri.

George Felos, however, moved quickly. Judge Greer had the power to "vacate" the automatic suspension—meaning that he could issue an order to put the suspended order back into effect. Felos ran to court with a motion to vacate the automatic suspension and revive the order forbidding Terri's seizure.

DCF's attorney was late to the midmorning hearing on George's motion. When the DCF attorney arrived, he asked Judge Greer to delay the ruling for a few hours. The judge said he would do so only if DCF would agree in the meantime to abide by the previous day's order not to grab Terri. The attorney wouldn't agree, so Judge Greer vacated the automatic suspension. At 11:25 A.M., the judge signed an order restoring the previous day's antiseizure order to "full force and effect."

What Judge Greer didn't know was that the governor had once again dispatched the FDLE agents for another try at seizing Terri and taking her to the hospital. The agents were staged near Terri's hospice, along with DCF personnel and a doctor. A showdown was brewing between state and local police. When someone from the FDLE called the local police to alert them that FDLE agents were on the way, the local police responded that "unless they had the judge with them when they came, they were not going to get in." As one official put it, "There were two sets of law enforcement officers facing off, waiting for the other to blink." Eventually, the FDLE backed off—evidently because of Judge Greer's 11:25 A.M. order.

Jeb Bush had blown it. DCF's 8:15 A.M. appeal had created a window of opportunity, but DCF failed to act in time to grab Terri before George Felos got Judge Greer to close the window. DCF lawyers later tried to get the Court of Appeal and the Florida Supreme Court to reinstate the automatic suspension, but those efforts also failed.

When I later tried to learn more about Governor Bush's attempts to grab Terri on March 23 and 24, I couldn't get anyone to talk. The hospital's attorney told me, "No employee at the hospital will speak to you or anyone else about that—if they talk it will be at the peril of losing their jobs." Lieutenant Riley first told my investigator, "I'm going to say no comment on that," then, "You're not going to get anyone to talk to you about that," and finally, "It's too sensitive." One hospice spokesperson told me, "I don't know anything about that"; another said, "I only know what I saw in the newspapers."

The next day—Friday, March 25—the Schindlers took one last shot at Judge Greer. This was the day the Schindlers announced they would give up on the federal court litigation, and I was winging my way from Washington back to Oakland. Gibbs filed a motion before Judge Greer requesting an immediate order for reinsertion of Terri's PEG tube, based primarily on an affidavit by Schindler attorney Barbara Weller recounting her visit with Terri a week earlier, when Terri had vocalized "Ahhhhhhh" and "Waaaaaaaa"—which Weller translated as "I want to live."

This motion included a few other affidavits that made some eye-popping claims. In one affidavit, an inventor named Lawrence J. Caldwell said he had "conceived of a device" that would "detect brain-waves that are equivalent to prevocalized thoughts" and could use computer software to "translate the thoughts to words"—a machine that might read Terri's mind. In another affidavit, a Dr. Elizabeth A. Schmidt, who hadn't practiced in years, said she had viewed the "video clips and reports on the internet" and concluded that Terri was not in PVS. In yet another, a Dr. George McClane claimed that "the circumstances surrounding her initial anoxic episode and her subsequent neurological status are consistent with a victim who has been strangled"—implying that Michael Schiavo was a would-be murderer.

That day, FBI agents arrested a North Carolina man who had offered, via e-mail, bounties of $250,000 for the killing of Michael Schiavo and $50,000 for the killing of Judge Greer.

On Saturday morning, March 26, Judge Greer issued his final ruling in the case, denying the Schindlers' motion. The judge's written order explained:

- Weller's account of Terri's vocalizations was "consistent with evidence presented at the 2002 trial" that Terri's "limited vocalizations" were "not a cognitive response" but were "random."

- The inventor of the mind-reading machine (kudos to the judge for keeping a straight face) admitted he "cannot render an opinion of the probability of success of this device."

- The videotape snippets and the implication of strangulation were nothing new and had already been considered.

The state court game was over. Later that day, the Florida Supreme Court denied a final request by the Schindlers to order Terri's immediate transportation to the hospital for reattachment of her feeding tube.

On Sunday, March 27, Gibbs said on the CBS television program *Face the Nation*, "Terri is declining rapidly. We believe she has, at this point, passed where physically she would be able to recover." She had been without sustenance for nine days.

Governor Bush said he was "sad that she's in the situation that she's in" but "I cannot violate a court order." In 2003, he hadn't had any compunction violating the constitutional separation of powers with "Terri's Law." In 2005, however, he was not willing to go to jail for her.

Randall Terry wasn't mollified. He fumed, "The governor blinked" and "If Governor Bush wants to be the man that his brother is, he needs to step up to the plate like President Bush did when the United Nations told him not to go into Iraq." Terry challenged Jeb Bush: "Be a man."

Terri Schiavo was approaching death.

Time Runs Out

Sunday, March 27. Easter Sunday. Monsignor Thaddeus Malanowski emerged from Hospice House Woodside after giving Terri Schiavo the last rites of the Catholic Church. He told reporters, "She is very calm now. She is very weak. To me, death is imminent." The night before, the Schindlers had urged the protestors outside the hospice to go home, but many had remained.

It was Terri's ninth day off her PEG tube. Michael Schiavo stayed at her side. He and his brother, Brian Schiavo, took up residence at the hospice in a room down the hall from Terri.

Monday, March 28. Michael's lead counsel, George Felos, announced that Terri was near death, although the end was not imminent. He said, "Her breathing is not labored. Her skin tone is fine." There was "no evidence" of "any bodily discomfort whatsoever."

According to Terri's sister, Terri had a look on her face that said, "Please help me." Bob Schindler said, "I have a great concern that they will expedite the process to kill her with an overdose of morphine."

In fact, Terri had been given a small amount of morphine by suppository—an unremarkable palliative measure in end-of-life care. As Wesley Smith wrote in his book on palliative care, "Continuing opioid medication as the patient is dying prevents the re-emergence of pain." Even Smith says it is "absolute rubbish" to suggest that palliation with morphine is deadly, and "rather than worrying unduly about morphine hastening death, the greater danger to human welfare is allowing this myth about opioids to result in untreated pain."

Tuesday, March 29. The Schindlers had announced four days previously, on March 25, that they were giving up on federal court litigation, where the last event had been the unanimous decision by the three-judge panel of the Eleventh Circuit refusing for the second time to order the reinsertion of Terri's PEG tube. If the Schindlers had been serious about giving up, they changed their minds on March 29, when Gibbs and Destro—again joined by Jay Sekulow of the American Center for Law and Justice—filed another petition for a rehearing by the Eleventh Circuit.

This petition tried something the Schindlers' lawyers had not previously attempted—an assault on the U.S. Supreme Court's ruling in *Cruzan* that the states *may* but *need not* require proof of end-of-life wishes by clear and convincing evidence. The petition argued that a few Supreme Court decisions predating *Cruzan* were in conflict with *Cruzan* and should be interpreted as requiring the higher standard of proof.

This assault on *Cruzan* was a springboard for a hidden agenda—a broader attack on all surrogate exercise of the right to refuse medical treatment. The Schindlers' lawyers argued that "oral testimony of the type provided by Michael Schiavo" could not constitutionally justify the removal of Terri's PEG tube. If that argument stood, it would be just a short leap to completely prohibiting the withholding or withdrawal of ANH from *anyone* under the bioethicists' substituted-judgment model for surrogate decision-making, which is usually based on prior conversations with relatives or friends. That would leave only one more target for the religious Right: surrogate decision-making on behalf of the few Americans who execute advance written directives.

This is the religious Right's ultimate goal: to take away the right to personal autonomy in all its manifestations.

While the Eleventh Circuit judges were coping with this new filing, the spectacle outside Terri's hospice was ongoing. Someone had erected a giant wooden cross bearing a bottle of water, grapes, and a loaf of French bread. Bagpipes were sounded. A woman blew on a shofar—a ritual horn sounded by the ancient Hebrews during battles. The Reverend Jesse Jackson showed up to support the Schindlers, saying Terri's "starvation to death" was "inhumane." Evidently Jackson, too, doesn't know about palliation and ketonemia. The protestors called to him, "Pray with us!" and "Jesse for president!" He declaimed, "We are all potentially Terris." This prompted a rebuff by a Florida legislator, Democrat Gary Siplin of Orlando, who said, "He's a pastor, and I'm a Christian, too. I believe in miracles. But if the Lord wanted to do something, he would do it."

Even Ralph Nader—another fringe presidential candidate—came to the Schindlers' defense. A few days earlier, Nader had issued a joint press release with Wesley Smith, saying, "A profound injustice is being inflicted on Terri Schiavo" and "Justice demands that Terri be permitted to live."

Ralph Nader and Wesley Smith? There is actually some logic to it. Smith was Nader's coauthor on four books about consumer issues. And they both share the attribute of taking money from political conservatives; Nader accepted contributions from wealthy Republicans during his 2004 presidential campaign.

Wednesday, March 30. The three-judge panel of the Eleventh Circuit denied the Schindlers' request for a rehearing. The next step was for the twelve judges of the appellate court to decide whether to grant a rehearing before all of them.

Outside Hospice House Woodside, the Pinellas Park police arrested a man for trespassing on hospice property carrying a plastic cup of water—evidently he meant to give it to Terri. A protestor held a poster saying, "We believe in miracles." A self-styled "evangelical" juggler arrived, saying, "God told me to come and juggle." Someone commented, "Now it really is a circus."

Meanwhile, except for the times when the Schindlers were visiting, Michael stayed constantly at Terri's bedside, accompanied by his brother, Brian, George Felos, or Debbie Bushnell.

Later that day, the full Eleventh Circuit ruled, denying a rehearing by a vote of 9 to 2 (with one judge not participating). Most of the judges remained silent, simply concurring in a one-sentence denial order. But one judge—Stanley F. Birch, Jr.—issued a thirteen-page opinion in which he blasted Congress and President Bush for acting "in a manner demonstrably at odds with our Founding Fathers' blueprint for the governance of a free people—our Constitution." Judge Birch said the congressional bill authorizing federal district court review of the Florida state court proceedings was "an unconstitutional infringement on the core principles of separation of powers." Citing Justice Scalia's opinion in the *Plaut* case, the judge explained that because the bill dictated "how a federal court should exercise its judicial functions," it "invades the province of the judiciary and violates the separation of powers principles."

The judge had this to say about the proper roles of the three branches of American government: "When the fervor of political passions moves the Executive and the Legislative branches to act in ways inimical to basic constitutional principles, it is the duty of the judiciary to intervene. . . . We must conscientiously guard the independence of our judiciary and safeguard the Constitution, even in the face of the unfathomable human tragedy that has befallen Mrs. Schiavo and her family and the recent events related to her plight which have troubled the consciences of many."

Judge Birch also had a few choice words about the proverbial "activist judge" of whom members of the religious Right so often complain—an epithet they were likely to hurl at the Eleventh Circuit. Birch defined an activist judge as "one who decides the outcome of a controversy before him or her according to personal conviction, even one sincerely held, as opposed to the dictates of the law as constrained by legal precedent and, ultimately, our Constitution." Birch said that if the courts were to "change the law" in the *Schiavo* case at the bidding of Congress and the Schindlers, then "an 'activist judge' criticism would be valid."

The judge's message was this: Those who attack the judicial branch for failing to do the bidding of the legislative and executive branches are asking for precisely the sort of "judicial activism" that they decry as repugnant to the Constitution.

Judge Birch is no liberal. He is a Republican appointed to the Eleventh Circuit by President George H. W. Bush. His appointment was vetted by Kenneth Starr. But he professes to put his personal politics aside when doing the work of a judge, choosing instead to uphold the law, regardless of where it leads. In a 2003 interview, he explained, "In this job I think we have a duty to maintain the purity of the law and where possible differentiate between the correct and the wrong by drawing the lines of legal demarcation as clearly as possible. . . . I have always viewed the courthouse as a temple of justice where our job is to keep the flame of the rule of law burning brightly."

Two other Eleventh Circuit judges—the ones who had signed the original majority opinion of the three-judge panel—wrote separately to address the notion that the court should reconsider the factual issues regarding Terri Schiavo's end-of-life wishes and medical condition. They said, "It is not the role of an appellate court to second-guess credibility determinations," and the evidence before Judge Greer "clearly was sufficient to meet the clear and convincing evidence standard, which the Florida courts had imposed and did apply in this case." In other words, putting the constitutional issues aside, the evidence supported Judge Greer's decision that Terri was in PVS and would not want ANH.

The Schindlers had one last legal move—another application to the U.S. Supreme Court for an order compelling the reinsertion of Terri's PEG tube. They filed the application immediately. And the Supreme Court denied it immediately. The legal battle was finally over.

Michael and Brian Schiavo stayed up all that night with Terri, sharing stories about their lives before her collapse.

Thursday, March 31. On this day, at 9:00 A.M., Terri died in Michael's arms.

A bit later, George Felos held a news conference to announce Terri's death. He said, "I just want to express my condolences to the entire Schiavo and Schindler family and all those in the country and around the world who are grieving Terri's loss." The Schindler family held a separate news conference and issued a statement saying, "After these recent years of neglect at the hands of those who were supposed to protect and care for her, she is finally at peace with God for eternity."

Public reaction from the Schindlers' supporters was swift. Monsignor Malanowski said, "Terri was murdered by the system, by legalism, and by the system's culture of death." A Vatican spokesman called the removal of Terri's PEG tube "an attack against God." Florida state senator Dennis Baxley, who had tried to get the Florida legislature to pass a "Terri's Law II," called Terri "a martyr." Jeb Bush said he was "heartbroken." President Bush issued a statement: "I urge all those who honor Terri Schiavo to continue to work to build a culture of life." One hospice protestor told a reporter, "This is indeed a culture war, a war between those who value life and those who do not value life." House majority leader Tom DeLay warned, "The time will come for the men responsible for this to answer for their behavior, but not today."

All of the amazing twists and turns of the previous weeks were finally over and done with. Battles had been fought on multiple fronts—in the Florida state courts, in the Florida legislature, in the U.S. Congress, in the federal courts, and in the hearts of the American people—in this "culture war" declared and funded by the religious Right. Legal scholars will spend years trying to make sense of the congressional legislation and the fantastically complex litigation strategies pursued by David Gibbs III, Robert Destro, Ken Connor, Pat Anderson, and all the other lawyers who worked for the Schindlers and Governor Jeb Bush.

Was there any winner? The Schindlers lost their beloved daughter. Michael Schiavo lost his wife and his privacy. Members of Congress lost the respect of the American people. Jeb Bush probably lost his shot at the presidency. The only true winner was the Constitution of the United States.

An editorial in the St. Petersburg Times said it best: "Ms. Schiavo is not a martyr, as one Florida legislator claimed after her death. She was simply the tragic victim of an ugly family dispute that robbed her of her privacy and brought out the worst impulses of government to meddle in the most private of moments. She had the right to determine her own fate and to die with dignity, as do we all. May she rest in peace."

PART THREE

Where It's Going

Vengeance

T erri Schiavo's autopsy report was publicly released on June 15, 2005. It undermines the claims by the Schindlers and their supporters about Terri's medical condition and the suggestions that Michael Schiavo might have strangled or otherwise physically abused her. The report concludes:

- Terri had severe brain damage from anoxia—in medical terms, a "marked global anoxic-ischemic encephalopathy resulting in massive cerebral atrophy."

- Her brain was half its normal weight—even more atrophied than Karen Ann Quinlan's had been.

- Her condition was irreversible. No amount of therapy or treatment could have regenerated the damaged parts of her brain.

- Her brain's vision center was dead, indicating she was blind.

- She had not been strangled. There was no evidence of any traumatic injury upon her hospital admission in 1990.

- A bone fracture detected in 1991 had been caused by osteoporosis—a common result of long-term immobility. There were no other bone fractures.

- She would not have been able to take nutrition or hydration orally. In fact, she would have aspirated it—that is, she would have choked to death.

- There were no traces of morphine in her body. She had been given only two doses of morphine—on March 19 and 26. Her death had not been hastened by opioids.

- She died of dehydration. She did not starve to death.

There was no truth to any of the outrageous statements made by the Schindlers, Governor Jeb Bush, Senate majority leader Bill Frist, and the rest of the Schindlers' advocates regarding Terri's medical condition and the cause of her collapse. She could not eat, drink, think, communicate, or see. She would not have benefited from any amount of treatment or therapy. Michael had not strangled or beaten her.

There were two questions the autopsy could not answer: whether Terri had been in PVS and whether she had suffered from bulimia.

On the PVS question, the report explained that "PVS is a clinical diagnosis arrived at through physical examination of living patients." In other words, the diagnosis of PVS is made by a patient's physician during her lifetime, not by a medical examiner after her death. Nothing discovered in the autopsy changed Terri's diagnosis of PVS.

On the bulimia question, the evidence was inconclusive. The autopsy report noted that although Terri's low potassium level when she was tested at the hospital was consistent with bulimia, it also could have been caused by a drug she was given before she was tested. The report noted there was no hard evidence of bulimia—such as accounts by relatives or friends that they had seen Terri vomiting—although Terri's massive tea drinking may have "played a role" in her collapse. Ultimately, the cause will never be known with medical certainty.

The autopsy report should have put the *Schiavo* case to rest. Certainly America's editorial writers thought it would. When the report was released, the nation's newspapers bristled with editorial headlines like

"Autopsy Vindicates Judges, Husband," "Autopsy Debunks Abuse," "Schiavo Autopsy Underscores Folly of Intervention," "Autopsy Reveals Much About Politicians," and "End of the Schiavo Case."

It isn't over yet, however. Not at all.

Politically, Jeb Bush—a presidential hopeful for 2008—is on the ropes because of the *Schiavo* case. The religious Right is livid at him for not following through on his March 23 and 24 efforts to grab Terri. Randall Terry has warned: "There will be hell to pay." He wasn't talking about the Democrats. He was aiming at Jeb Bush. And for the more moderate among us, Bush's political stature took a hit with the release of the autopsy report.

Bush is not alone in his political troubles. Senate majority leader Bill Frist—another 2008 presidential aspirant—is also at risk because of his claims in the Senate on March 17, 2005, about Terri's medical condition. Senator Frist's strategy after the autopsy was first to ignore history and then to rewrite it. His initial comment was, "It's time to move on." Later he insisted that, as he put it, he "never made" a diagnosis. But there's no ignoring or denying the transcripts of Dr. Frist's March 17 diagnosis in the Senate:

- "I have looked at the video footage. Based on the footage provided to me . . . she does respond."

- "Speaking more as a physician than as a U.S. Senator . . . I question [the PVS diagnosis] based on a review of the video footage which I spent an hour or so looking at. That footage, to me, depicted something very different than persistent vegetative state."

- "There is no question in the video that she actually looks up. She certainly seems to respond to visual stimuli."

What kind of doctor relies on a one-hour viewing of edited videotape to question an attending physician's diagnosis and say there were visual responses by a patient who turns out to have likely been blind—and then denies that he ever said it? How stupid or forgetful does Frist think the American people are?

Frist's colleague, Senator Mel Martinez—one of the architects of the congressional intervention—at least had the political acumen to express regret for the debacle he helped create. He conceded, "I really probably come to the view this has to be more resolved at the state level, seems like the kind of issue the state courts deal with."

Jeb Bush's strategy was different. As damaging as the autopsy report was to his political ambitions, he struck back by trying to use it as a springboard for continuing his attacks on Michael Schiavo. Two days after the report was released, Governor Bush faxed a letter to state prosecutor Bernie McCabe asking him to "take a fresh look at this case"—that is, to consider prosecuting Michael Schiavo for some un-specified crime.

The governor's letter claimed, "While the [autopsy] report clarifies many questions surrounding the case, it leaves some unanswered." The letter cited two such "unanswered" questions. First, Bush won-dered about the cause of Terri's 1990 collapse, saying that although the report "rules out any overt or blunt trauma," it "could not rule out or positively identify other causes," so that "the cause of her injuries is more in doubt than ever." Second, Bush claimed the report revealed a discrepancy regarding the timing of Michael Schiavo's 911 call after Terri's collapse: The call came at 5:40 A.M.; two years later, Michael testified, "I believe it was almost 5:00 A.M." when Terri collapsed; thirteen years later, he said in a 2003 television interview with Larry King that she collapsed at "about" 4:30 A.M. Bush's letter claimed there seemed to have been a forty- to seventy-minute "delay" before Michael called 911. Bush also told reporters that the delay was "a significant question that during this entire ordeal was never brought up."

It must have slipped the governor's mind that Bobby Schindler told him about the so-called delay *a year earlier*. On the day after Bush faxed his letter to McCabe, the *Miami Herald* reported that, according to Schindler attorney Barbara Weller, "The Schindlers had long held suspicions that Michael Schiavo delayed his call for help" and Bobby Schindler "has been keeping a log that he gave Bush more than a year ago."

In fact, Bobby and Michael had sparred publicly as far back as 2003 about the timing of events after Terri's collapse. In the 2003 Larry King interview, Michael said that after he found Terri lying "lifeless" in the hall, "I ran over, I called 911. Her brother [Bobby] happened to live in the same complex as we did. I called him." Bobby disputed Michael's account, saying that Michael first called Terri's father, Bob Schindler, and subsequently called 911.

If Weller is being truthful—and why wouldn't she be?—then Bush knew of the "delay" claim long ago. Yet he said nothing about it while Terri was still alive, even as he was sending the Florida Department of Children and Families to Judge Greer with bogus claims of physical abuse. Of all the attacks on Michael during Terri's lifetime, why would Bush hold back on this one until after her death? Perhaps it was because he knew the claim was too far-fetched to be useful—until the autopsy report put his political future on the line.

The most likely explanation for the "delay" is that there was none. Michael testified in 2000—long before the timing of his 911 call was at issue—that "I'm not good with dates and times." And who looks at the clock when their spouse has collapsed and is lying lifeless on the floor? Michael had more pressing things to do than to check the time. Does Jeb Bush really think a jury would convict Michael of some crime because he could only hazard a rough guess, years later, as to the time he called 911?

McCabe agreed to investigate, but he subsequently refused to pursue the matter further, saying that, despite any discrepancies, Michael Schiavo had been consistent in stating that he called 911 immediately after Terri's collapse and "this consistency, coupled with the varying recollections of the precise time offered by other interested parties, lead me to the conclusion that such discrepancies are not indicative of criminal activity." McCabe concluded that the most likely cause of Terri's collapse was an eating disorder. Governor Bush then declared an end to the state's inquiry into Terri's collapse.

It remains to be seen whether Governor Bush has something else up his sleeve. In the *Schiavo* case, no outrage is too implausible. After all, the Bush family's political handlers managed to tar two war heroes: John McCain as mentally unstable, and John Kerry as a cowardly liar.

Former Los Angeles police detective Mark Fuhrman has also demanded an investigation of Michael Schiavo's so-called delay in dialing 911. On June 28, 2005, Fuhrman released his book *Silent Witness* in which he urged Governor Bush to "call for a special prosecutor" because "Michael's missing forty minutes must be explained."

Ironically, Fuhrman's book is itself infused with date and time discrepancies. Fuhrman announces at the outset that he wrote the book at the behest of Fox News Channel talk show host Sean Hannity, saying, "A few days after Terri died, Sean Hannity called me" and "asked me, 'Will you investigate this case?'" Terri died on March 31, which would place Hannity's call in April. But Hannity seems to tell a different story; he is reported to have said he called Fuhrman in March.

Fuhrman also writes of Bob and Mary Schindler's "recollection" that "some twenty minutes" passed between Michael's 911 call and Terri's departure for the hospital. In fact, that period of time was approximately fifty-five minutes. The Schindlers were off by thirty-five minutes—almost as much as the "missing forty minutes" that Fuhrman insists "must be explained."

Is somebody lying here? Not likely. Fuhrman, Hannity, and the Schindlers are only human, not timepieces. Their errant date and time estimates are no more suspicious than Michael Schiavo's estimate of when his 911 call occurred.

Fuhrman also makes a strong case, albeit unwittingly, for Terri's being bulimic. He lists twenty-one factors that indicate bulimia and says only two were present in Terri's case. In fact, Fuhrman's book and other sources indicate the presence of at least eleven of those factors:

- Weight fluctuation (high of 250 pounds, low of 110 pounds, 126 pounds at time of collapse, twenty to twenty-five pound fluctuations reported by Michael).

- Irregular menstruation (reason for gynecologist consultation).

- Lethargy and fatigue (1990 police report indicated Terri had been "tired lately and not feeling well").

- Low potassium level (detected at hospital).

- Heavy eating (reported claim of "good metabolism" enabling her to eat much yet stay thin).

- Mood swings (reported by Bobby Schindler).

- Anxiety and depression (Bobby said Terri was "absolutely miserable" just before her collapse).

- Disappearing to the bathroom after meals (a friend of Terri's reported that after meals Terri would go to the bathroom with a toothbrush, toothpaste, and mouthwash, purportedly to clean her teeth).

- Excessive use of diuretics (massive quantities of iced tea).

- Periods of fasting (a doctor's report said "she frequently skips breakfast and lunch").

- Reluctance to socialize (Bobby called her "extremely timid").

Thus, if anything, Fuhrman's book breathes new life into the bulimia theory.

The entire religious Right is angry—very angry—about the outcome of the *Schiavo* case. Despite a legal and public relations effort backed by virtually unlimited financial resources, the think-tank machinery was unable to keep Terri Schiavo's PEG tube attached. The Republican leadership failed, despite Reagan-Bush speechwriter Peggy Noonan's warning that "you have to win on this" and "if you don't, you can't imagine how much you're going to lose."

It was bad enough that, after Terri's death, House majority leader Tom DeLay threatened that "the men responsible for this" will "answer for their behavior." Even worse was Texas Republican senator John Cornyn's suggestion that a point could come "where some people

. . . engage in violence" against judges who "are making political decisions yet are unaccountable to the public." Now we have members of Congress warning of revenge, even violence, against anyone who won't bend to their political will.

What is happening in America? Is this what has become of the right wing's culture wars—a war of vengeance?

The immediate consequence of the religious Right's ire was Governor Bush's continuing persecution of Michael Schiavo. But there will be other consequences that could threaten the rights of all Americans.

Smash the Third Branch

The leaders of the religious Right intend to use Terri Schiavo as a springboard for future attacks on America's judiciary:

- The Reverend Lou Sheldon, president of the Traditional Values Coalition (whose son, Phil Sheldon, brought Randall Terry into the *Schiavo* case), has expressed thanks for "the blessing that dear Terri's life is offering to the conservative Christian movement in America."

- Richard Lessner, executive director of the American Conservative Union, says: "I think the *Schiavo* case dramatized the need to do something to restrain the judiciary."

- Tony Perkins, current president of the Family Research Council, says: "It's a real showdown with the courts" and "the lasting dispute isn't going to be between Terri's parents and her estranged husband. It's going to be between the branches of government."

Indeed, throughout the Schiavo drama, the Schindlers' advocates have expressed hostility to the judiciary—called the "third branch" of American government because of its sequential position in the Constitution behind the legislative branch (Congress) and the executive branch (the president). Here are just a few examples:

- *James Dobson of Focus on the Family:* "The judicial system in this country is far too powerful and is totally out of control."

- *Lou Sheldon of the Traditional Values Coalition:* "Their power is illegitimate and must be restrained."

- *Wesley Smith, antieuthanasia advocate:* "This country is increasingly ruled by judges."

- *Bob Schindler, Terri's father:* "The judges are running this country."

- *Jay Sekulow, chief counsel of the American Center for Law and Justice:* "Those who are opposed to our values, our beliefs, our faiths, our practices know that their last best hope is the federal judiciary."

- *Tony Perkins of the Family Research Council:* "Just because someone dressed in black makes a decision, that is not the final word."

Pat Robertson, founder of the Christian Coalition and the American Center for Law and Justice, went so far as to suggest that America's judiciary is even more dangerous than the World Trade Center terrorists of September 11, 2001: "Over 100 years, I think the gradual erosion of the consensus that's held our country together is probably more serious than a few bearded terrorists who fly into buildings."

This isn't just talk. People such as James Dobson, Lou Sheldon, and Pat Robertson are turning their words into action, mobilizing on several fronts to break the back of the third branch and reshape it in their own image.

One line of attack is to strip the courts of their traditional authority to review the constitutionality of legislation—that is, the judicial power to overturn a law because it violates the U.S. Constitution. That power was enunciated by John Marshall, the fourth chief justice of the United States, in the 1803 case *Marbury v. Madison*, and it has survived intact for more than two hundred years. Now the religious Right wants to tinker with this fundamental tenet of American government. James Dobson has bemoaned *Marbury v. Madison* as giving judges "unrivaled imperial power" because it allows them "to rule on the constitutionality of every legal issue."

Falling in line with Dobson, a few members of Congress have recently introduced bills and resolutions in the House and Senate designed to subvert or restrict the judicial power of constitutional review in specific ways. For example:

- HR 2028 would forbid the courts from deciding any constitutional issues regarding recitation of the Pledge of Allegiance.

- House Resolution 568 would preclude the courts from making any reference to the laws of any other countries in reviewing the constitutionality of legislation (for example, to see how America's record on human rights compares with those of other nations).

- House Joint Resolution 39 would prohibit the courts from determining the constitutionality of laws against same-sex marriage.

- HR 2045 would require the courts to allow public displays of the Ten Commandments.

- S 520 would forbid the courts from deciding the constitutionality of any governmental "acknowledgment of God as the sovereign source of law, liberty, or government."

- S 489 would limit the duration of federal court orders prohibiting constitutional violations by state and local governments.

As of mid-2005, the two Senate bills (S 520 and S 489) were pending in the 109th Congress; the House bills and resolutions had failed in the 108th Congress but will undoubtedly return in one form or another.

Another line of attack is to create a congressional Office of Inspector General for the federal judiciary to act as a watchdog over the courts. This idea is a pet project of Wisconsin Republican representative F. James Sensenbrenner, who announced it in a May 9, 2005, speech at Stanford University.

Traditionally, an inspector general investigates governmental expenditures for waste, but that's not quite what Sensenbrenner has in mind. In his Stanford speech, he said:

- "The judiciary isn't supposed to write law."
- "If the courts are not spending their resources judiciously, the American people through their representatives are entitled to corrective action."
- Judges should "be punished in some capacity for behavior that does not rise to the level of impeachable conduct."
- Judges "must be accountable for their actions to co-equal branches of government."
- Judges are "not properly policing their behavior" and Congress will "step in if the federal judiciary [does] not do a better job discharging this responsibility."

Sensenbrenner even invoked the *Schiavo* case as one motivation, complaining that his "biggest beef with the federal judiciary's handling of the case" was that the courts did not conduct a "new, full and fresh review of the case's merits" at Congress's bidding.

Sensenbrenner's Office of Inspector General for the federal judiciary is plainly intended to do more than make sure judges don't spend too much on staff holiday parties. As Indiana University School of Law professor Charles Geyh observed, "Context is everything. In the abstract, there is nothing wrong with judges being accountable for the money they spend. But the backdrop here is a fairly carnivorous House trying to hold judges accountable for the decisions they make. This proposal is not made in the context of judges spending lavishly. It is being used as a proxy for [attacking] their decisions."

House majority leader Tom DeLay is more frank in what he would like to do—strangle the courts financially by choking off their funding: "We set up the courts. We can unset the courts. We have the power of the purse."

Yet another tactic is to revive the ultraconservative John Birch Society's 1960s campaign to impeach Earl Warren, the great mid-twentieth-century chief justice of the United States. In April 2005, James Dobson of Focus on the Family called for the impeachment of six (out of the nine) justices of the U.S. Supreme Court—Anthony Kennedy, Sandra Day O'Connor, Ruth Bader Ginsberg, David Souter, Stephen Breyer, and John Paul Stevens—singling out Kennedy as "the most dangerous man in America."

These six justices are not flaming liberals. They are moderate in every mainstream sense of the word.

Focus on the Family's Internet web site calls for "impeaching federal judges . . . as part of the fallout of the Terri Schiavo case." One of the group's senior officials suggests, "There needs to be some serious contemplation about what the role of the judiciary is, and what Congress's authority is, to try and bring it back under control, so that we do have a balance of power. As people look at that, impeachment may be one thing that is suggested."

A more stealthy approach is a proposal in Congress to split the Ninth Circuit Court of Appeals—the largest of the federal appellate courts—into two or three separate court systems. At first blush, this might seem innocuous, but there is a hidden agenda: the plan not only weakens the court but also would create new judicial positions to be filled by President George W. Bush.

Lou Sheldon's Traditional Values Coalition, voicing support for the proposed split, calls the Ninth Circuit "the most liberal court in the United States." James Dobson calls it a "troublesome" court, "which consistently issues off-the-wall rulings." He wants the Ninth Circuit to be "abolished and then staffed by different judges immediately." Moral Majority founder Jerry Falwell promises, "We're going to get rid of the

23 eggheads" on the Ninth Circuit. More obliquely, Representative Sensenbrenner says, "The Ninth's immense size is negatively affecting the quality of its legal decisions."

The conservative *National Review* openly acknowledges the purpose of the proposed split, calling the Ninth Circuit the "last empire of untrammeled judicial liberalism" and its justices "liberal suzerains," and observing that the split "can only help the broader cause of reining in" liberal judges.

The Family Research Council's Tony Perkins proposes flat-out disregard of some judicial pronouncements: "If necessary, and it shouldn't be often, the legislative and executive branch should refuse to acknowledge a judicial decision."

How often should that be? As often as Congress and the president don't like what a court has to say?

A solution proposed by right-wing constitutional scholar Bruce Fein is that "President George W. Bush should pack the United States Supreme Court with philosophical clones of Justices Antonin Scalia and Clarence Thomas and defeated nominee Robert H. Bork."

That is precisely what President Bush wants to do. During his second term, he will have the opportunity to make several appointments to the U.S. Supreme Court—perhaps as many as four. He wants to reshape the Supreme Court and the lower federal courts by appointing justices who, as he puts it, "understand that our rights are derived from God."

To implement this plan, President Bush is being advised by a group of four lawyers, nicknamed the "Four Horsemen," who hold weekly conference calls to plan strategy for the battle over judicial appointments. The "Four Horsemen" are Jay Sekulow, chief counsel at the American Center for Law and Justice and former attorney for the Schindlers; C. Boyden Gray, a director of the Reason Foundation, who personally donated nearly $1 million to the think-tank machinery in 1998–2003; former attorney general Ed Meese, now a fellow at the conservative Heritage Foundation; and the executive vice president of the Federalist Society, an association of conservative lawyers and law students that is amply funded by the right-wing foundations.

In the wake of Terri Schiavo's death, Senate Republicans threatened to eliminate the judicial filibuster power, which enables a minority of senators to block an appointment to the federal courts. The Democrats fought desperately to safeguard the filibuster, but ultimately a compromise was reached in mid-2005. The Republicans agreed to leave the filibuster power intact, and the Democrats conceded that they would virtually never use it. The result opened the door for a spate of ultraconservative appointments to the lower federal courts—judges who are being groomed for a short list of future Supreme Court appointments.

One of those judges is former California Supreme Court justice Janice Rogers Brown, now a judge on the federal Circuit Court of Appeals for the District of Columbia. Her appointment was confirmed in the Senate on June 8, 2005, as a result of the filibuster compromise. She is typical of what President Bush has in mind for future Supreme Court appointments.

Having argued six cases before Judge Brown when she sat on the California Supreme Court, I am quite familiar with her. I have always admired the writing style of her judicial opinions, and I respect her talent, sincerity, and integrity. In fact, when she was first nominated to the D.C. Circuit in October 2003, I wrote to the Senate Judiciary Committee in her support, saying: "I respectfully disagree with those of my political soulmates who view our disapproval of her political philosophy as grounds for opposing her confirmation, for I believe that an appointee's judicial qualifications, not political philosophy, should be the focus of the confirmation process." The White House liked my letter so much that it is quoted on President Bush's official web site.

I subsequently learned of some disturbing statements that Judge Brown made several years ago, off the bench, in obscure speeches about America's government and judiciary:

- "Where government moves in, community retreats, civil society disintegrates and our ability to control our own destiny atrophies. The result is: families under siege; war in the streets."

- "Where government advances ... freedom is imperiled; community impoverished; religion marginalized."

- "There are of course many reasons for our present difficulties, but some of our troubles can be laid at the feet of that most innocuous branch—the judiciary."

I began to wonder what sort of vision Judge Brown has for America. My answer came on April 25, 2005, when news reports appeared of a speech she gave the day before at a country club in Massachusetts. This was just a few weeks after Terri Schiavo's death, when the Senate was doing battle over Judge Brown's nomination to the D.C. Circuit.

On the constitutional right of personal autonomy, Judge Brown said that "atheistic humanism" has "handed human destiny over to the great god, autonomy, and this is quite a different idea of freedom. Freedom then becomes willfulness." Now we know of her disdain for autonomy rights, which courts across the land—including the U.S. Supreme Court—have said are constitutionally guaranteed. I'm not sure what Judge Brown means by "willfulness," but it's clear she doesn't like it—or autonomy.

Judge Brown also revealed herself to be a culture warrior of the religious Right: "There seems to have been no time since the Civil War that this country was so bitterly divided. It's not a shooting war, but it is a war.... These are perilous times for people of faith." She sounds very much like Focus on the Family's James Dobson, who said during that very same month, "Judicial hostility to faith, and especially Christianity has never been greater than today."

In May 2005, I wrote to the Senate Judiciary Committee to retract my endorsement of Judge Brown. Nevertheless, my 2003 comments about her remain on the president's web site.

For all of her talent, sincerity, and integrity, Judge Brown has attacked the U.S. Constitution itself, insofar as it guarantees the right of personal autonomy. That tells me she doesn't belong on the Supreme Court. She is part of the religious Right's plan to smash the third branch. Beware of more like her.

Indeed, President Bush's first nominee for the U.S. Supreme Court, John G. Roberts, has direct links to the ultraconservative think-tank machinery and the folks who were behind the effort to keep Terri Schiavo's PEG tube attached. He served on the Legal Advisory Council for the National Legal Center for the Public Interest, a right-wing think tank that has received at least $2 million from the Bradley and Scaife foundations, along with C. Boyden Gray, one of the Four Horsemen advising President Bush on judicial appointments. When Roberts was nominated for his 2003 appointment to the D.C. Circuit Court of Appeals, Ken Conner, then president of the Family Research Council, wrote a commentary praising Roberts as a "superbly qualified" nominee who should be supported by "those who value the sanctity of life." In November 2000, Roberts gave legal advice to Governor Jeb Bush in the Florida battle over the disputed presidential election. And in the early 1990s Roberts filed an amicus curiae brief in support of Randall Terry's Operation Rescue, and presented oral argument alongside Jay Sekulow—then representing Operation Rescue and later to represent the Schindlers and serve as another of the Four Horsemen—before the U.S. Supreme Court in *Bray v. Alexandria Clinic*, where a majority of the justices accepted arguments by Sekulow and Roberts that Operation Rescue and its members could not be sued for obstructing access to abortion clinics. After Roberts's nomination, Sekulow announced a "national campaign" by the American Center for Law and Justice "to ensure that Judge Roberts is confirmed." All this raises the question of where Roberts stands on the *Schiavo* case and surrogate exercise of the right to refuse medical treatment.

Congressional efforts to restrict the judiciary's power, the proposed congressional watchdog agency, threats of impeachment, and schemes to split the Ninth Circuit and pack the Supreme Court are all part of the religious Right's culture wars. Any doubt about that is dispelled by Lou Sheldon's Traditional Values Coalition, which recently announced on its Internet web site a "Battle Plan to Take Back Our Courts." The battle cry is: "We Must Defeat Our Robed Masters." Sheldon has budgeted $10 million for the campaign. The attack, says the web site, is five-pronged:

- A "nationwide media blitz through TV, radio and newspapers."
- "Voter mobilization mailings."
- "A major phone bank operation."
- A plan to "distribute 25,000,000 voter guides for the 2006 elections."
- "A nationwide Internet and email campaign."

The web site calls this "an all-out assault" on federal and state judges to "strip the courts of their tyrannical powers." Indeed it is.

The culture wars are throwing American constitutional law into disarray. The U.S. Supreme Court is riven with deep divisions between its conservative and moderate wings—divisions so deep that it is becoming increasingly difficult to say what the law is. With a single change in court personnel, today's 5 to 4 decision going one way could possibly become next year's 5 to 4 decision going the other way. A few Bush appointees could cut a broad swath across the entire landscape of constitutional law, laying waste to legal principles that have been settled for decades, even centuries.

The legal landscape is now so uncertain that Harvard constitutional law professor Laurence Tribe recently announced that he has abandoned work on the third edition of his monumental treatise, *American Constitutional Law*. He explained that "conflict over basic constitutional premises is today at a fever pitch," and "sharp splits on the Court reflect a much more fundamental and seemingly irreconcilable division within legal and popular culture that is not amenable to the treatment that a treatise might hope to give such cases."

It is alarming indeed that the nation's greatest constitutional scholar can no longer tell us what the law is.

President Bush says we need "judges who understand that our rights are derived from God." He might as well have taken his cue from the Internet web site of the Christian Law Association, which says: "Whether America thrives or flounders in the 21st Century could primarily depend upon who wins the battle for the courts in this generation. Will it be those judges who remember our Biblical roots or those who want to replace them with secular substitutes? . . . Supreme Court justices do not have the authority to contradict God's moral code and call it law. . . . God is the only superior able to impose moral laws on mankind."

Did the Founding Fathers really envision the United States of America as a place with "Biblical roots" to be guided by "God's moral code" as interpreted by the likes of Lou Sheldon, James Dobson, and the Christian Law Association?

Consider this 1785 statement by President James Madison, who is honored on President Bush's official web site as the "Father" of the Constitution: "What influence in fact have ecclesiastical establishments had on Civil Society? In some instances they have been seen to erect a spiritual tyranny on the ruins of the Civil authority; in many instances they have been seen upholding the thrones of political tyranny: in no instance have they been seen the guardians of the liberties of the people. Rulers who wished to subvert the public liberty, may have found an established Clergy convenient auxiliaries. A just government instituted to secure & perpetuate it needs them not." In 1822, Madison added, "I have no doubt that every new example will succeed, as every past one has done, in shewing that religion & Govt will both exist in greater purity, the less they are mixed together."

And consider this 1788 comment by President John Adams: "Although the detail of the formation of the American governments is at present little known . . . [i]t will never be pretended that any persons employed in that service had interviews with the gods, or were in any

degree under the influence of Heaven . . . ; it will forever be acknowledged that these governments were contrived merely by the use of reason and the senses." Adams signed the 1797 Treaty of Tripoli, which
stated, "The Government of the United States is not in any sense
founded on the Christian religion."

The Founding Fathers believed in God, but they kept God and his
earthly representatives out of the machinery of American government.
They feared the influence of politico-religious scoundrels.

America is neither Christian, nor Jewish, nor Muslim, nor Bud-
dhist, nor Hindu. It is a place where there is room for all, and its
supreme law is not the Bible but the Constitution. It has always been
that way. The religious Right wants to change that, starting with a
plan to make the judicial branch subservient to the legislative and executive branches. We cannot allow that.

We should all heed this warning by Alexander Hamilton: "The independence of the judges once destroyed, the Constitution is gone; it
is a dead letter."

Hand-to-Hand Combat

The judiciary is not the only front where post-*Schiavo* battles will be fought. The religious Right is also waging a state-to-state campaign to take away our personal autonomy rights—in particular, the right to refuse unwanted medical treatment. And it may soon be coming to a state house near you—if it's not already there.

One of the leaders in this assault is Father Frank Pavone, national director of Priests for Life, who ministered to the Schindler family. Claiming to speak for God, Father Pavone denies the moral legitimacy of a "right to die." He says the notion of such a right is erroneously based "on the idea of life as a 'thing we possess,'" whereas our lives are not ours to control but belong to God.

Thus, Father Pavone insists, nobody should *ever* be allowed to refuse artificial nutrition and hydration, either for themselves or as a surrogate on behalf of another. He says ANH "is always morally required" and we "are not morally permitted to request starvation and dehydration." He calls living wills "dangerous," saying that American culture "promotes the idea that as long as we say we want to die, we have the right to do so. But we have a basic obligation to preserve our own life. A person who leaves clear instructions that they don't want to be fed is breaking the moral law by requesting suicide."

This sort of thinking is common among members of the religious Right. Echoing Father Pavone, Rita Marker of the International Task Force on Euthanasia and Assisted Suicide says that the "type of

advance directive known as a 'living will' . . . is downright dangerous."
The web site for Operation Save America, one of many evangelical
antiabortion groups, says, "We are opposed to 'living wills' because
God Himself is opposed to them. He is sovereign. He is the One who
determines who lives and who dies—not us!"

The Christian Law Association has called for right-to-die legislation to be "reviewed in every state and on a national level." Former
Schindler lawyer Jay Sekulow, chief counsel for Pat Robertson's evangelical American Center for Law and Justice, likewise says that new
end-of-life legislation is needed in all states. Such efforts have, in fact,
been in the works for several years, with proposals for legislation like
the National Right to Life Committee's 2003 Model Starvation and
Dehydration of Persons with Disabilities Prevention Act.

NRLC's model act was the template for the efforts in the Florida
Legislature to pass another "Terri's Law" in March 2005, described in
Chapter 12 of this book. It's the legislative scheme I've subtitled "How
to Make It Virtually Impossible to Withhold or Withdraw ANH From
a PVS Patient." The NRLC model act does this by creating a legally
binding "presumption" that each and every one of us would want
ANH under all circumstances, and by prohibiting surrogate exercise of
the right to withhold or withdraw ANH except in three types of circumstances that are extremely unlikely to arise:

- When the provision of ANH is not medically possible or
  would hasten death or if the patient is incapable of digesting
  or absorbing ANH.

- When the patient made an advance directive containing a
  provision that specifically authorizes refusal of ANH and
  somehow overcomes the lawyer's trick that makes the provision effective only "to the extent the authorization applies."

- When there is clear and convincing evidence that shows the
  patient ruled out ANH and somehow overcomes the lawyer's
  tricks that make the refusal effective only "in the applicable

circumstances" and if it was "an understanding and enlightened decision."

NRLC's model law would wreak havoc with existing right-to-die legislation and lay waste to the fundamental principles of bioethics. And it's already on the march in several states.

During the last two months of Terri Schiavo's life, the NRLC model act was introduced either verbatim or nearly so in four state legislatures:

- *Georgia*: House Bill 1132, Starvation and Dehydration of Persons with Disabilities Prevention Act, introduced January 14, 2005.

- *Hawaii*: House Bill 1332 and Senate Bill 1809, Hawaii Starvation and Dehydration of Persons with Disabilities Prevention Act, introduced January 27, 2005.

- *Kentucky*: House Bill 501, An Act Relating to Life-Sustaining Medical Treatment for Persons with Disabilities, introduced February 14, 2005.

- *Alabama*: House Bill 592, Alabama Starvation and Dehydration of Persons with Disabilities Prevention Act, introduced March 8, 2005.

These proposed bills contain all the basic elements of the NRLC model act, including the legally binding presumption in favor of ANH and the lawyer's tricks making it virtually impossible to craft an effective advance directive to remove ANH or to meet NRLC's standard for proving "an understanding and enlightened decision."

In the month following Terri's death, NRLC's model act was introduced in four more state legislatures:

- *Minnesota*: Senate Bill 2184, A Bill for an Act Relating to Health; Creating a Presumption Directing Nutrition and Hydration Sufficient to Sustain Life, introduced April 11, 2005.

- *Iowa*: House Study Bill 302, Iowa Starvation and Dehydration of Persons with Disabilities Prevention Act, introduced April 20, 2005.

- *South Carolina*: House Bill 4013, South Carolina Starvation and Dehydration of Persons with Disabilities Prevention Act, introduced April 28, 2005.

- *Michigan*: House Bill 4743, Withholding or Withdrawal of Nutrition or Hydration, introduced May 5, 2005.

All eight of these bills were, in legislative parlance, "referred to committee"—which means they began the normal legislative process of analysis and consideration. That can take a while—months, sometimes even years. In South Dakota, a bill based on NRLC's model act—Senate Bill 187—was introduced on January 26, 2004, and a week later was referred to committee, where the bill languished.

As of mid-2005, no state had yet passed a version of the NRLC model act, and the proposals were a long way from success. Nevertheless, the battle lines had been drawn.

In four additional state legislatures, bills were introduced in versions quite different from the NRLC model act but with similar effects of subverting the right to refuse medical treatment:

- *Kansas*: Senate Bill 240, An Act Concerning Appointment of Guardians and Conservators," introduced March 2005. This bill would do something no state has ever done—prohibit surrogate exercise of the right to refuse ANH unless a guardian proves the patient's intent not just by clear and convincing evidence but *beyond a reasonable doubt* (the highest legal standard of proof, applicable in criminal trials) as determined by a *unanimous jury*.

- *Louisiana*: House Bill 675, Human Dignity Act, introduced April 15, 2005. This bill completely prohibits withholding or withdrawing ANH except where "death is imminent."

- *Ohio*: House Bill 216, "A bill" on "consent to the withholding or withdrawal of nutrition and hydration," introduced April 26, 2005. This one would prohibit the withholding or withdrawal of ANH if a close relative "disagrees" and presents "some evidence" disputing the patient's medical condition or wishes (i.e., a *Schiavo*-type scenario).

- *Florida*: House Bill 701, An Act Relating to Artificially Provided Sustenance and Hydration—the truncated version of the NRLC legislation that failed in the Florida legislature in March 2005—was reintroduced on May 6, 2005.

The Louisiana bill is the first to emerge victorious. Terri Schiavo's brother, Bobby Schindler, testified before a state Senate committee in support of the bill, saying that Terri had "suffered a slow death" and "we should err on the side of human life." The bill passed unanimously in both houses of the Louisiana legislature and was signed by the governor on July 11, 2005.

We might see similar federal legislation proposed in the U.S. Congress. On April 6, 2005, the Senate Health, Education, Labor and Pensions Committee—the same congressional committee that wrote to Michael and Terri Schiavo asking "both of you" to attend a March 28, 2005, committee hearing in Washington, D.C.—held a hearing to discuss whether federal legislation might be warranted in the wake of Terri's death. The committee chairman, Republican senator Michael Enzi, said: "Although Terri Schiavo very dramatically brought these issues to the attention of the nation, their importance did not fade or diminish with her loss."

At the committee hearing, the lead witness warned that "the slippery slope is slick and awaits us all," and he proposed a congressional bill allowing "federal intervention" in three situations:

1. The patient "is not near death" but will die if "treatment, hydration, or nutrition is withheld."

2. There is no "clear" advance directive or other "reliable" expression of the patient's wishes.

3. "There is irreconcilable disagreement among family members concerning the decision to be made."

This vision for a federal law has the potential for perpetuating ambiguities like those inherent in NRLC's model law—including all the lawyer's tricks designed to make it virtually impossible for a surrogate to exercise an incompetent patient's right to refuse ANH.

Bobby Schindler has moved to the vanguard of NRLC's hand-to-hand battle to get state legislatures to pass its model law. On June 16, 2005, he made an appearance at NRLC's annual convention, where a Franciscan monk who had advised the Schindlers asserted, "Terri's situation has been a loud wake-up call to the pro-life movement. I believe it's going to have a long-term effect." NRLC's web site contains a statement by Bobby Schindler advocating for "work to change the laws." He has taken over the foundation established by his parents to solicit donations, which he will use to help promote state-by-state legislative changes.

When asked to comment on recent proposals for legislation like NRLC's model act, bioethicist Ken Goodman, director of the bioethics program at the University of Miami, called them "preposterous." He said that although "end-of-life legislation can always be improved," changes "must be deliberate, incremental and cautious," and it's a "bad idea to tinker with state or federal law" based solely on the *Schiavo* case. He probably voices the sentiments of nearly every bioethicist in America.

I got a glimpse of the religious Right's true agenda years ago, at the time of the *Wendland* litigation, during an e-mail exchange I had with the antieuthanasia activist Wesley Smith in June 2001, a few weeks before Robert Wendland died:

Jon: "Wesley, if you were personally convinced that Robert's pre-accident wish was not to be sustained on artificial nutrition and hydration under his present circumstances, would you favor the removal of his jejunostomy tube?"

Wesley: "No, for a plethora of reasons."

That's the religious Right's agenda in a nutshell. They want to prevent all surrogate exercise of the right to refuse ANH, even when they *know* that the patient would not have wanted it.

Smith's favored vehicle for achieving his agenda is, not surprisingly, the NRLC model law. In one of his *Weekly Standard* articles, he endorsed the NRLC-based predecessor to Florida House Bill 701 as a "common sense law." In another article, he argued that surrogate decision-making should require "a well thought out, informed, and preferably written statement that not only indicates what is desired, but also shows that reasonable alternatives have been fully considered." There, again, is a lawyer's trick like in the NRLC model law—the insistence on proving that a patient's decision to refuse ANH was "enlightened," whatever that means.

It's not too late to prevent these state-by-state efforts to subvert the right to refuse unwanted medical treatment, but they will succeed unless there is a groundswell of opposition from the vast majority of Americans who value personal autonomy. E-mail campaigns are simple and effective—certainly the religious Right has figured that out. We in the majority need to use the same sort of weapons to fight back.

This really is a war, declared by the religious Right on a fundamental aspect of the American way of life. It brings to mind another war in American history and the cause for which my uncle, Bernard Eisenberg, gave his life.

My Uncle Bernie

In the small town of Draguignan in southern France, there is a U.S. military cemetery where lie the remains of 861 American soldiers. They died in the service of their country during World War II, in August 1944, during an assault from the beaches around Cannes that eventually met up with the June 1944 D-Day invaders from the north of France and then moved east to defeat Nazi Germany.

Scattered among the rows of Latin Cross grave markers are a few Jewish Stars of David. One of them bears the name of my father's older brother, my uncle and namesake—Bernard Eisenberg. My middle name is his.

Bernie overcame the poverty that hit my family hard during the years of the Great Depression, working his way through Los Angeles City College and UCLA, and was looking forward to a promising future with his wife, Peggy—perhaps teaching history, perhaps in business—when the war intervened. Bernie became a second lieutenant in the Army infantry, serving first in Italy and then in southern France. He was a "forward observer," which put him at the front lines. His job was to spot enemy soldiers and direct artillery fire at them. It put him smack in harm's way. When he first learned of his assignment, he told my father he probably would not survive.

Bernie was killed in combat on August 29, 1944. It was a grievous wound to my family that never healed. My grandfather never, ever, spoke to me of Bernie. To this day, my father, who had been an Army sergeant with a corps of radio operators in India, cannot bear to watch a war movie. Their younger sister, my aunt Lucy, is the keeper of a few mementos—Bernie's field jacket, the flag that draped his casket, some photographs. Before his stepmother died, she gave me a handful of letters he had sent home during the last months of his life.

In May 1991, my wife and I journeyed to Draguignan to visit Bernie's grave. No member of the family had ever been there. On the way from our hotel to the cemetery, we stopped at a street market and bought some flowers. I had with me the last letter Bernie had sent home from France, dated August 25, 1944—four days before he was killed.

Here's what Bernie wrote:

Dear folks,

Just a few lines to let you know that I'm doing well and feeling fine. You can tell all about my progress by watching the newspapers. You'll no doubt know more about the situation than I do.

I am going through some very beautiful country and really making quite a sightseeing tour. Of course, every now and then our vision is blocked by some swastikas, but we liquidate them as soon as they show up—not quite Russian style, but effectively enough. The French are really wonderful people. Oooh la la!

Even the men are nice.

Well, that's all for now. Will write again very soon.

Love, Bernie

At the cemetery, I laid the letter and the flowers on Bernie's grave and took a photograph for my father—close enough to show the inscription on the grave marker:

BERNARD EISENBERG

2LT 171 FA 45 DIV

CAL AUG 29, 1944

Shortly after the terrorist attacks of September 11, 2001, Ken Connor—Governor Bush's lawyer in the *Schiavo* litigation and former president of the evangelical Family Research Council—wrote on his group's web site: "Do you really think that when our troops from Delta Force crawl into Osama bin Laden's cave in Afghanistan or into the face of the muzzle of a terrorist machine gun, that they are doing it so that women can kill their children, so that pornographers can peddle their smut, so that people of the same sex can marry?"

I would ask this question somewhat differently: "Do you really think that when our troops in World War II, like Second Lieutenant Bernard Eisenberg, died to save the world from fascism, they did it to protect the reproductive rights of women, to secure the rights of free speech, and to prevent discrimination in all its forms?"

I'll speak for Bernie and say, "Yes."

Ken Connor and his ilk hold no monopoly on patriotism. I am a patriot, too. I am American to the core. I love my country, and I cherish the freedoms that are guaranteed by my Constitution—including the right of personal autonomy. That's one of the rights my uncle Bernie died for. I, too, will fight to keep it.

Across America, the *Schiavo* case has generated an unprecedented affirmation of the right of personal autonomy by people seeking to learn how to execute advance written directives. In March and early April 2005, Aging with Dignity, a nonprofit organization devoted to end-of-life issues, received requests for more than 800,000 copies of its "Five Wishes" advance directive—sixty times the group's normal rate of requests. In just two days, more than 17,000 people visited the New York State Bar Association's web site and downloaded information about living wills and health-care proxies. In Oklahoma, where the Oklahoma Bar Association normally receives perhaps one weekly request for its form advance directive, there were 150 requests during the week preceding Terri Schiavo's death. A lawyer there reported that 95 percent of the people were specifying that they did not want ANH if they were ever in PVS.

It's very easy to execute an advance written directive. You don't need a lawyer or a doctor. All you need is a form to fill out.

There are actually two different types of advance directives—the living will and the durable power of attorney for health care:

- A living will specifies the medical treatment you want to receive or don't want to receive under various circumstances, such as being comatose, in a persistent vegetative state, or in a minimally conscious state.

- A durable power of attorney for health care appoints an agent, surrogate, or proxy (terms that are generally interchangeable) to make health-care decisions on your behalf if you are unable to decide for yourself.

These days, most form advance directives combine the living will and the durable power of attorney for health care into a single document.

The legal requirements for these documents vary from state to state. In order to execute one properly, you need to obtain a form that is appropriate for the state in which you live. Many state bar associations and medical associations maintain web sites that will tell you how to easily get your hands on the right form for your state and how to fill it out. If you don't have access to the Internet, just give your state's bar or medical association a telephone call. You can also contact groups such as the American Association of Retired Persons (AARP), the American Bar Association, Compassion in Dying, or Aging with Dignity—on the Internet or by telephone—for form advance directives and other helpful information. Internet addresses are given in the Chapter Sources for this chapter.

Most advance directive forms call for appointment of an agent, surrogate, or proxy, such as a spouse, relative, or friend (that's the durable power of attorney for health care part of the form) and also have check boxes for you to indicate your health-care wishes (that's the living will part of the form). You can check a box to indicate whether you would want life-sustaining treatment such as a respirator, ANH, or cardio-pulmonary resuscitation (CPR) in any given circumstances. Alternatively, you can write in your own instructions saying what you want or don't want. You can even leave the check boxes blank and write in nothing, leaving it to your appointed agent to decide for you based on what he or she knows about your lifestyle, preferences, and values—the way I decided for my cousin Ros. Again, specific requirements can vary from state to state.

There is no hidden agenda behind these forms. They allow you to exercise the right of personal autonomy in any way you wish. You can say, "Do *nothing* to sustain my life," or you can say, "Do *everything* to sustain my life," or you can give instructions somewhere in between those two extremes. You can demand artificial nutrition and hydration under all circumstances just as easily as you can refuse it. It is your choice. That's what personal autonomy is all about.

And if you are among the relatively few Americans who would want to be kept on ANH no matter what the circumstances and are worried that the standard forms won't protect you sufficiently, then you can go to the National Right to Life Committee's web site and get a copy of its Will to Live, which plainly states, without any other option, "I direct my health care provider(s) and health care attorney in fact to provide me with food and fluids, orally, intravenously, by tube, or by other means." Rita Marker's International Task Force on Euthanasia and Assisted Suicide also offers what it calls a Protective Medical Decisions Document, which similarly contains a no-option directive to provide ANH under all circumstances.

You don't like forms? Well then, write your own advance directive. That can work, too. But it might be safer to use a form that is specially tailored to satisfy the law that applies in the state where you live.

The choice is yours. May it always remain so.

On May 21, 1944, as my uncle Bernie was preparing to ship out to Europe, he wrote to his father and stepmother from Washington, D.C., "All of my business affairs are settled so that if I should stop a bullet, my finances will proceed smoothly and Peggy will pick up the necessary funds. My will is made out to cover all exigencies. And now, I guess, I'm ready to go off to war."

I am quite certain that if Bernie had survived World War II and were still alive today, at the grand old age of eighty-nine, he would have executed an advance written directive for health care.

Appendix

Form **990**

Department of the Treasury
Internal Revenue Service

Return of Organization Exempt From Income Tax

Under section 501(c), 527, or 4947(a)(1) of the Internal Revenue Code (except black lung benefit trust or private foundation)

▶ The organization may have to use a copy of this return to satisfy state reporting requirements

OMB No 1545-0047

2003

Open to Public Inspection

A For the 2003 calendar year, or tax year beginning   **OCT 1, 2003**   and ending   **SEP 30, 2004**

B Check if applicable

- [ ] Address change
- [ ] Name change
- [ ] Initial return
- [ ] Final return
- [ ] Amended return
- [ ] Application pending

Please use IRS label or print or type. See Specific Instructions.

C Name of organization

FAMILY RESEARCH COUNCIL

Number and street (or P O box if mail is not delivered to street address) | Room/suite

801 G STREET, NW

City or town, state or country, and ZIP + 4

WASHINGTON, DC 20001

D Employer Identification number

52-1792772

E Telephone number

202-393-2100

F Accounting method [ ] Cash [X] Accrual [ ] Other (specify) ▶

● Section 501(c)(3) organizations and 4947(a)(1) nonexempt charitable trusts must attach a completed Schedule A (Form 990 or 990-EZ).

G Website: ▶WWW.FRC.ORG

J Organization type (check only one) ▶ [X] 501(c) (3) ◀ (insert no) [ ] 4947(a)(1) or [ ] 527

K Check here ▶ [ ] if the organization's gross receipts are normally not more than $25,000 The organization need not file a return with the IRS, but if the organization received a Form 990 Package in the mail, it should file a return without financial data Some states require a complete return.

L Gross receipts Add lines 6b, 8b, 9b, and 10b to line 12 ▶   **10,126,421.**

H and **I** are not applicable to section 527 organizations

H(a) Is this a group return for affiliates? [ ] Yes [X] No

H(b) If "Yes," enter number of affiliates ▶

H(c) Are all affiliates included?   N/A [ ] Yes [ ] No (If "No," attach a list)

H(d) Is this a separate return filed by an organization covered by a group ruling? [ ] Yes [X] No

I Group Exemption Number ▶

M Check ▶ [ ] if the organization is not required to attach Sch B (Form 990, 990-EZ, or 990-PF)

Part I   Revenue, Expenses, and Changes in Net Assets or Fund Balances

Revenue	1	Contributions, gifts, grants, and similar amounts received		
	a	Direct public support	1a	9,763,275.
	b	Indirect public support	1b	
	c	Government contributions (grants)	1c	
	d	Total (add lines 1a through 1c) (cash $ **9,763,275.** noncash $)	1d	9,763,275.
	2	Program service revenue including government fees and contracts (from Part VII, line 93)	2	230,115.
	3	Membership dues and assessments	3	
	4	Interest on savings and temporary cash investments	4	20,859.
	5	Dividends and interest from securities	5	
	6 a	Gross rents SEE STATEMENT 1	6a	34,390.
	b	Less rental expenses SEE STATEMENT 2	6b	16,024.
	c	Net rental income or (loss) (subtract line 6b from line 6a)	6c	18,366.
	7	Other investment income (describe ▶)	7	
	8 a	Gross amount from sales of assets other than inventory	(A) Securities 8a	(B) Other 8a 45,000.
	b	Less cost or other basis and sales expenses	8b	8b
	c	Gain or (loss) (attach schedule)	8c	8c 45,000.
	d	Net gain or (loss) (combine line 8c, columns (A) and (B)) STMT 3	8d	45,000.
	9	Special events and activities (attach schedule) If any amount is from gaming, check here ▶ [ ]		
	a	Gross revenue (not including $ of contributions	9a	
	b	Less direct expenses other than fundraising expenses	9b	
	c	Net income or (loss) from special events (subtract line 9b from line 9a)	9c	
	10 a	Gross sales of inventory, less returns and allowances	10a	
	b	Less cost of goods sold	10b	
	c	Gross profit or (loss) from sales of inventory (attach schedule) (subtract line 10b from line 10a)	10c	
	11	Other revenue (from Part VII, line 103)	11	32,782.
	12	Total revenue (add lines 1d, 2, 3, 4, 5, 6c, 7, 8d, 9c, 10c, and 11)	12	10,110,397.
Expenses	13	Program services (from line 44, column (B))	13	8,367,688.
	14	Management and general (from line 44, column (C))	14	1,126,017.
	15	Fundraising (from line 44, column (D))	15	704,767.
	16	Payments to affiliates (attach schedule)	16	
	17	Total expenses (add lines 16 and 44, column (A))	17	10,198,472.
Net Assets	18	Excess or (deficit) for the year (subtract line 17 from line 12)	18	-88,075.
	19	Net assets or fund balances at beginning of year (from line 73, column (A))	19	4,811,257.
	20	Other changes in net assets or fund balances (attach explanation)	20	0.
	21	Net assets or fund balances at end of year (combine lines 18, 19, and 20)	21	4,723,182.

RECEIVED FEB 2005 OGDEN

SCANNED FEB 2 4 2005

769

323001 12-17-03   LHA   **For Paperwork Reduction Act Notice, see the separate Instructions.**   Form **990** (2003)

FIG. 1. The first page of a 990 form, this one for the
Family Research Council.

SCHEDULE A (Form 990 or 990-EZ)	**Organization Exempt Under Section 501(c)(3)** (Except Private Foundation) and Section 501(e), 501(f), 501(k), 501(n), or Section 4947(a)(1) Nonexempt Charitable Trust Supplementary Information — (See separate instructions.)	OMB No 1545 0047 **2003**
Department of the Treasury Internal Revenue Service	► MUST be completed by the above organizations and attached to their Form 990 or 990-EZ.	

Name of the organization	Employer Identification number
CHRISTIAN LAW ASSOCIATION	34-1245065

Part I Compensation of the Five Highest Paid Employees Other Than Officers, Directors, and Trustees
(See instructions. List each one If there are none, enter 'None.')

(a) Name and address of each employee paid more than $50,000	(b) Title and average hours per week devoted to position	(c) Compensation	(d) Contributions to employee benefit plans and deferred compensation	(e) Expense account and other allowances
NONE				

Total number of other employees paid over $50,000 ► | | 0 | | |

Part II Compensation of the Five Highest Paid Independent Contractors for Professional Services
(See instructions. List each one (whether individuals or firms). If there are none, enter 'None.')

(a) Name and address of each independent contractor paid more than $50,000	(b) Type of service	(c) Compensation
GIBBS LAW FIRM PA 5666 SEMINOLE BLVD SUITE 2, SEMINOLE FL 33772	LEGAL SERVICES	1,908,689.

Total number of others receiving over $50,000 for professional services ► | | 0 |

BAA For Paperwork Reduction Act Notice, see the Instructions for Form 990 and Form 990-EZ. Schedule A (Form 990 or 990-EZ) 2003

TEEA0401L 08/28/03

FIG. 2. A page from Christian Law Association's 990 form for 2003, showing payments to Gibbs Law Firm

---

Calamas, Christa

From:	Calamas, Christa
Sent:	Thursday, January 27, 2005 8:40 AM
To:	DiPietre, Jacob; Faraj, Alia
Subject:	FW: Schiavo OpEd

OpEd Schiavo -
JS SupCt.doc (2..

-----Original Message-----
From: Ken L. Connor [mailto:KConnor@wilkesmchugh.com]
Sent: Wednesday, January 26, 2005 6:22 PM
To: rockyrodriguez@msn.com; christa.calamas@myflorida.com
Subject: FW: Schiavo OpEd

Here is an op ed I drafted for Dan Webster which should appear in USA Today tomorrow. I an working one one for the Wash. Times which will follow.

Ken

> -----Original Message-----
> From: Ken L. Connor
> Sent: Wednesday, January 26, 2005 12:43 PM
> To: 'mat@lc.org'; 'astaver@lc.org'; 'jon@johnsonandassociates.com'
> Cc: Jim Wilkes; Steve Vancore
> Subject: Schiavo OpEd
>
> Final draft with 350 word target.
>
> > <<OpEd Schiavo - US SupCt.doc>>
>
> Kenneth L. Connor
> Wilkes & McHugh, P.A.
> 50 Catoctin Circle NE, Ste. 203
> Leesburg, VA 20176-3101
> 703-669-3377
> 703-669-8311-Fax
> kconnor@wilkesmchugh.com
>
>

****
This message has been scanned by Wilkes & McHugh IT Department.
****

1

FIG. 3. Ken Connor's e-mail transmitting the op-ed piece he wrote for Senator Webster.

S. 529, The Incapacitated Person's Legal Protection Act

- Teri Schiavo is subject to an order that her feeding tubes will be disconnected on March 18, 2005 at 1p.m.

- The Senate needs to act this week, before the Budget Act is pending business, or Terri's family will not have a remedy in federal court.

- This is an important moral issue and the pro-life base will be excited that the Senate is debating this important issue.

- This is a great political issue, because Senator Nelson of Florida has already refused to become a cosponsor and this is a tough issue for Democrats.

- The bill is very limited and defines custody as "those parties authorized or directed by a court order to withdraw or withhold food, fluids, or medical treatment."

- There is an exemption for a proceeding "which no party disputes, and the court finds, that the incapacitated person while having capacity, had executed a written advance directive valid under applicably law that clearly authorized the withholding or withdrawal of food or fluids or medical treatment in the applicable circumstances."

- Incapacitated persons are defined as those "presently incapable of making relevant decisions concerning the provision, withholding or withdrawal of food fluids or medical treatment under applicable state law."

- This legislation ensures that individuals like Terri Schiavo are guaranteed the same legal protections as convicted murderers like Ted Bundy.

Fig. 4. Memo by counsel for Senator Mel Martinez on how to exploit the Schiavo case politically. (The author of this memo, Brian Darling, misidentified the bill number and misspelled Terri's name.)

Appendix

ONE HUNDRED NINTH CONGRESS

Congress of the United States

House of Representatives

COMMITTEE ON GOVERNMENT REFORM

2157 RAYBURN HOUSE OFFICE BUILDING

WASHINGTON, DC 20515–6143

March 18, 2005

Mrs. Theresa Marie Schiavo
The Hospice of the Florida Suncoast
6774 102nd Avenue
Pinellas Park, FL 33782

Dear Mrs. Schiavo:

Attached please find a subpoena to appear on Friday, March 25, 2005 at 10:00 a.m., at the Hospice of the Florida Suncoast for the Committee on Government Reform.

The Committee has initiated an inquiry into the long term care of incapacitated adults, an issue of growing importance to the federal government and federal healthcare policy. The hearing will review the treatment options provided to incapacited patients to advance the quality of life by examining the procedures, practices, methods, and equipment used by health care professionals. Additionally, the Committee will examine nutrition and hydration which incapacited patients receive as part of their care. Further, the Committee seeks to understand the issues raised by the legislative proposals contained in H.R. 1332, Protection of Incapacitated Persons Act of 2005 and S. 539, Incapacitated Persons Legal Protection Act of 2005. Your appearance at the hearing would be central to the Committee's understanding of these matters.

Thank you in advance for your participation in this important hearing. If you have any questions regarding this hearing, please contact the Committee at (202) 225-5074.

Sincerely,

Tom Davis
Chairman

cc: The Honorable Henry A. Waxman
Minority Ranking Member

FIG. 5. Representative Tom Davis's letter to Terri Schiavo telling her to appear at a congressional hearing.

SUBPOENA

**BY AUTHORITY OF THE HOUSE OF REPRESENTATIVES OF THE
CONGRESS OF THE UNITED STATES OF AMERICA**

To Theresa Marie Schiavo

You are hereby commanded to be and appear before the Committee on Government Reform

of the House of Representatives of the United States at the place, date and time specified below.

☑ to testify touching matters of inquiry committed to said committee or subcommittee; and you are not to depart without leave of said committee or subcommittee.

> Place of testimony: Hospice of the Florida Suncoast, 6774 102nd Avenue, Pinellas Park, FL 33782
>
> Date: March 25, 2005   Time: 10:00 AM

☐ to produce the things identified on the attached schedule touching matters of inquiry committed to said committee or subcommittee; and you are not to depart without leave of said committee or subcommittee.

> Place of production:
>
> Date: Time:

To U.S. Marshals Service or any authorized staff member

_____ to serve and make return.

Witness my hand and the seal of the House of Representatives of the United States, at the city of Washington, this 18 day of March , 2005 .

_____
Chairman or Authorized Member

Attest:

Clerk

FIG. 6. The subpoena commanding Terri Schiavo to appear and "testify" at the congressional hearing.

From: Destro, Robert A
Sent: Sat 3/19/2005 10:50 AM
To: Philip.Kiko@mail.house.gov
Subject: Private Bill Concerns

Dear Phil:

You have asked me to state my concerns about the Senate's "private bill" aspects. I am happy to do so.

The biggest problem facing Governor Bush in the Supreme Court of Florida was that court's unshakable perception that "Terri's Law", Florida Statutes Chapter 2003-418, violated both state and federal principles of separation of powers. Relying on this Court's decisions in Plaut v. Spendthrift Farm, Inc., 514 U.S. 211 (1995) and Landgraf v. USI Film Products, 511 U.S. 244 (1994) <http://www.westlaw.com/Find/Default.wl?rs=++++1.0&vr=2.0&DocName=511US244&F indType=Y&ReferencePositionType=S&ReferencePosition=269> , the Florida court held that legislative authorization for the Governor to assume protective jurisdiction of an incapacitated person denied nutrition and hydration pursuant to a judicial decree prior to his or her death violates the separation of powers. In the Florida Circuit Court's view, Chapter 2003-418 "clearly attaches new legal consequences to Mrs. Schiavo's previously adjudicated privacy right", and the creation of a new, post-judgment review process constituted a "clear" case of legislative and executive "intrusion into judicial functions".

The Florida Supreme Court affirmed, holding that, under the principles enunciated in Plaut and relevant Florida cases applying them, "the Act, as applied in this case, resulted in an executive order that effectively reversed a properly rendered final judgment and thereby constituted an unconstitutional encroachment on the power that has been reserved for the independent judiciary." The practical result was that it became impossible to litigate the federal claims before the Florida courts.

My concern about a private bill is twofold. First, it will inevitably be viewed as an attempt by Congress to overturn the judgment of a state court. That is why we suggested an approach centered on habeas corpus. Chairman Sensenbrenner quite rightly suggested that, even if we were able to get into a habeas court, we would be faced judicial hostility on grounds of federalism, issue and claim preclusion, and the "prisoner-centric" language of the habeas statutes.

The orders of Judge Moody issued last night (copies attached) make it clear that every single one of the Chairman's worst fears has come to pass.

· The judge ruled that we were issue and claim precluded under the Rooker-Feldman Doctrine (which does not even apply to habeas proceeding.

· He ruled that Terri Schiavo is not a "person in custody pursuant to the judgment of a State court," even though her husband's only power over her person or the interests of his wife comes from his appointment as her statutory guardian under Florida Statutes § 765.401; and

· He ruled that Mr. and Mrs. Schindler have no standing to raise the legality of their daughter's confinement - thus implicitly deciding one of the key factual issues to be decided in the case: i.e. whether Terri was "effectively represented" by her guardian and by his counsel.

· Lastly, he ruled that we have stated no significant federal claims - a claim belied by the claims Governor Bush argued in the Florida Supreme Court and in his Petition for Certiorari in Bush v. Schiavo. See Petition for Certiorari, Bush v. Schiavo, No. 04-757

4

Fig .7. Robert Destro's e-mail advising Philip Kiko, chief counsel for the House Judiciary Committee, how to draft the Congress's Schiavo bill. Other participants in this e-mail chain include Bill Wichterman, senior aide to Senate majority leader Bill Frist; Burke Balch, medical ethics director for the National Right to Life Committee; Brian Darling, former counsel for Senator Mel Martinez and the source of the anonymous memo on the political exploitation of Terri Schiavo; and Jeb Bush lawyer Ken Connor.

(October Term, 2004), cert denied 125 S.Ct. 1086 (2005) (copy attached).

Thus, my clients are left in a significant bind. Unless the House and Senate conferees can agree on language that makes it clear that Congress is simply trying to afford Terri her existing remedies under federal law, it is going to look like it is creating new ones just for her. That, in my view, would be a disaster of immense proportions, and would complicate the lives of her now-extremely-tired legal team enormously.

There may be several ways to solve the problem. The bills proposed by the Senate and the Chairman are trying to do the same thing: get Terri the federal hearing to which she is entitled. A recent Supreme Court case explicitly affirms the right of Congress to provide her with that remedy, and clearly outlines the differences between a habeas and 1983 remedy.

These cases, taken together, indicate that a state prisoner's § 1983 <http://www.westlaw.com/Find/Default.wl?rs=dfa1.0&vr=2.0&DB=1000546&DocName= 42USCAS1983&FindType=L> action is barred (absent prior invalidation)--no matter the relief sought (damages or equitable relief), no matter the target of the prisoner's suit (state conduct leading to conviction or internal prison proceedings)--if success in that action would necessarily demonstrate the invalidity of confinement or its duration.

Wilkinson v. Dodson, 2005 WL 516415 at *5 (emphasis in the original)

In our case, the Petitioners are explicitly seeking review of the procedures that led to the Ward's confinement by Respondent, Judge Greer, and the guardian he appointed, Respondent, Michael Schiavo, under the authority granted to him by the State of Florida. By citing the Rooker-Feldman doctrine - which is inapplicable to habeas corpus proceedings - the District Court inadvertently proves the very problem that Chairman Sensenbrenner's bill sought to avoid: i.e. that the federal courts are hostile to habeas cases generally, and that they would treat Terri like they do prisoners.

This is what happened here. A private bill might accomplish the goal of getting us into court and eliminating the hostility, but it will, in my professional judgment, create a constitutional crisis before a Supreme Court that is in no mood to brook dissent from its views that Congress may not overturn a settled judgment of any court, Plaut v. Spendthrift Farm, Inc., 514 U.S. 211 (1995); Landgraf v. USI Film Products, 511 U.S. 244 (1994) <http://www.westlaw.com/Find/Default.wl? rs=++++1.0&vr=2.0&DocName=511US244&F indType=Y&ReferencePositionType=S&ReferencePosition=269> .

I trust your judgment, and that of counsel for the Senate, to solve this tricky problem. On behalf of my clients, and of the whole legal team, we thank the conferees and the entire Congressional staff, for the help and concern you have shown under very trying circumstances.

From: Wichterman, Bill (Frist) [mailto:Bill_Wichterman@frist.senate.gov]
Sent: Sat 3/19/2005 8:50 AM
To: Destro, Robert A
Subject: Re: Judge Moody's latest

Bob, why do you believe the Martinez private relief bill passed by the Senate would not save Terri? Do you realize the bill has no habeas hook in it (unlike earlier versions of it, which did)?

Bill Wichterman
Policy Advisor

Senate Majority Leader Bill Frist
Washington, DC 20510
202-224-3741

-----Original Message-----
From: Destro, Robert A <DESTRO@law.edu>
To: Philip.Kiko@mail.house.gov <Philip.Kiko@mail.house.gov>; kconnor@wilkesmchugh.com
<kconnor@wilkesmchugh.com>; bbalch@nrlc.org <bbalch@nrlc.org>; Darling, Brian M. 64DARLING
<64DARLING@cua.edu>; Wichterman, Bill (Frist) <Bill_Wichterman@frist.senate.gov>
Sent: Fri Mar 18 22:07:54 2005
Subject: Judge Moody's latest

Judge Moody appears to have reconsidered his Rooker Feldman ruling. He now
says:
1) We have no standing
2) She's not "in custody"
3) No issues; and
4) No Certificate of appealability.

He's wrong, but we need to prove it to the 11th Cir. Tonight we do the application for the COA.
Tomorrow the appeal brief (assuming we get the COA). We need a statute!!!

This tells me that Moody a) does not want to cast aspersions on his fellow "jurist" (Greer); and b)
does not want to have to grapple with this case in the worst way. He's afraid of it-- so much so that
he's telling the 11th Circuit that they have to force him to hear it.

Bob

6

6A   THE PALM BEACH POST • SATURDAY, MARCH 26, 2005

Agents readied in case 'legal window' opened

By DARA KAM
Special to The Palm Beach Post

TALLAHASSEE — Gov. Jeb Bush on Wednesday asked Florida Department of Law Enforcement agents in Clearwater to stand ready to seize Terri Schiavo should a "legal window of opportunity come," an FDLE spokesman said Friday.

An attorney for Michael Schiavo said his legal team was informed that officials from FDLE and the Department of Children and Families were en route to take the brain-damaged woman from her Pinellas Park hospice to Morton Plant Hospital Wednesday, so they went to Pinellas Circuit Judge George Greer, who ordered the state officials to stay away.

"There was no plan," she said. "We were working through the legal process. We were hopeful that the new information would raise enough doubt to give her another opportu-

---

'We were hopeful that the new information would raise enough doubt to give her another opportunity.'

ALIA FARAJ, Bush spokeswoman

---

nity."

Jon Eisenberg, one of Michael Schiavo's attorneys, spoke Friday of a telephone conversation between a hospital attorney and George Felos, who also represents Michael Schiavo. The hospital attorney said the governor's office "had contacted the hospital and said DCF was preparing to seize Terri Schiavo at 4 p.m. (Wednesday) and take her to the hospital for placement of an IV and some tests," Eisenberg said.

A Morton Plant Hospital spokeswoman confirmed Friday that hospital attorneys also filed a motion Wednesday for "declaratory relief" in Pinellas Circuit Court after concluding that Schiavo might soon be a patient. At the time, Schiavo had been without her feeding tube for

five days.

"We were under the impression that the patient might be brought to our hospital and we were concerned that we might be in a situation of receiving a patient that had conflicting legal orders," hospital spokeswoman Beth Hardy said Friday. "We wanted direction from the court as to how we were supposed to proceed should we receive that patient."

Hardy said she did not know why the hospital was under the impression Schiavo was to be brought there. The motion filed Wednesday does not say why, either, other than to note a story posted on *The Palm Beach Post* Web site Wednesday that said state officials "say they are considering removing Terri Schiavo

from the hospice, by force if necessary."

The motion asks a judge for an order "declaring (the hospital's) rights and status because they are insecure and uncertain as to their rights and responsibilities pertaining to their actions as they relate to the care and treatment of Theresa Schiavo."

After receiving the call from the hospital, Felos sent another attorney, Debbie Bushnell, to the hospice, while he went to Greer's court. Bushnell told the Pinellas Park Police Department and the Pinellas County Sheriff's Office, the two agencies guarding the hospice, what Felos had been told but, they had heard nothing about it, Eisenberg said.

But someone from one of those departments contacted FDLE, then told Bushnell that FDLE would be accompanying DCF to seize Schiavo, Eisenberg said.

FDLE spokesman Tom Berlinger said Friday: "At the request of the governor's office, we had a spe-

cial agent supervisor and a couple of agents on standby for some time Thursday and for some time Wednesday, along with folks from DCF and a doctor.

"Had a legal window of opportunity come, where they would have been allowed to proceed to the hospice and rehydrate Ms. Schiavo, they were ready and prepared to do that. Unfortunately, that legal window never came."

Although the agents were staged at a nearby Clearwater office, Berlinger said they did not go to the hospice.

"There was apparently some discussion" about taking Schiavo to Morton Plant Hospital, Berlinger said. But by Thursday, "they felt she was too ill to be moved."

Faraj said Bush "did everything he could within the law, and we were faced with defeats in the judicial process even though we felt we had compelling new information about Terri's medical condition."

Staff writers Thomas R. Collins and S.V. Dáte contributed to this story.

Fɪɢ. 8. *Palm Beach Post* account of Governor Jeb Bush's attempts to abduct Terri Schiavo.

My cousin Ros at the base of Yosemite Falls.

My uncle Bernie's grave at the American military cemetery
in Draugignan, France.

Acknowledgements

My thanks go to my wife, Linda Hillel, for her invaluable support while I wrote this book; my parents, Harold and Myra Eisenberg, just for being my parents; my friend Don Putterman, for reviewing the manuscript; my literary agent, Carole Bidnick, for making this happen; my editor, Roger Freet at Harper San Francisco, for allowing me to write the book I wanted to write; executive managing editor Terri Leonard and Claudia Boutote, Helena Brantley, and Margery Buchanan in publicity and marketing at Harper San Francisco, for all their hard work; my colleagues at my law firm, Horvitz & Levy LLP, for their support throughout my involvement in the *Schiavo* case; Professor Laurence Tribe, for teaching me a few things about American constitutional law; my law firm colleague Peder Batalden, for research support during those frantic days in March 2005; bioethicists Tom Shannon, Jim Walter, and Kevin O'Rourke, for guiding me through the thicket of Catholic thought on end-of-life care; Florida bioethicists Bill Allen, Kathy Cerminara, and Jeffrey Spike, for steering me toward helpful resources during March 2005; Bonnie Eskenazi and Bert Fields, for legal assistance; investigators Eric Mason, Shanti Michaels, and Amanda Malkovich, for help on the money trail; Alexis Wright and Sophea Nop, for extensive research assistance; Berkeley bioethicist Sue Rubin, for her crucial role in putting together the group of bioethicists for whom I filed the amicus curiae briefs in the *Wendland* and *Schiavo* cases; San Francisco attorney Jim Braden, for pulling me into the *Wendland* case; and Debbie Bushnell and George Felos, counsel for Michael Schiavo, for the privilege of working with them.

I would also like to acknowledge John Kenneth Galbraith's 1975 book *Money: Whence it Came, Where it Went*, which has absolutely nothing to do with the *Schiavo* case but was my inspiration for the three-part structure of this book.

Chapter Sources

CHAPTER 1: MY COUSIN ROS

On hospital ethics committees, see B. Minogue, *Bioethics: A Committee Approach* (Jones & Bartlett, 1996); and M. Kuczewski and R. Pinkus, *An Ethics Casebook for Hospitals: Practical Approaches to Everyday Cases* (Georgetown University Press, 1999).

CHAPTER 2: A FAMILY TRAGEDY

Factual background on the life of Terri Schiavo and the *Schiavo* litigation prior to the October 2003 passage of "Terri's Law" in Florida may be found in court documents from the case and in numerous newspaper articles. These include: Judge Greer's 2000 order for discontinuance of Terri's ANH—*Guardianship of Theresa Marie Schiavo*, Circuit Court for Pinellas County, Florida, Probate Division, File No. 90-2908GD-003, order dated February 11, 2000; the four published appellate opinions in the *Schiavo* case that appeared between 2001 and 2003—*Guardianship of Schiavo* (Fla. Ct. App., Jan. 24, 2001) 780 So.2d 176, *Guardianship of Schiavo* (Fla. Ct. App., July 11, 2001) 792 So.2d 551, *Guardianship of Schiavo* (Fla. Ct. App., Oct. 17, 2001) 800 So.2d 640, and *Guardianship of Schiavo* (Fla. Ct. App., June 6, 2003) 851 So.2d 182; the 2003 guardian ad litem's report on Terri Schiavo pursuant to the requirements of "Terri's Law"—J. Wolfson, "A Report to Governor Jeb Bush and the 6th Judicial Circuit in the Matter of Theresa Marie Schiavo" (Dec. 1, 2003); and the following newspaper articles—R. Mishra, "Struggle for acceptance, then a tragic turn," *Boston Globe*, Apr. 1, 2005; J. Frey, "Terri Schiavo's unstudied life," *Washington Post*, March 25, 2005; A. Hull, "Who was Terri Schiavo?" *Grand Rapids Press*, Apr. 1, 2005; L. Copeland and J. Lawrence, "Feud may be as much over money as principle," *USA Today*, March 24, 2005; and W. Levesque, "Schiavo clash is rooted in cash," *St. Petersburg Times*, Nov. 23, 2003.

For a description of the persistent vegetative state, see Multi-Society Task Force on PVS, "Medical aspects of the persistent vegetative state," *New England Journal of Medicine*, vol. 330, no. 21 (May 26, 1994): 1499.

CHAPTER 3: THE RIGHT TO DIE

The judicial opinions discussed in this chapter are *Matter of Quinlan* (N.J. Superior Ct. 1975) 348 A.2d 801; *Matter of Quinlan* (N.J. 1976) 355 A.2d 647; *Cruzan v. Director, Missouri Department of Health* (1990) 497 U.S. 261; *Superintendent of Belchertown State School v. Saikewicz* (Mass. 1977) 370 N.E.2d 417; *Barber v. Superior Court* (1983) 147 Cal.App.3d 1006; *Bartling v. Superior Court* (1984) 163 Cal.App.3d 186; *Bouvia v. Superior Court* (1986) 179 Cal.App.3d 1127; *Conservatorship of Drabick* (1988) 200 Cal.App.3d 185; *Conservatorship of Morrison* (1988) 206 Cal.App.3d 304; *Thor v. Superior Court* (1993) 5 Cal.4th 725; *Guardianship of Browning* (Fla. 1990) 568 So.2d 4; *In re Martin* (Mich. 1995) 538 N.W.2d 399; *Conservatorship of Wendland* (2001) 26 Cal.4th 519.

On right-to-die law generally, see A. Meisel and K. Cerminara, *The Right to Die: The Law of End-of-Life Decisionmaking* (3d ed. 2004). On the *Wendland* case, see J. Eisenberg and J. Clark Kelso, "Legal implications of the *Wendland* case for end-of-life decision making," *Western Journal of Medicine*, vol. 176 (March 2002): 124; L. Nelson and R. Cranford, "Michael Martin and Robert Wendland: Beyond the vegetative state," *Journal of Contemporary Health Law and Policy*, vol. 15 (1999): 427; and M. Dolan, "Out of a coma, into a twilight," *Los Angeles Times*, Jan. 2, 2001.

The *Time* magazine article quoted in this chapter was in the edition of March 26, 2001, p. 62. The *People* magazine article was in the edition of June 4, 2001, p. 99.

The California legislation on end-of-life decision-making is in California Probate Code, sections 2350 et seq. and 4600 et seq.; the Florida legislation is in Florida Statutes, sections 765.101 et seq.; the Texas legislation is in Texas Statutes, sections 166.001 et seq.; the quoted portion of the Uniform Health-Care Decisions Act is in West's Uniform Laws Annotated (1999), Uniform Health Care Decisions Act, section 5, subdivision (f).

CHAPTER 4: THE BIOETHICISTS

Books, articles, and reports I consulted on bioethics generally, its four fundamental values, its three models for surrogate decision-making, the hierarchy of preferred surrogates, tube-feeding and its withdrawal, and hospital ethics committees include Hastings Center, *Guidelines on the Termination of Life-Sustaining Treatment and the Care of the Dying* (Indiana University Press, 1987); J. Lynn, ed., *By No Extraordinary Means: The Choice to Forgo Life-Sustaining Food and Water* (Indiana University Press, 1989); B. Minogue, *Bioethics: A Committee Approach* (Jones & Bartlett, 1996);

R. Dworkin, *Limits: The Role of the Law in Bioethical Decision Making* (Indiana University Press, 1996); H.-M. Sass, R. Veatch, and R. Kimura, *Advance Directives and Surrogate Decision Making in Health Care: United States, Germany, and Japan* (Johns Hopkins University Press, 1998); M. Kuczewski and R. Pinkus, *An Ethics Casebook for Hospitals: Practical Approaches to Everyday Cases* (Georgetown University Press, 1999); C. Baron, "Assuring 'detached but passionate investigation and decision': The role of guardians ad litem in *Saikewicz*-type cases," *American Journal of Law & Medicine*, vol. 4, no. 2 (1978): 111; President's Commission for the Study of Ethical Problems in Medicine and Biomedical and Behavioral Research, "Deciding to forgo life-sustaining treatment: A report on the ethical, medical, and legal issues in treatment decisions" (March 1983); M. Solomon et al., "Decisions near the end of life: Professional views on life-sustaining treatments," *American Journal of Public Health*, vol. 83, no. 1 (Jan. 1993): 14; Letters, "Tube feeding in patients with advanced dementia," *Journal of the American Medical Association*, vol. 285, no. 12 (March 22/29, 2000): 1563; and B. Rich, "The ethics of surrogate decision making," *Western Journal of Medicine*, vol. 176 (March 2002): 127.

On the minimally conscious state, see R. Cranford, "What is a minimally conscious state?" *Western Journal of Medicine*, vol. 176 (March 2002): 129; and L. Nelson and R. Cranford, "Michael Martin and Robert Wendland: Beyond the vegetative state," *Journal of Contemporary Health Law and Policy*, vol. 15 (1999): 427.

The study on end-of-life practice in the Detroit hospital appears in M. Campbell et al., "Experience with an end-of-life practice at a university hospital," *Critical Care Medicine*, vol. 25, no. 1 (1997): 197. The survey of physicians fearing lawsuits appears in S. McCrary et al., "Treatment decisions for terminally ill patients: Physicians' legal defensiveness and knowledge of medical law," *Law, Medicine & Health Care*, vol. 20 (Winter 1992): 364.

The hierarchy of preferred surrogate decision-makers is prescribed in Florida Statutes, section 765.401; the Texas statute is Texas Statutes, section 166.039. For an explanation of how Florida law allows a patient's surrogate to refer a health-care decision to the circuit court, see *Guardianship of Schiavo* (Fla. Ct. App., Jan. 24, 2001) 780 So.2d 176, 179, and *Guardianship of Browning* (Fla. 1990) 568 So.2d 4, 16.

On the infrequency of advance directives, see California Law Revision Commission, "Recommendation: Health care decisions for adults without decisionmaking capacity," *Cal. Law Revision Com. Rep.*, vol. 29 (1998): 16. California's statutory definition of "health care decision" appears in California Probate Code section 4617. The American Medical Association ethics opinion on physician acceptance of a surrogate's decision to forgo treatment is Opinion E-2.20 of the opinions of the American Medical Association's Council on Ethical and Judicial Affairs (1996).

On attitudes in other countries regarding advance directives and surrogate decision-making, see H.-M. Sass, R. Veatch, and R. Kimura, *Advance Directives and Surrogate Decision Making in Health Care: United States, Germany, and Japan* (Johns Hopkins University Press, 1998); and P. Ford, "World divided on ethics of Terri Schiavo case," *Christian Science Monitor*, March 25, 2005.

CHAPTER 5: THE WORD OF GOD

The two statements by Bishop Stephen E. Blaire on the *Wendland* case are Diocese of Stockton, "Statement from Stephen E. Blaire, Bishop of Stockton regarding case of Robert Wendland," December 1, 2000; and Diocese of Stockton, "Statement by the Most Reverend Stephen E. Blaire, Bishop of Stockton: The case of Robert Wendland," June 7, 2001. The quotation from Catherine Short, legal director of Life Legal Defense Fund, can be found on the Internet at http://www.angelfire.com/ca7/robertsangels/ShortStatement. html.

Articles I consulted on the Catholic tradition regarding life-sustaining treatment and ANH include T. Shannon and J. Walter, "Assisted nutrition & hydration and the Catholic tradition: The case of Terri Schiavo," *Theological Studies*, vol. 66 (Sept. 2005); R. Hamel and M. Panicola, "Must we preserve life?" *America*, Apr. 19–26, 2004, p. 6; G. Coleman, "Take and eat: Morality and medically assisted feeding," *America*, Apr. 5, 2004, p. 16; K. O'Rourke and P. Norris, "Care of PVS patients: Catholic opinion in the United States," *Linacre Quarterly*, vol. 68, no. 3 (Aug. 2001): 201; K. O'Rourke, "Development of church teaching on prolonging life," *Health Progress*, Jan.–Feb. 1988; J. Paris and R. McCormick, "The Catholic tradition on the use of nutrition and fluids," *America*, May 2, 1987, p. 356; and J. Paris, "The Catholic tradition on the use of nutritions," in K. Wildes, ed., *Birth, Suffering and Death* (Kluwar, 1992), p. 189.

The 1980 Declaration on Euthanasia by the Congregation for the Doctrine of the Faith can be found on the Internet at http://www.vatican.va/ roman_curia/congregations/cfaith/documents/rc_con_cfaith_doc_19800505_ euthanasia_en.html. Pope John Paul II's 1996 encyclical letter "Evangelium Vitae" can be found on the Internet at http://www.vatican.va/holy_father/ john_paul_ii/encyclicals/documents/hf_jp-ii_enc_25031995_evangelium-vitae_ en.html. The "Ethical and Religious Directives for Catholic Health Care Services," published by the United States Conference of Catholic Bishops, can be found on the Internet at http://www.usccb.org/bishops/directives.htm.

For discussions of deontology, see R. Popkin and A. Stroll, *Philosophy Made Simple* (Broadway Books, 2d ed. rev., 1993); and A. Lacy, *A Dictionary of Philosophy* (Routledge, 3d ed., 1996).

Pope John Paul II's allocution of March 20, 2004 can be found on the In-

ternet at http://www.vatican.va/holy_father/john_paul_ii/speeches/2004/
march/documents/hf_jp-ii_spe_20040320_congress-fiamc_en.html. For defi-
nitions of "allocution," "ex cathedra," "papal constitution," and "encyclical,"
see Rev. P. Stravinskas, ed., *Our Sunday Visitor's Catholic Encyclopedia* (Our
Sunday Visitor, rev. ed. 1991); and the *Catholic Encyclopedia* on the Internet
at http://www.newadvent.org.

The quotations and comments from Catholic theologians on the pope's al-
locution are from T. Shannon and J. Walter, "Artificial nutrition, hydration:
Assessing papal statement," *National Catholic Reporter*, Apr. 16, 2004; Shannon
and Walter, "Implications of the papal allocation on feeding tubes," *Hastings
Center Report*, July–Aug. 2004, p. 18; L. Greene, "At the pope's word, new
Schiavo cases?" *St. Petersburg Times*, May 2, 2004 (Paris and Strynkowski); J.
Thavis, "Experts say pope's speech on feeding tubes settles some issues,"
Catholic News Service, Apr. 7, 2004 (Faggioni and Sgreccia); C. Grossman,
"Pope's edict on life support stuns Catholic caregivers," *Chicago Sun-Times*,
Apr. 2, 2004 (Hamel); S. Vegh, "3 local hospitals weigh pope's words on feed-
ing tubes," *Virginian-Pilot*, May 4, 2004 (Reese); and e-mail from Father Kevin
O'Rourke to me dated July 13, 2004. For the Catholic Health Association's
news release on the pope's allocation, see Catholic Health Association of the
United States, "Statement on the papal allocation on persistent vegetative
state" (Apr. 1, 2004). For a newspaper account of the upcoming papal document on bioethical issues, see S. Dolbee, "Official says Vatican working on
new bioethics document," *San Diego Union Tribune*, Apr. 13, 2005.

The Schindlers' written arguments for reconsideration of Judge Greer's decision in light of the pope's allocation are in *Guardianship of Theresa Marie
Schiavo*, Circuit Court for Pinellas County, Florida Probate Division, File No.
90-2908GD-003, "Motion for Relief from Judgment and Motion to Reconsider," filed July 20, 2004, and "Respondents' Memorandum of Law in Support of Motion for Relief from Judgment and Motion to Reconsider," filed
Sept. 10, 2004. Judge's Greer's decision on the motion is in the court's file,
"Order" dated October 22, 2004.

For a discussion of the Jewish tradition on end-of-life care, see Rabbi E.
Dorff, "A Jewish approach to end-stage medical care," *Proceedings of the Committee on Jewish Law and Standards/1986–1990*, p. 65; see also M. Nevins,
"Perspectives of a Jewish physician," in J. Lynn, ed., *By No Extraordinary
Means: The Choice to Forgo Life-Sustaining Food and Water*, (Indiana University Press, 1989), p. 99. The comments on the *Schiavo* case by Rabbi Dorff
and Scott B. Rae are reported in T. Watanabe and L. Stammer, "Religious
ethicists are divided on Schiavo case," *Los Angeles Times*, March 24, 2005.
Rae discusses the removal of ANH from PVS patients in S. Rae, *Moral
Choices: An Introduction to Ethics*, (Zondervan, 2d ed., 2000), pp. 200–205;
the quotation is from page 205. The quotation from Rabbi Dorff on the

disabled and quality-of-life assessments is in "A Jewish approach to end-stage medical care," p. 104.

CHAPTER 6: THE SLIPPERY SLOPE

Information about Not Dead Yet and Diane Coleman can be found on Not Dead Yet's Internet web site at www.notdeadyet.org. The 1999 article in the online edition of *Ragged Edge Magazine* is M. Johnson, "Busy—But Not Dead Yet," *Electric Edge: Online Edition of Ragged Edge Magazine*, July/August 1999; it is on the Internet at http://www.ragged-edge-mag.com/0799/ c799ft2.htm. Coleman shared her thoughts with me in e-mail exchanges in late September through mid-October 2004. She also wrote publicly about the *Schiavo* case in D. Coleman, "Statement of Diane Coleman on Terri Schiavo," *MCIL [Memphis Center for Independent Living] Journal*, Nov. 14, 2003; D. Coleman, "Terri Schiavo case is really about disability rights," *MCIL Journal*, Aug. 30 2004; and D. Coleman, "Terri Schiavo case is really about disability rights," *Tallahassee Democrat*, Aug. 31, 2004.

The quotations from Autonomy Inc.'s mission statement are from the group's former Internet web site, which is no longer online. Andrew Batavia's 1997 article is A. Batavia, "Disability and physician-assisted suicide," *New England Journal of Medicine*, vol. 336, no. 23 (June 5, 1997): 1671. The 2002 Harris poll is H. Taylor, "2-to-1 majorities continue to support rights to both euthanasia and doctor-assisted suicide" (Harris Interactive, 2002). The quotation from the New Jersey quadriplegic is in C. Connolly, "Schiavo raised profile of disabled," *Washington Post*, Apr. 2, 2005.

The quote from Molly Ivins is in M. Ivins, "The disconnect in Bush's mind," *San Francisco Chronicle*, May 31, 2005.

CHAPTER 7: THE VOICE OF THE PEOPLE

The *Los Angeles Times* article about Tom DeLay's father is W. Roche and S. Verhovek, "DeLay's own tragic crossroads: Family of the lawmaker involved in the Schiavo case decided in '88 to let his comatose father die," March 27, 2005. Other accounts appear in W. Saletan, "Deathbed conversion: The lesson of Tom DeLay's moral hypocrisy," *Slate*, online at http:// slate.msn.com/id/2115879/; and S. Stolberg, "Years ago, DeLay's father was taken off life support," *New York Times*, March 27, 2005.

The CNN/USA Today/Gallup poll was reported in D. Sharp, "Schiavo lawyers challenge 'Terri's Law,'" *USA Today*, Oct. 29, 2003. The *St. Petersburg Times/Miami Herald* poll was reported in A. Smith, "Voters: Schiavo law was bad move," *St. Petersburg Times*, Dec. 7, 2003. The Fox News Channel poll was reported in D. Blanton, "Majority would remove Schiavo's feeding tube," on the Fox News Channel Internet web site, available online at http://www.foxnews.com/story/0,2933,101826,00.html. The CBS News poll was reported in "Political fallout over Schiavo" on the CBS News Internet web site, available online at http://www.cbsnews.com/stories/2005/03/23/politics/main682619.shtml. The ABC News poll was reported in G. Langer, "Poll: No role for government in Schiavo case," on the ABC News Internet web site, available online at http://abcnews.go.com/Politics/PollVault/story?id=599622&page=1. The Harris Poll taken after Terri Schiavo's death is Harris Interactive, "The Terri Schiavo case," Harris Poll #29, April 15, 2005, available online at http://harrisinteractive.com/harris_poll/index.asp?PID=558. The National Right to Life Committee press release containing the Wilson Research Strategies poll, entitled "National survey shows that more Americans support Terri Schindler-Schiavo's right to life" and dated Aug. 18, 2004, was on the Schindlers' Internet web site at http://www.terrisfight.org.press/081804.html, but is no longer.

The 1992 medical journal survey on public support of right-to-die legislation is in R. Blendon et al., "Should physicians aid their patients in dying?" *Journal of the American Medical Association*, vol. 267, no. 19 (May 20, 1992): 2658. The 2000 medical journal survey of nursing home residents is in M. Gillick, "Rethinking the role of tube feeding in patients with advanced dementia," *New England Journal of Medicine*, vol. 342, no. 3 (Jan. 20, 2000).

The *San Francisco Chronicle* articles are "Two cents: Ending life support," March 23, 2005, and "Two cents: The Schiavo case," March 21, 2005. The quote from Bill Moyers is in M. Matousek, "The last taboo," *Modern Maturity*, Sept.–Oct. 2000, p. 50.

CHAPTER 8: THE END OF LIFE

The quotation from Wesley Smith on the bioethicists is in W. Smith, *Culture of Death: The Assault on Medical Ethics in America* (Encounter Books, 2000), p. ix. Smith's biography is on his Internet web site at http://www.wesleyjsmith.com. His description of terminal dehydration is in W. Smith, *Forced Exit: The Slippery Slope from Assisted Suicide to Legalized Murder* (Times Books, 1997), p. 50, where Smith quotes Dr. William Burke; a footnote on page 262 attributes the quotation to "interview with author." Dr. David Stevens's description of terminal dehydration can be found in "Dehydration death called 'cruel, agonizing': Experts debunk 'myth' of no food, water being painless way to die," March. 24, 2005, on the Internet web site for *World Net Daily*, at http://worldnetdaily.com/news/article.asp?ARTICLE_ID=43467.

On kenotemia, see S. Winter, "Terminal nutrition: Framing the debate for the withdrawal of nutritional support in terminally ill patients," *American Journal of Medicine*, vol. 109 (Dec. 15, 2000): 723; I. Byock, "Patient refusal of nutrition and hydration: Walking the ever-finer line," *American Journal of Hospice & Palliative Care* (March/April 1995): 8; R. McCann et al., "Comfort care for terminally ill patients: The appropriate use of nutrition and hydration," *Journal of the American Medical Association*, vol. 272, no. 16 (Oct. 26, 1994): 1263; L. Printz, "Terminal dehydration, a compassionate treatment," *Archives of Internal Medicine*, vol. 152 (April 1992): 697; and D. Brock and J. Lynn, "The competent patient who decides not to take nutrition and hydration," in J. Lynn, ed., *By No Extraordinary Means: The Choice to Forgo Life-Sustaining Food and Water* (Indiana University Press, 1989), p. 202.

The National Hospice and Palliative Care Organization's definition of palliative care can be found on the organization's Internet web site at http://www.nhpco.org. On palliation for terminal dehydration, see I. Byock, "Patient refusal of nutrition and hydration: Walking the ever-finer line," *American Journal of Hospice & Palliative Care* (March/April 1995): 8; R. McCann et al., "Comfort care for terminally ill patients: The appropriate use of nutrition and hydration," *Journal of the American Medical Association*, vol. 272, no. 16 (Oct. 26, 1994): 1263; L. Printz, "Terminal dehydration, a compassionate treatment," *Archives of Internal Medicine*, vol. 152 (April 1992): 697; and P. Schmitz and M. O'Brien, "Observations on nutrition and hydration in dying cancer patients," in J. Lynn, ed., *By No Extraordinary Means: The Choice to Forgo Life-Sustaining Food and Water* (Indiana University Press, 1989), p. 30. On terminal sedation, see T. Quill and I. Byock, "Responding to intractable terminal suffering: The role of terminal sedation and voluntary refusal of foods and fluids," *Annals of Internal Medicine*, vol. 132, no. 5 (March 7, 2000): 408; and T. Quill et al., "Palliative treatments of last resort: Choosing the least harmful alternative," *Annals of Internal Medicine*, vol. 132, no. 6 (March 21, 2000): 488.

The 1994 study of terminal dehydration in conscious patients is in R. McCann et al., "Comfort care for terminally ill patients: The appropriate use of nutrition and hydration," *Journal of the American Medical Association*, vol. 272, no. 16 (Oct. 26, 1994): 1263. The 2003 study of nurses' perceptions of terminal dehydration is in L. Ganzini et al., "Nurses' experiences with hospice patients who refuse food and fluids to hasten death," *New England Journal of Medicine*, vol. 349, no. 4 (July 24, 2003): 359. Dr. Byock's article discussing the 1994 report is I. Byock, "Patient refusal of nutrition and hydration: Walking the ever-finer line," *American Journal of Hospice & Palliative Care* (March/April 1995): 8. Dr. Byock's endorsement of Wesley Smith's book on palliative care—E. Chevlen and W. Smith, *Power over Pain: How to Get the Pain Control You Need* (International Task Force 2002)—is on the back cover of the book and also can be found on Smith's Internet web site at http://www.wesleyjsmith.com. Smith's November 2003 article in the *Weekly Standard* is W. Smith, "A 'painless' death?" *Weekly Standard*, Nov. 12, 2003.

CHAPTER 9: THE THINK-TANK MACHINERY

For a description of the think tanks, their history, and their assets, see J. Russell, "Funding the culture wars" (National Committee for Responsive Philanthropy, January 2005); L. Lapham, "Tentacles of rage: The Republican propaganda mill, a brief history," *Harpers Magazine*, September 2004, p. 31; the Internet web site of People for the American Way at http://www.pfaw.org; the Internet web site of Media Transparency at http://www.mediatransparency.org; the Internet web site of the Philanthropy Roundtable at http://www.philanthropyroundtable.org; B. Bradley, "A party inverted," *New York Times*, March 30, 2005; M. O'Keefe, "Conservative group adds might to the right," *Newark (N.J.) Star-Ledger*, Sept. 21, 2003; and R. Reeves, "The politics (and money) of ideas," *Tulsa World*, July 10, 2002. For the Ahmanson quote, see T. Rubin, "Religion out abroad, in at home," *Philadelphia Inquirer*, March 23, 2005. The quote from National Committee for Responsive Philanthropy is J. Krehely et. al., "Axis of Ideology," p. 5 (National Committee for Responsive Philanthropy, March 2004).

The money flow from Christian Law Association to the Gibbs Law Firm and the other Gibbs-related firm is detailed in the CLA's 990 forms for 1997–2003. A transcript containing David Gibbs III's "for nothing" comment to Larry King is online at http://cnnstudentnews.cnn.com/TRANSCRIPTS/0409/27/lkl.00.html. Gibbs's comments to the Associated Press reporter are in M. Stacy, "Money evaporating in Terri Schiavo right-to-die battle," Associated Press, March 16, 2005.

Payments to Pat Anderson from Alliance Defense Fund and Life Legal Defense Foundation are reported on LLDF's Internet web site—http://www.lldf.org—including a press release dated October 22, 2003, and a solicitation letter from Bob Schindler; and in D. Kam, "State investigating Schiavo foundation," *Palm Beach Post*, Feb. 8, 2005 ("six figures"). Grants received by LLDF in 1996–2002 are reported on its 990 forms for 2002 and 2000. Alliance Defense Fund's grants to LLDF are reported on ADF's 990 form for 2002.

Robert Destro's biography, including his publication history, is on the web site for Catholic University of America, Columbus School of Law, at http://law.cua.edu. His "Marriage Law Project" and its funding are described in J. Feuerherd, "Joining forces to battle same-sex marriage," *National Catholic Reporter*, March 26, 2004. The grants to his publishers are reported on the Media Transparency web site. Alliance Defense Fund's grants to Destro's law school are reported on ADF's 990 form for 2002.

The American Center for Law and Justice and its chief counsel, Jay Sekulow, are described on the ACLJ's web site at http://www.aclj.org. Its 2003 budget is reported on the People for the American Way web site. Alliance Defense Fund's grants to ACLJ are reported on ADF's 990 form for 2002.

Alliance Defense Fund's contributions from the DeVos and Grewcock foundations are reported on the Media Transparency web site.

Grants to Judicial Watch (with whom Berliner and Wood were affiliated) are reported on the Media Transparency web site.

Wesley Smith's fellowship at Discovery Institute for Public Policy is described on Discovery's Internet web site—http://www.discovery.org—which also posts his numerous articles on bioethical issues. The description of him as an "informal advisor" to the Schindlers occasionally appears in *San Francisco Chronicle* articles on the *Schiavo* case by Smith's wife, Debra J. Saunders. Saunders's article about LLDF's Mary Riley is "A family of jailbirds," *Jewish World Review*, Feb. 8, 2001. Discovery's 1997–2003 grants are reported on its 990 forms for 2001–2003. Financial contributions to the Collier-Horowitz entities are reported on the Media Transparency web site. On Discovery's neocreationist "intelligent design" advocacy, see H.A. Orr, "Devolution," *New Yorker*, May 30, 2005, p. 40.

Contributions to Family Living Council and its payments to Rita Marker and her husband are detailed in FLC's 990 forms for 1998–2003. Randolph Foundation's contribution to International Task Force on Euthanasia and Assisted Suicide is reported on the Media Transparency web site.

Ken Connor's biography is online at http://www.wilkes-mchugh.com/bios/lv_connor.html. His 2001–2002 salary from Family Research Council is reported on FRC's 990 forms for those years. Grants to FRC are reported in J. Russell, "Funding the culture wars" (National Committee for Responsive Philanthropy, January 2005), and on the Media Transparency web site. The self-describing quote from FRC is on its web site at http://www.frc.org/get.cfm?c=abOUT_FRC. Tony Perkins's purchase of David Duke's mailing list is reported in M. Blumenthal, "Justice Sunday preachers," *Nation*, April 26, 2005, online at http://www.thenation.com/docprint.mhtml?i=20050509&s=blumenthal.

The think-tank contributions to the National Organization on Disability and the World Institute on Disability are reported on the Media Transparency web site.

For a description of Tom DeLay's Values Acton Team and how it was organized, see D. Batstone and M. Wexler, "The right stuff," *Soujourners Magazine*, July 2004. For Representative Pitts's description of how the VAT was started at the request of the Family Research Council, see FRC's web site at http://www.frc.org/get.cfm?i=QU03E01. The connection between Martinez/Darling/DeLay and the Alexander Strategy Group is discussed in K. Tumulty, "DeLay and company," *Time*, March 21, 2005. Funding by Americans for a Republican Majority for the Alexander Strategy Group is reported on the Internet at http://www.public-i.org/527/search.aspx?act=com&orgid=11. Funding by the Koch foundations for Americans for a Republican Majority is reported on the Internet at http://www.politicalfriendster.com/showPerson.php?id=1200&name=Americans-for-a-Republican-Majority. On Tom DeLay's ethics troubles because of the 2001 junket to Korea, see M. Allen and R.J. Smith, "S. Korean group sponsored delay trip," *Washington Post*, March 10, 2005.

The Schindler foundation's 2003 donations are reported in its registration papers, belatedly filed with the state of Florida in February 2005. The Schindlers' legal troubles in failing to register are reported in D. Kam, "State investigating Schiavo foundation," *Palm Beach Post*, Feb. 8, 2005; and D. Kam, "Schiavo parents fined, must register foundation," *Palm Beach Post*, Feb. 9, 2005. The Schindlers' attempt to sell their donor list is reported in D. Kirkpatrick and J. Schwartz, "List of Schiavo donors will be sold by direct-marketing firm," *New York Times*, March 29, 2005; and B. Berkowitz, "Deathbed dollars," at mediatransparency.org, April 18, 2005. National Right to Life Committee's connection with Bobby Schindler is reported in M. Allen, "Conservative groups' support steady," *Washington Post*, March 24, 2005.

The partial payment of Felos's and Bushnell's attorney fees is described in M. Stacey, "Money evaporating in Terri Schiavo right-to-die battle," Associated Press, March 16, 2005. The ACLU of Florida's 2004 assets are documented in its 2003 annual report.

CHAPTER 10: JEB STRIKES OUT

For descriptions of Randall Terry's and Phil Sheldon's 2003 involvement in the *Schiavo* case, see W. Levesque, "Schiavo's family ends legal fight," *St. Petersburg Times*, Oct. 15, 2003; W. Levesque, "Battle ends with quiet removal of feeding tube," *St. Petersburg Times*, Oct. 16, 2003; W. Levesque, "Effort to intervene for Schiavo falls short," *St. Petersburg Times*, Oct. 18, 2004; A. Goodnough, "Victory in Florida feeding case emboldens the religious Right," *New York Times*, Oct. 24, 2003; C. Gray, "Grassroots effort turned legal tide in Schiavo case," *Philadelphia Inquirer*, Nov. 7, 2003; D. Machacek, "Interminable," *Religion in the News*, vol. 7, no. 3 (Winter 2005, published by the Leonard E. Greenberg Center for the Study of Religion in Public Life, Trinity College, Hartford, CT); and B. Miner, "Randall Terry resurfaces," *In These Times*, Nov. 24, 2003. The quotations from the October 15 press release are in the Machacek article. Bob Schindler's "carte blanche" quotation and the reference to "Terry's Law" are in the Miner article. Terry's "feet to the fire" quotation is in the Gray article. The quotation from Pat Anderson is in the Levesque article of October 16. The quotation from Governor Bush's spokesman is in the Levesque article of October 18. For Randall Terry's own account, see http://societyfortruthandjustice.com/prod01.htm.

The Florida politics behind "Terri's Law" and the quotations from the Florida legislators are described in S. Bousquet, "How Terri's Law came to pass," *St. Petersburg Times*, Nov. 2, 2003; A. Ulferts et al., "House votes to save Schiavo," *St. Petersburg Times*, Oct. 21, 2003; "Fla. Gov. to restore feeding tube?" cbsnews.com, Oct. 21, 2003; "Another indignity" (editorial), *St. Petersburg Times*, Oct. 22, 2003; and A. Goodnough, "Victory in Florida feeding case emboldens the religious Right," *New York Times*, Oct. 24, 2003. The quotations from the members of Congress can be found on the Internet at http://www.miami.edu/ethics2/schiavo/timeline.htm, at the entry for October 21, 2003, "Statements by some House members." A transcript of President Bush's October 28, 2003, press conference can be found on the Internet at http://www.whitehouse.gov/news/releases/2003/10/20031028–2.html. The quotations from Wesley Smith and Bill Allen are in M. Roig-Franzia, "Woman's feeding tube is ordered reinstated: Gov. Bush gains power to override courts," *Washington Post*, Oct. 22, 2003. The quotations from Professors Little and Tribe are in M. Stacy, "Jeb Bush ripped for right-to-die intervention," *Chicago Sun-Times*, Oct. 23, 2003. The quotation from Senator Lee is from the Goodnough article. The quotation from Senator King is from the *St. Petersburg Times* editorial. The quotation from Representative Gelber is from the Ulferts article.

"Terri's Law" is Florida Senate Bill HB 35-E, Oct. 21, 2003, Florida Statutes, Chapter 2003-418. Governor Bush's order for reinsertion of Terri Schiavo's feeding tube pursuant to "Terri's Law" is Executive Order 03-201, Oct. 21, 2003. The circumstances of the feeding tube's reinsertion are described in D. Sommer et al., "Schiavo back on life support," *Tampa Tribune*, Oct. 23, 2003.

Justice Scalia's opinion on the constitutional separation of powers is *Plaut v. Spendthrift Farm, Inc.* (1995) 514 U.S. 211.

The "Terri's wish" quotation from Michael Schiavo can be found in V. Chachere, "Husband rips in-laws in right-to-die case," *Atlanta Journal-Constitution*, Oct. 28, 2003. Michael's lawsuit against Governor Bush began as *Schiavo v. Bush*, "Petition for Declaratory Judgment and Request for Temporary Injunction," Circuit Court for Pinellas County, Florida, Civil Division, Case Number 03-008212-CI-20, filed Oct. 21, 2003. The federal court lawsuit by the disability rights organization was *Advocacy Center for Persons with Disabilities v. Schiavo*, U.S. Dist. Court, Middle Dist. of Fla., Tampa Division, Case No. 8:03-cv-2167-T-23EAJ; the judge's order is dated Oct. 21, 2003.

Judge Greer's order prohibiting public dissemination of the videotapes is in *Guardianship of Theresa Marie Schiavo*, Circuit Court for Pinellas County, Florida, Probate Division, Case Number 90-2908-GD3, dated June 27, 2002. The *St. Petersburg Times* article describing the videotapes is S. Nohlgren, "Schiavo tapes: Snippets, then not much," *St. Petersburg Times*, Nov. 10, 2003. Judge Greer's 2002 written opinion in *Guardianship of Theresa Marie Schiavo*, entitled simply "Order," is dated Nov. 22, 2002. Wesley Smith's 2003 article is W. Smith, "Life, death, and science: Why the media elites won't tell the full story on Terri's prognosis and Michael Schiavo," *Daily Standard*, Oct. 31, 2003; his 2004 article is W. Smith, "The assault on Terri Schiavo continues: Michael Schiavo won his fight to have his wife killed by dehydration. Now he won't even allow her parents to sit by her side," *Weekly Standard*, Apr. 30, 2004.

For a description of the various legal maneuvers by Governor Bush's lawyers during the early stages of *Bush v. Schiavo*, see the timeline assembled by Kathy Cerminara of Nova Southeastern University, Shepard Broad Law Center, and Kenneth Goodman of the University of Miami Ethics Programs, "Key events in the case of Theresa Marie Schiavo," on the Internet at http://www.miami.edu/ethics2/schiavo/timeline.htm. The Court of Appeal opinion on the motion to disqualify Judge Baird is *Bush v. Schiavo* (Fla. Ct. App., Dec. 10, 2003) 861 So.2d 506; the opinion on the motion to take depositions is *Bush v. Schiavo* (Fla. Ct. App., Feb. 13, 2004) 866 So.2d 136; the opinion on the venue motion is *Bush v. Schiavo* (Fla. Ct. App., Apr. 23, 2004) 871 So.2d 1012. For a sampling of news articles describing the early legal maneuvers, see W. Levesque, "Judge calls Terri's Law intrusive," *St. Petersburg Times*, Nov. 15, 2003; K. Virella, "Court issues stay in Terri's Law case," *St. Petersburg Times*, Nov. 16, 2003; "Appeals court removes stay so Schiavo case can proceed," *St. Petersburg Times*, Nov. 19, 2003; W. Levesque, "Jury trial sought to decide what Schiavo wanted," *St. Petersburg Times*, Nov. 20, 2003; W. Levesque, "Judge ready to rule on validity of Terri's Law," *St. Petersburg Times*, Dec. 24, 2003; and "Guardian casts doubt on Fla. woman's recovery chances," *Andrews Nursing Home Litigation Reporter*, vol. 6, no. 13 (Dec. 30, 2003): 10.

Professor Wolfson's guardian ad litem report is J. Wolfson, "A Report to Governor Jeb Bush and the 6th Judicial Circuit in the Matter of Theresa Marie Schiavo" (Dec. 1, 2003).

The *St. Petersburg Times* article about the legislators' regret over voting for "Terri's Law" is A. Smith, "Regret plagues King after Schiavo vote," *St. Petersburg Times*, Feb. 10, 2004. The failed 2004 Florida Senate bill was S.B. 692.

Judge Baird's opinion on the unconstitutionality of "Terri's Law" is in *Schiavo v. Bush*, Circuit Court for Pinellas County, Florida, Civil Division, Case Number 03-008212-CI-20, "Order Granting Petitioner's Motion for Summary Judgment," dated May 5, 2004. My amicus curiae brief, "Amicus Curiae Brief in Support of Michael Schiavo as Guardian of the Person of Theresa Marie Schiavo" on behalf of "55 Bioethicists and Autonomy Inc.," was filed in the Florida Supreme Court, Number SC04-925, on July 28, 2004. Newspaper accounts of the oral argument before the Florida Supreme Court can be found in A. Goodnough, "Comatose woman's case heard by Florida court," *New York Times*, Sept. 1, 2004; and J. Hallifax, "Florida's high court hears Schiavo right-to-die case," Associated Press, Aug. 31, 2004. The Florida Supreme Court's opinion is *Bush v. Schiavo* (Fla. 2004) 885 So.2d 321.

On Pat Anderson's withdrawal from the case, see W. Levesque, "Lead lawyer for Schiavo's parents quits," *St. Petersburg Times*, Sept. 30, 2004. Ken Connor's comment that "this matter is now at an end for the governor" is quoted in M. Newmann, "Court rejects challenge in feeding tube standoff,"

New York Times, Jan. 25, 2004. The op-ed article Connor drafted for Senator Webster is D. Webster, "'Death sentence' is unjust," *USA Today*, Jan. 26, 2005.

CHAPTER 11: JUDGE GREER TOUGHS IT OUT

For newspaper profiles of Judge Greer and the quotations from him and his campaign worker, see W. Levesque, "Quiet judge persists in Schiavo maelstrom," *St. Petersburg Times*, March 6, 2005; A. Goodnough, "In Schiavo feeding-tube case, notoriety finds unlikely judge," *New York Times*, March 17, 2005; and A. Samuels, "Schiavo judge, church part ways," *St. Petersburg Times*, March 31, 2005. For accounts of Judge Greer's 2004 reelection campaign, see W. Levesque, "Lawyer is judge's first challenger," *St. Petersburg Times*, May 8, 2004; and W. Levesque, "Pinellas-Pasco Circuit Court: Schiavo rulings do no harm to Greer," *St. Petersburg Times*, Sept. 1, 2004. Wesley Smith's attack on Judge Greer is in W. Smith, "The assault on Terri Schiavo continues: Michael Schiavo won his fight to have his wife killed by dehydration. Now he won't even allow her parents to sit by her side," *Weekly Standard*, Apr. 30, 2004. Randall Terry's February 16, 2005, press release can be found on the Internet at http://www.earnedmedia.org/tf0215.htm.

Judge Greer's written order of February 25 is in *Guardianship of Theresa Marie Schiavo*, Circuit Court for Pinellas County, Florida, Probate Division, Case Number 9-2908-GD-003, "Order" dated February 25, 2005.

The court filings by Gibbs on February 25, 2005, before Judge Greer in *Guardianship of Theresa Marie Schiavo* are "Respondents' Fla.R.Civ.P. 1.540(b)(5) Motion for Relief from Judgment Pending Contemporary Medical/Psychiatric/Rehabilitative Evaluation of Theresa Marie Schiavo," and "Petition for Extraordinary Authority for the Ward to Undergo Experimental Treatment."

The court filings by Gibbs on February 28, 2005, before Judge Greer in *Guardianship of Theresa Marie Schiavo* are "Emergency Expedited Motion to Permit Theresa Schiavo to Receive the Rite of Extreme Unction in Compliance with Her Religious Faith"; "Emergency Expedited Petition for Extraordinary Authority for the Ward to Divorce Her Husband"; "Emergency Expedited Motion to Compel the Deposition of Michael Schiavo and [Name Omitted for Privacy Purposes]"; "Emergency Expedited Motion for Permission to Provide Theresa Schiavo with Food and Water by Natural Means"; "Emergency Expedited Motion to Permit Mrs. Schiavo to Be Buried in Florida Without Cremation"; "Emergency Expedited Motion for Limited Media Access to Mrs. Schiavo and Visits with Her Family"; "Emergency Expedited Motion to Allow Theresa Schiavo to Die at Home"; "Emergency Expedited Motion to Not Remove Feeding Tube When Nutrition and Hydration of Theresa Schiavo Are Terminated"; "Emergency Expedited Motion for Family

Access to Theresa Schiavo While She Is Dying"; "Emergency Expedited Motion for Permission to Photograph and Videotape Mrs. Schiavo with Her Family"; "Emergency Expedited Motion to Request Appointment of Medical Witness"; and "Request for Oral Argument." A list of all fifteen pending motions and petitions and the request for forty-eight hours of court hearing time are in a letter from David C. Gibbs III to Judge Greer, filed in the guardianship case on February 28, 2005. A newspaper account of the motions and petitions can be found in W. Levesque, "Last rites, cremation part of Schiavo battle," *St. Petersburg Times*, March 1, 2005. The provision in the Catechism of the Catholic Church on cremation is 2301; see also Canon 1176 of the 1983 Code of Canon Law.

Judge Greer's order addressing the new treatment and swallowing issues is in *Guardianship of Theresa Marie Schiavo*, dated March 9, 2005.

The DCF's February 23, 2005, motion to intervene in *Guardianship of Theresa Marie Schiavo* is entitled "Notice to Court Pursuant to Section 415.1055(9), F.S. and Petition/Motion for Intervention, Stay of Order of the Probate Court, Appointment of Legal Counsel for Theresa Marie Schiavo and Sealing of the Proceedings." Judge Greer's order denying the motion is dated March 10, 2005. The Court of Appeal's order on the DCF's appeal is in *Department of Children & Family Services v. Schiavo*, District Court of Appeal of the State of Florida, Second District, Case Number 2D05-1300, dated March 16, 2005; the Florida Supreme Court's order is in *Florida Department of Children and Families v. Schiavo*, Supreme Court of Florida, Case Number SC05-443, dated March 17, 2005. For a newspaper account of the DCF motion, see W. Levesque, "Source of claims in Schiavo case was abuse hotline," *St. Petersburg Times*, March 4, 2005.

Excerpts from the publicly disclosed DCF reports can be found on the Internet at http://www.miami.edu/ethics2/schiavo/timeline.htm, at the entry for April 15, 2005. For newspaper accounts of the disclosure and documents, see "Report on Schiavo finds no abuse," *New York Times*, Apr. 16, 2005; "Schiavo was not abused, DCF finds," *Brandenton Herald*, Apr. 16, 2005; "Florida found no abuse of Schiavo," *New Jersey Record*, Apr. 17, 2005; "Abuse claims unsubstantiated," *St. Petersburg Times*, Apr. 20, 2005; "Schiavo myth collapses," *Palm Beach Post*, Apr. 24, 2005; and C. Tisch and C. Krueger, "Schiavo abuse claims were old," *St. Petersburg Times*, June 4, 2005.

The Court of Appeal's last opinion in the *Schiavo* case is *Guardianship of Schiavo* (March 16, 2005) 2005 Westlaw 600377. The U.S. Supreme Court order denying an immediate stay, issued by Justice Anthony Kennedy, is in *Schindler v. Schiavo*, Number 04A801, dated March 17, 2005.

The Schindlers' federal district court pleading in *Schiavo v. Greer* is "Emergency Petition for Temporary Injunction and Petition for a Writ of Habeas Corpus," United States District Court, Middle District of Florida, Tampa Division,

Case Number 8:05-cv-522-T-30TGW, filed March 18, 2005. The district court judge's quotation is from the order in that case filed later that day.

CHAPTER 12: THE FLORIDA LEGISLATURE BOWS OUT

The National Right to Life Committee's Model Starvation and Dehydration of Persons with Disabilities Prevention Act is on the Internet at http://www.nrlc.org/euthanasia/modelstatelaw.html. The NRLC's mission statement is at http://www.nrlc.org/Missionstatement.htm.

Senate Bill 692 and its legislative history can be found on the Internet at http://www.flsenate.gov/session/index.cfm?BI_Mode=ViewBillInfo&Mode=B ills&SubMenu=1&Year=2004&billnum=692. House Bill 701 and its legislative history, including the various versions of the bill, can be found at http://www.myfloridahouse.gov/bills_detail.aspx?Id=16262. Senate Bill 804 and its legislative history can be found at http://www.flsenate.gov/session/ index.cfm?Mode=Bills&Submenu=1&BI_Mode=ViewBillInfo&Billnum= 0804&Year=2005. The Florida bioethicists' analysis of HB 701 is "Florida Bioethics Leaders' Analysis on HB 701," March 7, 2005.

The quotations from various Florida lawmakers and citizens, and accounts of HB 701 and SB 804 generally, are in the following newspaper articles: S. Bousquet, "Lawmakers push another bill to keep Schiavo alive," *St. Petersburg Times*, March 9, 2005 (Baxley, Bense, and Lee); J. Follick, "Bill could save woman in case over right to die," *Gainsville Sun*, March 10, 2005 (Baxley and Stargel); S. Bousquet, "Bill sets rules for all like Schiavo," *St. Petersburg Times*, March 10, 2005 (Baxley); S. Bousquet, "Schiavo bill a race against time," *St. Petersburg Times*, March 15, 2005; S. Bousquet and C. Johnson, "End-of-life bills reveal divide over how far law should go," *St. Petersburg Times*, March 16, 2005 (King and Lee); S. Gross, "Florida effort to keep Terri Schiavo alive hits roadblock," Associated Press, March 17, 2005 (King and Bush); C. Johnson, "Schiavo bill loses GOP backers," *St. Petersburg Times*, March 18, 2005 (Jones, Dean, Russell, and Justice); A. Kumar et al., "Terri Schiavo: Decision day," *St. Petersburg Times*, March 18, 2005 (Bush); editorial, "Terri's Life series," *St. Petersburg Times*, March 18, 2005; A. Ulferts and C. Johnson, "Pressure builds, time grows short," *St. Petersburg Times*, March 23, 2005 (King and Argenziano).

CHAPTER 13: THE TUBE COMES OUT

Judge Greer's last-minute refusal to postpone the removal of Terri Schiavo's PEG tube and George Felos's announcement are described in A. Goodnough and M. Newman, "Schiavo's feeding tube removed at judge's order," *New York Times*, March 18, 2005. The scene outside Hospice House Woodside is described in "Schiavo feeding tube removed," cbsnews.com, March 18, 2005, on the Internet at http://www.cbsnews.com/stories/2005/03/18/national/main

681495.shtml; "Bush signs Schiavo legislation," Associated Press, March 21, 2005; and J. Hannigan, "Pictures from Woodside Hospice," March 24, 2005, on the Internet at http://www.floridabaptistwitness.com/4081.article.

President George W. Bush's press release is "President's Statement on Terri Schiavo," Office of the Press Secretary, March 17, 2005, on the Internet at http://www.whitehouse.gov/news/releases/2005/03/20050317-7.html. Governor Jeb Bush's lamentation is reported in "Roadblocks frustrate Jeb Bush," Associated Press, March 25, 2005. Arthur Caplan's statement on MSNBC is A. Caplan, "The time has come to let Terri Schiavo Die," MSNBC News, March 18, 2005, on the Internet at http://www.msnbc.msn.com/id /7231440/. The blogger's comment, "Terri died a long time ago," can be found on the Internet at http://www.blogsforterri.com/archives/2005/03/tube_is_out _mic.php.

The statement by Richard Land is reported in M. Foust and T. Strode, "Terri Schiavo feeding tube removed; Congress still working," *BP News*, March 18, 2005, on the Internet at http://www.bpnews.net/bpnews.asp? ID=20384. The statements by Troy Newman and the editors of the *New Pantagruel* can be found on the Internet at http://www.freerepublic.com/focus/f-bloggers/1365998/posts. The statement by Wesley Smith can be found on the Internet at http://www.tothesource.org/3_23_2005/3_23_2005_printer.htm. The Internet bloggers' postings calling for the killing of Michael Schiavo are at http://www.blogsforterri.com/archives/2005/03/tube_is_out_mic.php. The blogger's warning of a second Civil War is at http://www.freerepublic.com/ focus/f-bloggers/1365998/posts. Bo Gritz's "Citizen's Arrest Warrant" and press release are on the Internet at http://almightywind.com/terri/050316 totherescue.htm.

Peggy Noonan's warning to congressional Republicans is in P. Noonan, "'Don't kick it': If Terri Schiavo is killed, Republicans will pay a political price," *Wall Street Journal*, March 18, 2005, on the Internet at http://www. opinionjournal.com/columnists/pnoonan/?id=110006442. Robert Destro's plea is in his letter to the Honorable James Sensenbrenner, Chairman, Committee on the Judiciary, United States House of Representatives, dated March 20, 2005. Kenneth Connor's call for House agents to reinsert Terri Schiavo's feeding tube is reported in M. Foust, "Connor: House should send in agents to save Terri Schiavo, protect subpoenaing power," *BP News*, March 23, 2005, on the Internet at http://www.bpnews.net/bpnews.asp?ID=20418.

The statement by Frist and Hastert is reported in M. Foust and T. Strode, "Terri Schiavo feeding tube removed: Congress still working," *BP News*, March 18, 2005, on the Internet at http://www.bpnews.net/bpnews.asp? ID=20384; and M. Roig-Franzia and W. Branigin, "Doctors remove Schiavo's feeding tube," *Washington Post*, March 18, 2005. DeLay's speech to the Family Research Council is reported in K. Tumulty, "Tom DeLay: 'It is more than just

Terri Schiavo,'" *Time*, March 23, 2005. Randall Terry's warning to the Republicans is described in A. Goodnough and M. Newman, "Schiavo's feeding tube removed at judge's order," *New York Times*, March 18, 2005.

The *News Hour with Jim Lehrer* debate between Bill Allen and Dave Weldon is on the Internet at http://www.pbs.org/newshour/bb/congress/jan-june05/schiavo_3–18.html. Cardinal Martin's comment is reported in W. Moore, "Vatican official enters Schiavo feeding tube fray," *St. Petersburg Times*, Feb. 26, 2005. Bishop Wenski's statement can be found on the Internet at http://www.orlandodiocese.org/our_diocese/wenski/columns/terri_schiavo_18mar05.htm. Barbara Weller's account of her March 18 visit to Terri Schiavo's bedside is in B. Weller, "My last visit with Terri Schiavo," *Christianity Today*, March 21, 2005, on the Internet at http://www.christianitytoday.com/ct/2005/112/32.0.html.

CHAPTER 14: THE DEMOCRATS BAIL OUT

The e-mail exchanges among staff for Governor Bush and members of Congress are reported in D. Kam, "Governor, lawmakers in daily contact on Schiavo, e-mails show," *Palm Beach Post*, May 24, 2005. The Martinez memo is reported in C. Shaw, "Blogs debate politics of Schiavo case," *St. Paul Legal Ledger*, March 31, 2005; M. Allen, "Counsel to GOP senator wrote memo on Schiavo," *Washington Post*, April 7, 2005; and R. Schultz, "Memo to Martinez: Cover blown," *Palm Beach Post*, April 10, 2005. Debra J. Saunders's comment on the memo is in her *San Francisco Chronicle* column for April 7, 2005. The connection between Martinez/Darling/DeLay and the Alexander Strategy Group is discussed in K. Tumulty, "DeLay and company," *Time*, March 21, 2005. Funding by Americans for a Republican Majority to the Alexander Strategy Group is reported on the Internet at http://www.public-i.org/527/search.aspx?act=com&orgid=11. Funding by the Koch Foundation to Americans for a Republican Majority is reported on the Internet at http://www.politicalfriendster.com/showPerson.php?id=1200&name=Americans-for-a-Republican-Majority.

The press release by DeLay and Hastert announcing the House subpoenas is "Joint Statement of Speaker of the House J. Dennis Hastert, House Majority Leader Tom DeLay and Government Reform Committee Chairman Tom Davis," March 18, 2005. The subpoenas themselves, and their cover letters, can be found on the Internet at http://www.miami.edu/ethics2/schiavo/031805-USHousePetition%20SCt.pdf. The citation to the *Barenblatt* case is *Barenblatt v. United States* (1959) 360 U.S. 109. The House committee's attempt to intervene in the *Schiavo* guardianship proceeding is *Guardianship of Theresa Marie Schiavo*, Circuit Court for Pinellas County, Florida, File No. 90-2908-GD-003, "Motion to Intervene of the Committee on Government Reform of the U.S. House of Representatives" and "Motion of the Committee on Government Reform of the U.S. House of Representatives to Modify February 25, 2005 Order," filed March 18, 2005.

The House and Senate bills, and their legislative histories, can be accessed on the Internet through http://thomas.loc.gov. The floor debates and votes are recorded in the *Congressional Record* for their respective dates. The six representatives' opposition to unanimous consent in the House is described on the Internet blog of Representative John Conyers at http://www.conyers-blog.us/archives/archive–032005.htm. The Frist-Hastert press release announcing the compromise bill and thanking Senator Reid is on the Internet at http://speaker.house.gov/library/misc/050319schiavo.shtml.

Newspaper reports about the events in Congress and the various quotations from the law professors, President Bush, Governor Bush, Michael Schiavo, and the *New York Times* editorial are in A. Kumar, "Schiavo's case lands in Congress," *St. Petersburg Times*, March 11, 2005; G. Earle, "GOP bill to save life of Schiavo," *Hill*, March 16, 2005; A. Liptak, "With Schiavo subpoenas, lawmakers leap into contested territory," *New York Times*, March 19, 2005 (Fried and Tribe); editorial, "The Schiavo case," *New York Times*, March 19, 2005 ("ghoulish gimmick"); R. Toner and C. Hulse, "Congress ready to approve bill in Schiavo case," *New York Times*, March 20, 2005; M. Allen and M. Roig-Franzia, "Congress steps in on Schiavo case," *Washington Post*, March 20, 2005; C. Hulse and D. Kirkpatrick, "Congress passes and Bush signs legislation on Schiavo case," *New York Times*, March 21, 2005 (President Bush statement); C. Hulse and M. Newman, "Judge hears Schiavo arguments, but does not rule yet," *New York Times*, March 21, 2005 (President Bush's "err on the side of life" comment); "Terri Schiavo bill becomes law," CBS News online, March 21, 2005 (Michael Schiavo quote), on the Internet at http://www.cbsnews.com/stories/2005/03/21/national/main681849 .shtml; "House passes Schiavo Bill," CNN.com, March 21, 2005, online at http://www.cnn .com/2005/LAW/03/20/schiavo/ (Governor Bush quote); M. Roig-Franzia, "Schiavo case goes to federal judge," *Washington Post*, March 22, 2005; D. Milbank, "Legal experts say parents are unlikely to prevail," *Washington Post*, March 22, 2005 (Bruce Fein comment).

Howard Dean's comment on upcoming elections is reported in "Dean: Schiavo case to be used against GOP elections," *USA Today*, April 16, 2005. Wesley Smith's blog comment is at http://www.wesleyjsmith.com/blog/2005/ 04/dean-says-schiavo-case-partisan-issue.html.

CHAPTER 15: THE JUDGES SPEAK OUT

The federal lawsuit filed by the Schindlers is *Schiavo ex rel. Schindler v. Schiavo*, United States District Court, Middle District of Florida, Tampa Division, No. 8:05-CV-530-T-27TBM, "Plaintiff's Complaint for Temporary Restraining Order, Declaratory Judgment, and Preliminary and Permanent

Injunctive Relief," filed March 21, 2005. The Schindlers' injunction request in the district court is "Plaintiff's Motion for Temporary Restraining Order" and "Memorandum in Support of Motion for Temporary Restraining Order," filed March 21, 2005. Michael Schiavo's written opposition in the district court is "Opposition to Motion for Injunction," filed March 21, 2005. Judge Whittemore's March 22 opinion denying the injunction is *Schiavo ex rel. Schindler v. Schiavo* (March 22, 2005) 357 F.Supp. 1378.

The Schindlers' two Eleventh Circuit filings on March 22, 2005 are "Brief for Plaintiff-Appellant" and "Appellant's All Writs Petition for Emergency Injunctive Relief to Preserve Meaningful Appeal," filed in *Schiavo ex rel. Schindler v. Schiavo*, Eleventh Circuit Court of Appeals, No. 05-11556 and No. 05-11556-D. Michael Schiavo's opposing briefs are "Brief for Respondents-Appellees" and "Opposition to Appellants' All Writs Petition" filed on March 22, 2005. The three-judge panel's decision affirming Judge Whittemore is *Schiavo ex rel. Schindler v. Schiavo* (March 23, 2005) 403 F.3d 1223.

The Schindlers' petition for a rehearing en banc by the Eleventh Circuit is "Petition for *Expedited* Rehearing En Banc," Eleventh Circuit Court of Appeals, No. 05-11517-A, filed March 23, 2005. Michael Schiavo's opposing brief is "Brief for Respondent-Appellee in Opposition to Petition for Rehearing En Banc," filed March 23, 2005. The en banc decision denying a rehearing is *Schiavo ex rel. Schindler v. Schiavo* (March 23, 2005) 403 F.3d 1261.

The Schindlers' application to the U.S. Supreme Court is *Schiavo ex rel. Schindler v. Schiavo*, United States Supreme Court, No. 04A-825, "Emergency Application for Stay of Enforcement of the Judgment Below Pending the Filing and Disposition of a Petition for a Writ of Certiorari to the Circuit Court of Appeal of the United States for the Eleventh Circuit," filed March 23, 2005. Michael Schiavo's opposition brief in the Supreme Court is "Respondent Michael Schiavo's Opposition to Application for Injunction," filed March 24, 2005. The Supreme Court's March 24 order denying the Schindlers' application is reported at 125 S.Ct. 1692.

The Schindlers' first amended pleading filed in the district court is "Plaintiff's First Amended Complaint for Temporary Restraining Order, Declaratory Judgment, and Preliminary and Permanent Injunctive Relief," filed March 22, 2005. Their second amended pleading is "Plaintiff's Second Amended Verified Complaint for Temporary Restraining Order, Declaratory Judgment, and Preliminary and Permanent Injunctive Relief," filed March 24, 2005. For an account of the Thursday night hearing before Judge Whittemore, see W. Levesque et al., "Schiavo's parents left with few options," *St. Petersburg Times*, March 25, 2005. Judge Whittemore's March 25 opinion is *Schiavo ex rel. Schindler v. Schiavo* (March 25, 2005) 358 F.Supp.2d 1161.

The Schindlers' Eleventh Circuit Filing on March 25 is "Brief for Plaintiff-

Appellant," filed March 25, 2005. The Eleventh Circuit's same-day opinion ruling against the Schindlers is *Schiavo ex rel. Schindler v. Schiavo* (March 25, 2005) 403 F.3d 1289.

CHAPTER 16: JEB CHICKENS OUT

DCF's March 23 intervention motion is "Notice to Court Pursuant to Section 415.1055(9), F.S. and Petition/Motion for Intervention," *In re Guardianship of Theresa Marie Schiavo*, Pinellas County Circuit Court, Probate Division, No. 90-2908GD-003, filed March 23, 2005. Dr. Cheshire's affidavit is attached to the intervention motion.

For a description of Dr. Cheshire and his position at the Center for Bioethics and Human Dignity, see http://www.cbhd.org/aboutcbhd/staff/ cheshire.htm. For a description of Kilner's attack on Michael Schiavo, see http://www.cbhd.org/resources/endoflife/schiavo_focus_2005–03–08.htm. For the pronouncements on ANH by the Christian Medical Association's Ethics Commission, see http://www.cmdahome.org/index.cgi?BISKIT=294053362 &CONTEXT=art&art=367. For descriptions of the positions of Dr. Cheshire and Wesley Smith at the Center for Bioethics and Culture, see http:// www.thecbc.org/redesigned/cbc_bod_cheshire.php and http://www.thecbc.org/ redesigned/cbc_sc.php.

The March 23 and 24 attempts to seize Terri Schiavo and the Hadi news conference are described in C. Miller, "Terri Schiavo case: Police 'showdown' averted," *Miami Herald*, March 26, 2005; D. Kam, "Agents readied in case 'legal window' opened," *Palm Beach Post*, March 26, 2005; and D. Kam, "Judge bars agency from taking custody," *Palm Beach Post*, March 23, 2005. The October 2003 legal arguments solicited by Randall Terry can be found on the Internet at http://societyfortruthandjustice.com/serv03.htm. Judge Greer's March 23 antiseizure order is "Amended Emergency Order Enforcing Mandate," *In re Guardianship of Theresa Marie Schiavo*, Pinellas County Circuit Court, No. 90-2908-GD-3, March 23, 2005.

The quotations from March 24 are in M. Schneider, "Terri Schiavo's parents: No federal appeals court review," *Palm Beach Post*, March 25, 2005 (Bob Schindler); S. Ertelt, "Governor Jeb Bush pressured to take Terri Schiavo into custody," LifeNews.com, March 25, 2005 (Keyes); S. Bousquet, "Bush's powers fall short of beliefs," *St. Petersburg Times*, March 25, 2005 (capitol protestor's sign and Governor Bush); and G. White, "Pressure put on Bush to defy court," *Atlanta Journal-Constitution*, March 24, 2005 (Lt. Riley).

Judge Greer's March 24 orders denying DCF's intervention motion and refusing to change the original judgment are both entitled "Order," *In re Guardianship of Theresa Marie Schiavo*, Pinellas County Circuit Court, No. 90-2908-GD-3, March 24, 2005. The judge's order of the same day vacating the March 23 antiseizure order is "Order Vacating Rule 9.310 Stay." The quotation from the local police is reported in C. Miller, "Terri Schiavo case: Police 'showdown' averted," *Miami Herald*, March 26, 2005.

The Schindlers' March 25 motion, with attached affidavits, is "Emergency Motion for Injunction and Immediate Relief," *In re Guardianship of Theresa Marie Schiavo*, Pinellas County Circuit Court, No. 90-2908-GD-3, filed March 25, 2005. The FBI arrest for the death threats is reported in "Man arrested in alleged Schiavo case murder plot," CNN.com, March 25, 2005.

Judge Greer's ruling on the Schindlers' March 25 motion is "Order," *In re Guardianship of Theresa Marie Schiavo*, Pinellas County Circuit Court, No. 90-2908-GD-3, filed March 26, 2005. Governor Bush's "sad" comment is quoted in "Backers of Schiavo's parents head to Washington," CNN.com, March 27, 2005. Randall Terry's quotes are in L. Copeland, "Anger at Bushes as time grows short for Schiavo," *USA Today*, March 27, 2005; and D. Kam, "Case proves a quagmire for governor," *Palm Beach Post*, March 26, 2005.

CHAPTER 17: TIME RUNS OUT

The March 27 quote from Monsignor Malanowski is in J. Riley and A. Metz, "Ready to let her go," *Newsday*, March 28, 2005. The March 28 quotes from George Felos, Terri's sister, and Bob Schindler are in S. Nohlghen et al., "Father: 'Still fighting to hold on to life,'" *St. Petersburg Times*, March 29, 2005. The quotes from Wesley Smith are in E. Chevlen and W. Smith, *Power over Pain: How to Get the Pain Control You Need* (International Task Force, 2002), pp. 43 and 121.

The Schindlers' March 29 petition in the Eleventh Circuit is "Emergency Petition for Rehearing and Rehearing En Banc and for Emergency Injunctive Relief," *Schiavo ex rel. Schindler v. Schiavo*, United States Court of Appeals for the Eleventh Circuit, No. 05-11628D, filed March 29, 2005. Accounts of the scene at Hospice House Woodside and Jesse Jackson's appearance are in S. Nohlgren, "'I'm here because I care,' Jackson tells crowd," *St. Petersburg Times*, March 30, 2005; and A. Metz, "Finding common ground in Schiavo case," *Newsday*, March 30, 2005. Ralph Nader's joint press release with Wesley Smith is at http://www.usnewswire.com. An account of Nader's financial contributions from Republicans is in C. Marinucci, "GOP donors funding Nader," *San Francisco Chronicle*, July 9, 2004.

The March 30 ruling by the three-judge panel of the Eleventh Circuit is *Schiavo ex rel. Schindler v. Schiavo* (March 30, 2005) 404 F.3d 1282. The ruling by the full Eleventh Circuit denying a rehearing, including the concurring opinions, is *Schiavo ex rel. Schindler v. Schiavo* (March 30, 2005) 404 F.3d 1270. The 2003 interview with Judge Birch is on the Internet at http://legalaffairs.org/howappealing/20q/2003_10_01_20q-appellateblog_archive .html. The U.S. Supreme Court's order denying the Schindlers' final application is reported at 125 S.Ct. 1722. The March 30 events at Hospice House Woodside are described in W. Levesque et al., "For Schiavo, 'It's getting real late,'" *St. Petersburg Times*, March 31, 2005. The evangelical juggler is described in J. Thompson, "Juggler says, 'God told me to come,'" *St. Petersburg Times*, March 31, 2005.

The March 31 quotes are in T. Lush, "Memorial praises Terri," *St. Petersburg Times*, April 1, 2005 (Malinowski); T. Zucco et al., "For two families, even grief is divided," *St. Petersburg Times*, April 1, 2005 (Vatican spokesman, Baxley, Governor Bush, and President Bush); T. Lush et al., "Protesters' hope faded as Schiavo neared end," *St. Petersburg Times*, April 1, 2005 ("culture war" protestor); and W. Allison, "Recess quiets Washington's response," *St. Petersburg Times*, April 1, 2005 (DeLay).

The *St. Petersburg Times* editorial is "Terri's legacy," April 1, 2005.

CHAPTER 18: VENGEANCE

The report on Terri Schiavo's autopsy, dated June 13, 2005, can be accessed online at http://www.sptimes.com/2005/06/15/schiavoreport.pdf. For news reports on the autopsy, see M. Stacy, "Schiavo autopsy shows massive brain damage," *St. Petersburg Times*, June 15, 2005; and B. Watson, "Autopsy report synopsis," *St. Petersburg Times*, June 15, 2005.

The quoted editorial headlines: "Autopsy vindicates judges, husband," *Kansas City Star*, June 17, 2005; "Autopsy debunks abuse, doesn't end exploitation," *Palm Beach Post*, June 18, 2005; "Schiavo autopsy underscores folly of intervention," *Worcester Telegram & Gazette* (Massachusetts), June 19, 2005; "Autopsy reveals much about politicians," *St. Petersburg Times*, June 19, 2005; and "End of the Schiavo case," *Boston Herald*, June 17, 2005.

The Randall Terry "hell to pay" quote is in M. Roig-Franzia, "Long legal battle over as Schiavo dies," *Washington Post*, April 1, 2005. The Frist quotations in the Senate are in the *Congressional Record*. The Frist "time to move on" quote is reported in "End of the Schiavo case," *Boston Herald*, June 17, 2005. The Frist "never made" a diagnosis quote is reported in "Autopsy debunks abuse, doesn't end exploitation," *St. Petersburg Times*, June 18, 2005. The Martinez quote is reported in "Autopsy reveals much about politicians," *St. Petersburg Times*, June 19, 2005.

The Jeb Bush letter to prosecutor Bernie McCabe, dated June 17, 2005, was released to the public by the governor's office. The Bush statement that the delay "was never brought up" before is reported in A. Goodnough, "Gov. Bush seeks another inquiry in Schiavo case," *New York Times*, June 18, 2005. For Barbara Weller's statement that Bobby Schindler told Bush about the delay a year previously, see N. Bierman et al., "State attorney to probe time of husband's call to 911," *St. Petersburg Times*, June 18, 2005.

Michael Schiavo's 2003 Larry King interview is reported in W. Levesque, "Schiavo: 'Nothing's going to stop me,'" *St. Petersburg Times*, Oct. 28, 2003.

Bobby Schindler's version of the events after Terri's collapse is reported in D. Lynne, "Michael Schiavo pleads case on CNN," *World Net Daily*, Oct. 28, 2003; and D. Lynne, "The whole Terri Schiavo story," *World Net Daily*, March 24, 2005. The Fuhrman book references are to M. Fuhrman, *Silent Witness*, (2005): when Hannity called, p. xi; bulimia factors, pp. 53–54; weight fluctuations, pp. 62, 107; irregular menstruation, pp. 55, 103–4; skipping breakfast and lunch, p. 56; disappearing to bathroom after meals, p. 57; timidity, p. 107; mood swings, anxiety, and depression, p. 110; "Michael's missing forty minutes," p. 172; Bob and Mary Schindler's "recollection," p. 181; call for special prosecutor, p. 224; and lethargy and fatigue, p. 238.

Peggy Noonan's warning to the Republican leadership is in P. Noonan, "'Don't kick it': If Terri Schiavo is killed, Republicans will pay a political price," *Wall Street Journal*, March 18, 2005. Senator Cornyn's comments are in the *Congressional Record*.

CHAPTER 19: SMASH THE THIRD BRANCH

Lou Sheldon's thanks for the "blessing" of the *Schiavo* case is reported in D. Kirkpatrick, "The Schiavo case: The money," *New York Times*, March 25, 2005. The Perkins "showdown" and "lasting dispute" quotes are reported in L. Feldmann and W. Richey, "The Terri Schiavo legacy," *Christian Science Monitor*, April 1, 2005; and W. Allison, "Courts may feel Schiavo impact," *St. Petersburg Times*, April 4, 2005. The Lessner quote is in the Allison article.

Dobson's "totally out of control" quote is in from his *Action Newsletter* of April 2005, on the Internet at http://www.focusaction.org/articles/A0000066.cfm. Sheldon's "must be restrained" quote is from his Internet web site at http://www.ourbattleplan.com/why.php. Coleman's quote is from W. Smith, *Forced Exit: The Slippery Slope from Assisted Suicide to Legalized Murder* (Times Books, 1997), p. 184. Smith's quote is from W. Smith, "Death plays the name game," *Weekly Standard*, Aug. 16, 2004. Bob Schindler's quote is reported in T. R. Goldman, "Full-court pressure," *Legal Times*, March 28, 2005. Jay Sekulow's "last best hope" quote is reported in J. Cummings, "Lawyer rallies evangelicals on filibuster issue," *Wall Street Journal*, May 17, 2005. The Pat Robertson quote is reported in J. Holland, "Judge asks Senate to help tone down jurists' critics," Associated Press, May 19, 2005.

Dobson's criticism of *Marbury v. Madison* is from his April 2005 *Action Newsletter*. HR 2045 was introduced in the 108th Congress, First Session; HR 2028 and HR 568 were introduced in the 108th Congress, Second Session; House Joint Resolution 39, S 489 and S 520 were introduced in the 109th Congress, First Session.

Sensenbrenner's proposal for an Office of Inspector General for the federal judiciary and the comment by Professor Geyh are reported in P. MacLean, "Does the judiciary need a watchdog?" *National Law Journal*, May 23, 2005.

Sensenbrenner's Stanford speech can be read online at http://judiciary.house
.gov/media/pdfs/stanfordjudgesspeechpressversion505.pdf. DeLay's "power of
the purse" comment is reported in R. Chernow, "Chopping off the weakest
branch," *New York Times*, May 6, 2005.

Dobson's call for impeachment is in his April 2005 *Action Newsletter*.
Focus on the Family's call for impeachment is on its Internet web site at
http://www.family.org/cforum/fnif/news/a0036121.cfm.

Lou Sheldon's attack on the Ninth Circuit is from his Internet web site.
Dobson's attack on the Ninth Circuit is in his April 2005 *Action Newsletter*.
The Falwell quote is from a sermon he gave at his Thomas Road Baptist
Church on December 19, 2004. The Sensenbrenner quote on the Ninth Cir-
cuit is from his Stanford speech. The *National Review* quote is from A.
Thomas, "Split decision," Sept. 16, 2003. Perkins's call to disregard judicial
pronouncements is reported in W. Allison, "Courts may feel Schiavo impact,"
St. Petersburg Times, April 4, 2005.

Bruce Fein's "pack the court" proposal is in B. Fein, "Pack the Supreme
Court," *Washington Lawyer*, February 2005. The "Four Horsemen" advisory
group is described in J. Cummings, "Lawyer rallies evangelicals on filibuster
issue," *Wall Street Journal*, May 17, 2005. C. Boyden Gray's donations are reported in J. Krehely et. al., "Axis of Ideology," p.39 (National Committee for
Responsive Philanthropy, March 2004).

The White House quotation from my 2003 letter regarding Judge Brown is
online at http://www.whitehouse.gov/infocus/judicialnominees/brown.html.
The quotations from Judge Brown's speeches are online at http://www.pfaw
.org/pfaw/general/default.aspx?oid=12751. Justice Brown's country club
speech is reported in J. Nickerson, "Red Mass breakfast visited by filibuster
controversy," *Stamford Advocate*, April 25, 2005.

The Traditional Values Coalition's "Battle Plan" can be viewed online at
http://www.ourbattleplan.com/.

Professor Tribe's comments are published in 8 Green Bag 2d 292 (Spring
2005).

President Bush's pronouncement is reported in "Bush calls pledge ruling
'out of step,'" *USA Today*, June 27, 2002. The quotation from the Christian
Law Association's Internet web site can be found online at http://www.chris-
tianlaw.org/christian_america.html.

The 1785 Madison statement is in his *Memorial and Remonstrance Against
Religious Assessments*. The 1822 Madison statement is in his letter to Edward
Livingston dated July 10, 1822. The 1788 Adams quote is from his *Defence of
the Constitutions of Government of the United States of America*. The Hamilton
quote is from a speech to the New York City bar in February 1802; it is mentioned in R. Chernow, "Chopping off the weakest branch," *New York Times*,
May 6, 2005.

CHAPTER 20: HAND-TO-HAND COMBAT

The quotes from Father Pavone are from the Priests for Life Internet web site, http://www.priestsforlife.org, and from a press release issued by Father Pavone, available online at http://www.earnedmedia.org/pfl0407.htm. The Rita Marker quotation is from the Internet web site for the International Task Force on Euthanasia and Assisted Suicide, at http://www.internationaltask-force.org/adneeds.htm. The Internet web site for Operation Save America is http://www.operationsaveamerica.org. The quotation from the Christian Law Association is on its Internet web site at http://www.christianlaw.org/schi-avo.html. The Sekulow comment is reported in J. Price, "Terri Schiavo's legacy: Death raises questions on end-of-life intervention," *Washington Times*, April 10, 2005.

The NRLC model law is online at http://www.nrlc.org/euthanasia/model-statelaw.html.

The bills in the various state legislatures can be accessed on the Internet web sites for each state: Georgia—http://www.legis.state.ga.us; Hawaii—http://www.capitol.hawaii.gov; Kentucky—http://www.lrc.ky.gov; Alabama—http://alisdb.legislature.state.al.us; Minnesota—http://www.revisor.leg.state.mn.us; Iowa—http://coolice.legis.state.ia.us; South Carolina—www.scstatehouse.net; Michigan—http://legislature.mi.gov/; South Dakota—http://legis.state.sd.us; Kansas—http://www.kslegislature.org; Louisiana—http://www.legis.state.la.us.; Ohio—http://lsc.state.oh.us; and Florida—http://myfloridahouse.gov. The quotations from Bobby Schindler's testimony before the Louisiana state Senate committee are reported in S. Ertelt, "Louisiana Bill Protecting Disabled Patients Heads to Gov. Blanco," Lifenews.com, June 22, 2005.

The quotation from Senator Enzi appears in J. Price, "Terri Schiavo's legacy: Death raises questions on end-of-life intervention," *Washington Times*, April 10, 2005. The quoted testimony before the Senate Health, Education, Labor and Pensions Committee is online at http://help.senate.gov/testi-mony/t231_tes.html.

Bobby Schindler's appearance before the NRLC convention, the quotation from the monk, and Bobby's takeover of his parents' foundation are reported in M. Lohn, "National Right to Life Committee: Schiavo case grabs spotlight, abortion foes gather in Twin Cities," *Grand Forks Herald* (North Dakota), June 17, 2005. Bobby's statement on NRLC's web site is at http://nrlc.org/euthanasia/willtolive/BobSchindlerjrstatement.html. Ken Goodman's comments are quoted in J. Price, "Terri Schiavo's legacy: Death raises questions on end-of-life intervention," *Washington Times*, April 10, 2005.

The quoted articles by Wesley Smith are W. Smith, "Beyond Terri's Law: What we can learn from the Schiavo case," *Weekly Standard*, Jan. 19, 2004; and W. Smith, "The consequences of casual conversations," *Weekly Standard*, Oct. 27, 2003.

CHAPTER 21: MY UNCLE BERNIE

The Ken Connor quote is from an article posted on Family Research Council's web site on October 2, 2001; the article is no longer on FRC's web site but is reported on the People for the American Way web site at http://www.pfaw.org/pfaw/general/default.aspx?oid=4211. The 800,000 requests for advance directives from Aging with Dignity are reported in J. Schwartz and J. Estrin, "Many still seek one final say on ending life," *New York Times*, June 17, 2005. The 17,000 visits to the New York State Bar Association's web site are reported in "17,000 download living wills from NY State Bar Assn. website," *Daily Record (Rochester, NY)*, March 30, 2005. The requests to the Oklahoma Bar Association and the 95 percent rate of directives against ANH are reported in J. Shottenkirk, "Drama over Schiavo case spurs action in living wills," *Journal Record (Oklahoma City)*, March 31, 2005.

The AARP Internet web site is http://www.aarp.org. The American Bar Association web site is http://www.abanet.org. The Compassion in Dying web site is http://www.compassionindying.org. The Aging with Dignity web site is http://www.agingwithdignity.org. The National Right to Life Committee web site is http://www.nrlc.org. The International Task Force on Euthanasia and Assisted Suicide web site is http://www.internationaltaskforce.org.